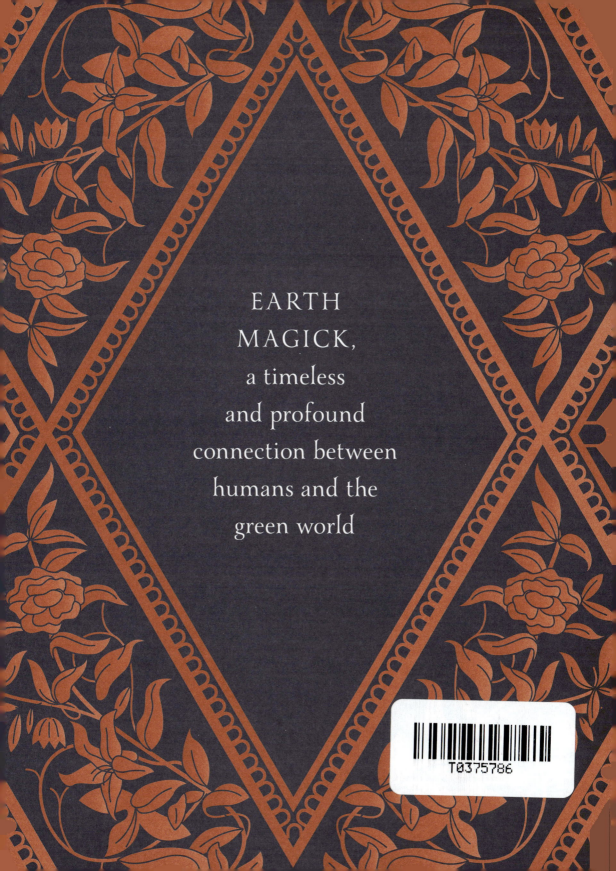

EARTH
MAGICK,
a timeless
and profound
connection between
humans and the
green world

Earth

Magick

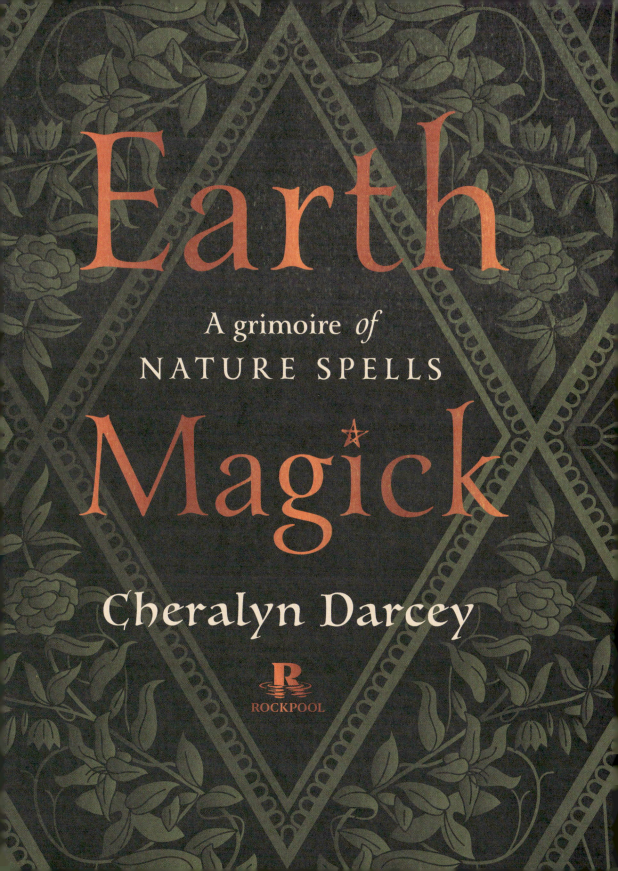

A Rockpool book
PO Box 252
Summer Hill
NSW 2130
Australia

rockpoolpublishing.com
Follow us! f 🅾 rockpoolpublishing
Tag your images with #rockpoolpublishing

First published as *The Book of Flower Spells*, ISBN 9781925682250 (2018), *The Book of Herb Spells*, ISBN 9781925682267 (2018) and *The Book of Tree Spells*, ISBN 9781925682885 (2019).

This collected edition published in 2025 by Rockpool Publishing

ISBN: 9781923208308

Copyright text © Cheralyn Darcey 2025
Copyright design © Rockpool Publishing 2025

All rights reserved. No part of this publication may be reproduced, stored in a retrieval system, or transmitted in any form or by any means, electronic, mechanical, photocopying, recording or otherwise, without the prior written permission of the publisher.

Design and typesetting by Sara Lindberg, Rockpool Publishing

The information presented in this book is intended for general inquiry, research and informational purposes only and should not be considered as a substitute or replacement for any trained medical advice, diagnosis, or treatment.

All preparations and information about the usage of botanicals presented in this book are examples for educational purposes only. Always consult a registered herbalist before taking or using any preparations suggested in this book.

No responsibility will be accepted for the application of the information in this book.

 A catalogue record for this book is available from the National Library of Australia

Printed and bound in China
10 9 8 7 6 5 4 3 2 1

Contents

Introduction	1
How to Use This Book	5

FLOWER SPELLS   13

Flower Spells *for* Relationships and Love	16
Flower Spells *for* Happiness and Harmony	31
Flower Spells *for* Success and Prosperity	47
Flower Spells *for* Protection and Clearing	63
Flower Spells *for* Health and Healing	79
Flower Spells *for* Transition and Change	95

HERB SPELLS   113

Herb Spells *for* Love, Relationships and Friendship	116
Herb Spells *for* Home, Family and Pets	132
Herb Spells *for* Study, Career and Money	148
Herb Spells *for* Protection, Clearing and Banishment	163
Herb Spells *for* Health, Self-Care and Happiness	178
Herb Spells *for* Spirituality, Faith and Divination	193

TREE SPELLS 209

Tree Spells *for* Balance and Harmony 212

Tree Spells *for* Modern Problems 228

Tree Spells *for* Relationships and Love 243

Tree Spells *for* Change and Empowerment 258

Tree Spells *for* Purpose and Paths 273

Tree Spells *for* the Earth and Life 288

How to Create Your Own Spells 305

Glossary 319

Bibliography 323

About the Author 327

Introduction

In the embrace of an ancient forest or nestled in a blooming garden, there is a language spoken not in words but in whispers, fragrances and delicate movements. It is the language of Earth Magick, a timeless and profound connection that exists between humans and the green world around us. This is your invitation to step into the botanical realm.

In a world that often moves too fast, we can forget the old ways – the methods by which our ancestors communed with Nature, not only to heal the body but to mend the spirit and guide the soul. This book is a way back to that place, a gentle yet powerful guidebook that teaches you how to work with plants as allies in your magickal practice. From lush forests to humble houseplants, each leaf and petal holds within it the essence of the earth's energy, waiting for a willing heart to awaken its potential.

This collection of spells lays the groundwork for understanding the magick that resides in the natural world. Each will share with you the history of plant-based practices, while touching on ancient rituals that have sustained generations of healers, witches and wise folk. But this book is not just about history; it is a call to integrate that wisdom into your modern practice. Whether you live in the sprawling countryside or a bustling city with only a single pot of herbs on your windowsill, the magick of plants is accessible to you.

You will gain deep insights into cultivating relationships with plants while learning ways to integrate their properties into your life. As you work through the spells within, you will enhance the energy in your life and deepen your spiritual resonance with Earth Magick. This collection of spells is based on time-honoured folklore that will help you weave a tapestry of knowledge that connects each plant to its magickal properties.

Beyond the profiles of plants, I'll teach you the art of creating your own rituals and spells based on mine. With clear instructions, I'll guide you in crafting herbal charms, teas, incense and anointing oils, each one tailored to enhance specific intentions such as love, protection, healing and clarity. These practices are not just exercises; they are ways to deepen your bond with the earth and harness its energies in a mindful and respectful manner.

An essential part of the book is understanding the ethics of working with Nature. Make sure you study the additional notes included with each spell, as they will remind you to practice Earth Magick with great respect for the earth itself. Within are tips on wildcrafting with care and finding harmony in a reciprocal relationship with the natural world.

With this book in hand, you will not only learn about the magickal properties of plants but how to invite their energies into your life in a transformative and practical way. *Earth Magick* is a guide, a companion and an invitation to remember that Nature is not just a backdrop but a partner in your spiritual journey. Prepare to awaken your senses, nourish your soul and step into the ancient dance of Earth Magick that continues to unfurl, one leaf at a time.

Bunches of best wishes,

Cheralyn Darcey

How to Use This Book

It's never an easy task to create a book of magick instruction to suit everyone. We are all on different paths, with different beliefs and varying levels of experience, and I do not believe that these things should bar anyone from experiencing or practising Nature Magick. In order to be safe and work safely for others and your environment, you must first educate yourself in these ways of working. Make sure you read through all the sections of this introduction as they will give you this knowledge. It is simple but vital when creating and casting spells.

Those more experienced in spellcrafting and casting, or who have dedicated and defined paths in their own beliefs, may be able to skim the following instruction pages and dive straight into the spells, experimenting and exploring new paths which may open up, enhance or complement their work. However, I suggest that everyone read through this section in order to familiarise themselves with the foundations on which I have presented this book of Earth Magick. Whether you are a complete beginner or have some experience, this chapter will provide a good grounding in safe and best practice when creating and casting spells. It also explains, in detail, what a spell is and how it works.

In this collection of earth magick spells, I have shared 180 spells that I have written over my life. They focus on plants and their energies. Divided into Flower Spells, Herb Spells and Tree Spells, they are further arranged in short chapters by their use so that you can quickly find a spell that suits your needs. Make sure you observe the instructions I have given and any instructions you already use each time you are creating and casting spells.

All steps to using each spell are clearly explained along with simple, everyday ingredients and tools to create them. I also share additional interesting and helpful tips with each spell to enrich your experience working with Nature.

Sourcing Plants for Magickal Work

GROWING PLANTS

A garden, a magickal garden, can be anything from a vast estate to a pot plant. The most important thing is that you grow your plants organically and with a positive intention.

To teach you how to garden is beyond the scope of this book but I would suggest that you seek out resources close to your home. Your local garden centre not only contains plants to purchase but people who know your area and what will grow there. They will also help you with any challenges you may encounter. Most can also order in plants for you – ones that may not be on display.

Local councils, land and environment bodies and gardening clubs are all sources of local plant knowledge. The best people of all, however, are your gardening neighbours, who might provide good information about suppliers and other contacts.

When planting, be sure that you are not growing anything that is considered an invasive weed in your area. Be very careful when considering plants that may be toxic to others, especially wildlife or pets. Planning your garden is important as is soil preparation, seasonal considerations and your climate zone.

MAGICK HARVEST

When obtaining botanical ingredients for magick – or plants and their treasures for any use – you should always follow these steps:

+ Never harm the plant.
  Learn how to harvest each type of plant properly.
+ Never take more than you need or have a use for.
  Leave some for the next person, animal or time.
+ Never harvest more than the plant can sustain sharing.
  You may need to find another plant or source.
+ Step lightly in the environment you find yourself in.
  Be mindful of your actions and their possible outcomes.
+ Give back to Nature more than you take.
  Plant more than you take or help Nature in some way.
+ Share what it is you have been blessed with.
  You could share your harvest, creation or knowledge.

WHAT IF YOU DON'T HAVE ACCESS TO YOUR OWN PLANTS?

As wonderful as it would be to access every plant on earth, no matter where you found yourself, the reality is that you cannot. I have given you alternate plants that you may be able to source and that hold similar energies, but I would also encourage you to dry your own plants when they are available and create or source essences, candles, incenses and other botanical treasures from trusted suppliers, so you always have a magickal apothecary to rely on.

WHAT IF YOU DON'T HAVE PLANTS AT ALL?

To further focus energy or to connect with plants when you do not have access to them, imagery in the form of artwork, photos, your sketches or oracle cards can be used. I feel it is very important to see the plant to connect with its unique energy.

What Is a Spell and How Does It Work?

A spell is a combination of ingredients, tools, actions and focus, which come together energetically to create change. Timings (*when you cast your spell*) can also be observed to ensure added power.

TIMINGS

I have included simple and broad timings in these spells, which include Moon Phase, Day of the Week and Time of the Day. These are the times that you put spells together and cast them. You can observe these to give your spellwork a boost because working in line with the time of Nature is working in synchronicity with what is going on around you and provides stronger focus for your intentions. See pages 306–7 for a list of simple timings, but you can also explore deeper, seasonal timings – ones associated with traditional pagan celebrations and observances and ones that are unique to your area and people as well as being open to other people's.

How to Use This Book ✦ 7

INGREDIENTS

The ingredients you gather to create the spell will have correspondences to your intention. In a way, they illustrate what it is that you want to happen. They will support the things you wish to happen because they have similar meanings and energies. These meanings and energies may also assist you in removing something. These correspondences are important because they also help us find substitute ingredients for our spells when what is prescribed is not available. I will give you my suggestions with each spell.

TOOLS

Tools are additional items that you can use to help you create your spell. These are just a few examples of tools used in spellcrafting and casting:

+ cloths to set your spell up on (usually in colours which align with the energy of the spell)
+ wands and staffs to direct and enhance energies
+ divination tools such as tarot and oracle cards, crystal balls, pendulums and runes to provide clarity
+ drums and bells (musical instruments and music express your intentions)
+ practical items such as glasses, cups, vases, bowls and cutting tools.

The way you put a spell together, the words you may recite, the things you actually do to cast your spell are the actions that bring it all together. These focus your intention, put you squarely in the path of the outcome and strengthen the relationship between the energies of the ingredients and the tools you are using. The combination of all these things raises the energy for magick to happen.

OBTAINING INGREDIENTS AND TOOLS

Tools and magickal ingredients can be obtained from bricks-and-mortar stores and online, but always be guided by your feelings when making purchases. Make sure you feel comfortable and positive about these businesses because their energies will transfer. Anything that comes into your space to use for spellwork has passed through various other hands and should be magickly cleansed. Do this by placing the items under running water, smudging with smoke or placing them underground in suitable wrapping or a container for a night.

Why Wouldn't a Spell Work?

Not many things in life work all the time. External factors influence them; maybe they are not put together properly; sometimes it is just not meant to be.

You cannot change another person's free will and this is also why spells do not work at times. Perhaps the consequence of the spell will adversely affect another or counter their stronger will, which you might not even be aware of. Another reason a spell may not work is because other energies have greater strength at that moment or they may in fact be leading you to a better eventual outcome.

Spells work because the person creating and casting them fully believes in what they are doing and has a strong, focused intention with a good connection to the energies of their spell and the outcome. While perhaps changing things for personal benefit, the outcome is still generally in keeping with a good outcome for all involved without forcibly changing anyone's free will.

How to Create and Cast a Spell

When you are using the spells in this book, please ensure you do so safely – and by this I don't just mean keeping burning candles attended to. Working with energies to create magick requires you to take responsibility for what you are doing, for yourself and the world you live in. There are many ways you can do this, just as there are many ways of life and beliefs with their own rituals, which ensure safety and power in spellcasting. Most safety measures include a way to protect yourself and those around you. A way to mark the beginning of the spell or opening the space comes next. There will be words, meditation, music, chants or actions which will help you focus on the task at hand, and then there will be a way to release the energy, perhaps give thanks and to close the space. This is a simple and safe way to cast a spell.

PROTECT AND OPEN

Before you can begin it's important to establish protection from negative energies. There are various ways you can achieve this, but whatever way you use make sure you always protect yourself before casting. You may wish to use a smudging method, by burning sage or other plants, or by spraying the room with a smudging mist. You can also visualise or draw a circle around you and your spell with your finger in the air, then fill your circle with white light.

If you are aligned with certain deities, elementals or guides, you may wish to ask for their assistance in providing protection. A very simple and effective protection method is to light a white candle while visualising the light cleansing, clearing and protecting you.

FOCUS INTENTION

Sit or stand still for a long moment and imagine your outcome. Really see it in your mind and complete your picture with exact times, places and events. You may like, at this time before you cast your spell, to write down your intention and say it out loud to get yourself fully focused and your energy aligned with what it is you are about to create.

CAST SPELL

In each of the spells I have shared with you, I have set out very specific steps to create your spell and I have explained why I've used these steps. In the final section, I've provided instruction on creating your own spells. Casting your spell is simply what you do to make the spell happen. While casting your spell, you must maintain your focus on your intention.

RELEASE, CLOSE AND GROUND

Once you have completed your spell, you will need to release the power you have raised in creating it. I will provide a way to release the spell for each spell I share with you, but you can also simply say: 'I release the power I have raised' or 'It is done' or by putting out your white candle if lit.

Grounding is the way you bring yourself back from your spellcasting time. Clapping your hands, ringing a bell or placing your bare feet or hands on the earth are all ways to ground yourself.

Magickal Correspondences

You may wish to create a bath, essence, tea, mandala – anything at all that will be in itself an action related to the energy of the spell. Items required for this should be aligned with your outcome. These are usually called *correspondences* or *magickal correspondences*.

Expand your knowledge in areas that you do not have experience with by seeking out resources that specialise in the correspondence you wish to include, such as astrological, colours and crystals. See page 305 for a list of correspondences.

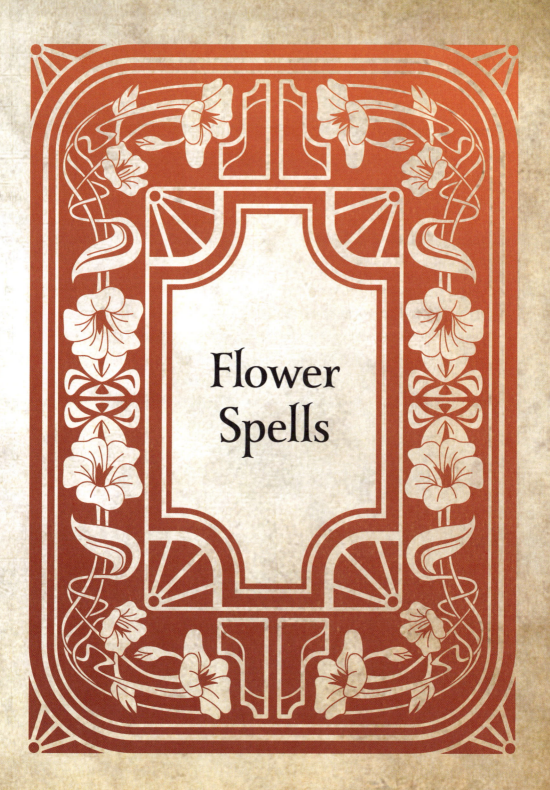

Flower Spells

Introduction

This section will help you live magickally with flowers. Before we even begin, though, I want to make sure that you understand flowers and how to respectfully use them to create real magick.

Flowers are the reproductive organs of a plant and, as such, they are emotional in nature. They attract pollinators in a variety of ways, including using their looks, fragrance and texture as well as their energy. Along with their physical attributes, this energy is how we can connect with flowers to share their magick. Flowers illicit an emotional response from us, which connects us directly to their energy and, in doing so, makes them more desirable. We will acquire, tend, protect and assist what pleases or seems to help us, and this ensures the flowers' continuance.

To discover what the individual energy of each flower is, we look at the way it behaves, its appearance, the things it provides. Lavender, for example, produces a fragrance that is naturally calming and cleansing. The colour indicates restfulness, and even the soft texture of the leaves and flowers leads us to a certain understanding of the energy of this plant.

I have written these flower spells in a way that will assist you in understanding why each flower is included, and sprinkled throughout the spells are tips, ideas, fascinating facts and a little bit of mythical magick.

Flowers for Spells

As this is a collection of flower spells, you will need to find a way to obtain the flowers. Of course the very best way would be to grow them but I know it is not possible for everyone to garden, nor is it possible to grow everything in every place all the time.

When purchasing fresh flowers, try to support your local florist and growers. Try your local markets or farmers' markets and look out for local signage.

14 ✦ Earth Magick

Selecting fresh flowers should be done with care. Make sure you are purchasing flowers that look and feel energetic and positive then take them home swiftly and look after them. Remove excess foliage that may turn water brown. Snip stems at an angle to remove dried ends and enable them to easily take a long fresh drink. Place in water with a little sugar or feeder. Change water completely every two to three days and snip stems as required.

One solution to purchasing fresh flowers is to keep dried flowers – something I've been doing successfully for decades and a practice that enables me to have supplies all year round. You can easily dry most flowers by tying in loose bundles and hanging in a cool, dry space. Single blossoms can also be dried on racks or pressed, and for those particularly dedicated there are various food dehydrators on the market that work very well. Another popular flower drying method is the use of silica gel. Flowers are placed in containers layered with the gel in bead form and this dries out flowers over a number of weeks.

Once dry, keep your flowers in a cool, dry place, out of direct sunlight in airtight jars. Label by flower type. You may also like to add place, time or season in which the flower was harvested. Ensure that your flowers are completely dry before bottling or they will grow mould.

AM I KILLING THE FLOWER IF I USE IT IN A SPELL?

Flowers are part of the lifecycle of plants, which we harvest and enjoy and regrow throughout the year – just like the vegetables you had in your last salad, which may have included parts of plants and maybe also flowers and what could have been flowers taken too soon (*put that artichoke down!*). You are not killing a flower; you are using a part of a plant at the end of its own lifecycle. To use flowers in spells, be respectful. Don't over harvest, don't uproot whole plants unnecessarily and try to observe the tips I have given above.

Flower Spells ✛ 15

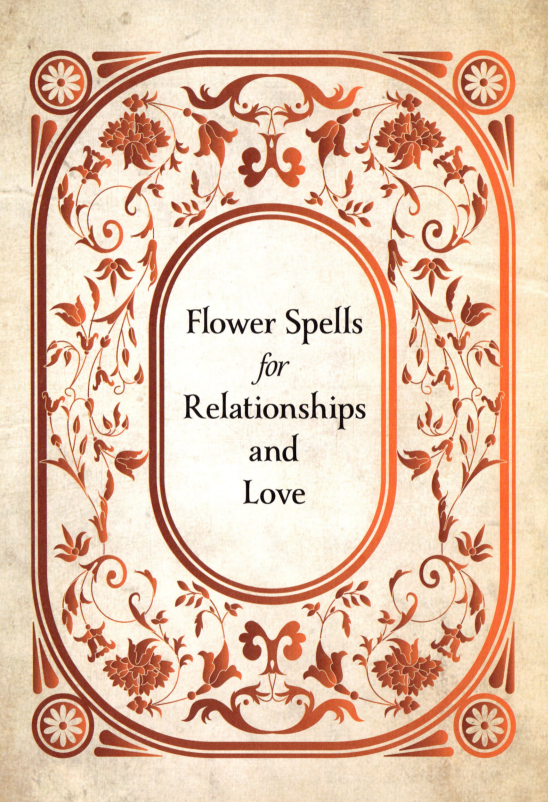

Flower Spells *for* Relationships and Love

Lisianthus and Red Rose New Love Spell

If you are looking for a new love, one that will lead to a long-term partnership/relationship/marriage, then this spell will help you. Lisianthus will create an atmosphere of desire and open up the possibilities for commitment. Pink and Red Roses will help bring love your way.

Timings: New Moon, Friday, Sunrise

Find and Gather

- a Lisianthus flower (*Eustoma grandiflorium*)
- a Red Rose flower (*Rosa*)
- a red candle
- a pink candle
- a map of an area you would find your new love in (*your local area or even the world*)

The Spell

Set a protected space and place your map upon a flat surface.

Light your red and your pink candle and place one on either side of your map while imagining the qualities that you would like in your new love.

Gently remove the petals of the Lisianthus and the Rose and let each drift down onto your map until all petals are removed while reciting the following words continuously:

Within the corners of this map,
My new love will be found.

Take your petals outside and, dropping them one by one, form a path from your front door. Once you've dropped the last of your petals, walk slowly back and say the following words over and over until you return:

The path is set to bring you to me,
On the steps of roses let our new love now be.

Once your candles have burned down, take them outside and bury them in the earth. Keep your map and repeat the spell each New Moon until your new love arrives.

Alternate Flowers

Pink Rose (*Rosa*), Red Carnation (*Dianthus caryophyllus*), Morning Glory (*Ipomoea purpurea*), Lady's Mantle (*Alchemilla vulgaris*), Cornflower (*Centaurea cyanus*)

Fuchsia and Agapanthus Rekindle Love Spell

To reconnect with your love you can bake a ring cake, which symbolises the unbroken circle. The element of fire via the heat of the oven will help you light the spark of renewal into a current relationship and can assist with relationships you are attempting to mend. Fuchsia releases emotions and helps people express their true feelings. Agapanthus will affirm your own commitment to love and help prevent the love from fading.

Timings: Full Moon, Sunday, Morning

Find and Gather

- a Fuchsia flower (*Fuchsia magellanica*)
- an Agapanthus flower (*Agapanthus praecox*)
- a ring cake pan (*or be prepared to cut a hole in the centre of your cake*)
- a favourite cake recipe that you both enjoy
- a lovely small vase
- a beautiful pink cloth

The Spell

Make your cake with your loved one, if possible. Set your flowers in their vase next to where you are cooking but do not add these flowers to your mix – they are not edible. Imagine a happier future together while making your cake and, as you do the final mixing, be sure to give it a good stir and say:

> *Together we blend our hearts,*
> *Together we mend.*
> *Within our new circle,*
> *Love stronger with flame.*

Earth Magick

Once you have baked your cake, create a beautiful setting upon your pink cloth, which will encourage healing and peaceful and romantic energies to surround you both. Place your vase of flowers in the centre and share your magickal cake together.

Dry your flowers and add to mojo bags, perhaps with a little rose quartz for love.

Place under your pillows at times when you want a little extra spark in your relationship.

Mojo bags are small fabric bags containing magickal items, which are either worn or placed in areas to emit their energies.

Alternate Flowers

Fuchsia » Poinsettia (*Euphorbia pulcherrima*), Delphinium (*Delphinium*)
Agapanthus » Ambrosia (*Ambrosia*), Cactus (*Cactaceae*)

If a Bride wears Fuchsias in her hair she will then be assured of the blessings of the Heavens.

The botanical name Agapanthus has a Greek origin: 'Agape', which means love, and 'anthos', meaning flower.

Peruvian Lily and Yellow Rose Friendship Spell

Peruvian Lily helps communicate genuine offers of friendship and expresses devotion to another. Yellow Rose is a flower that not only supports friendships but also helps create space for new beginnings. Creating this offering of refreshments and making a circle is a way of inviting new friends into your life. Make sure you focus on bringing positive souls into your life and go out there in the world to seek them. This spell will help you shine with happy and positive friendship energy.

Timings: Waxing Moon, Friday, Evening

Find and Gather

- a Peruvian Lily (*Alstroemeria*)
- a Yellow Rose (*Rosa*)
- a tiny jar of honey
- a small glass of milk

- a very lovely cupcake/biscuit
- items that represent interests your new friends may share with you

The Spell

Find a welcoming outdoor space and place your treasures, which your new friends may find a common bond with you over, upon the ground. If you love gardening, perhaps you might add a gardening tool; if it is crystals, you could add your favourite ones; or maybe you want to find friends who share your enthusiasm for animal protection so you might add images of animals.

Holding your flowers, slowly circle your 'friendship treasures' in a clockwise direction, while gently loosening the petals and letting them drift to the earth. Repeat until all petals have been released and your circle is formed. Repeat the following words:

> *The circle of friendship grows,*
> *New folks I will know.*
> *Good friends of warm heart,*
> *Welcome to our new hearth.*

Dip a tiny dash of honey in the milk. Sit and enjoy your milk and sweet treat while imagining your new friendships. You should also be open to messages and ideas that might come to you to help you find avenues to make these lovely new friends.

Once you have finished, gather the petals and bury them under a favourite tree for protection of your spell and future friendships.

Alternate Flowers

Cornflower (*Centaurea cyanus*), Phlox (*Phlox*), Shasta Daisy (*Leucanthemum maximum*), Periwinkle (*Vinca minor*), Pink Rose (*Rosa*)

The Peruvian Lily is also known as 'The Lily of the Incas'. It has a very long vase-life and can easily last a month.

The Ancient Romans planted roses when a member of the family went away to war or on a long voyage. to ensure their safe return.

Cosmos Communication Improvement Spell

Cosmos flowers provide opportunities for communication and coherency. They also offer peace and tranquility, which is obviously beneficial when communication is difficult due to raised emotions. This spell is very helpful at times when you feel you are not being clearly heard by another person/s or even an institution or company. While you cannot energetically change their opinion, you can raise energy to ensure you are better understood so that a fair outcome is more likely.

Timings: Full Moon, Wednesday, Dusk

Find and Gather

- a small bunch of Cosmos (*Cosmos*)
- two bells
- a blue cloth
- pen and paper
- a clear vase
- a beautiful bottle
- rain/distilled water
- glycerin

The Spell

Lay your cloth out neatly and create a bridge-like pattern with your flowers. This should look roughly like an arch. At either end of the arch, place a bell.

Take out your pen and paper and write whatever it is that you need understood. Be as clear as possible. It is okay to rewrite this a few times until you are happy with it.

Ring the first bell and then say:

Bell, take my words,

Loud, clear and true.

Then read what you have written.

Ring the second bell and say:

So may they be heard

Loud, clear and true.

Place the flowers in a clear vase (this will ensure clarity of your words) with fresh water and place it on top of your message. When the flowers are spent, put them with your folded message into a beautiful bottle with 4/5 rain/distilled water and 1/5 glycerin. Seal the bottle. Whenever you wish your message to be heard, ring a bell and shake your bottle.

Alternate Flowers

Stephanotis (*Stephanotis*), Delphinium (*Delphinium*), Hippeastrum (*Hippeastrum*)

Cosmos, comes from the Greek word 'kosmos', which means 'order of the world'.

Originating in Mexico, Spanish explorers carried Cosmos plants across to Spain in the 16th century. Cosmos flowers have been used since pre-Columbian times to create orange and yellow dyes.

Red Tulip and Rosewater Passion Spell

All Tulips hold the energy of passion, desire and love, but Red Tulips will help those who wish to stoke a passionate fire! They also firmly declare your love for another. In this spell, we will be using rose oil, which has been a favourite passion-inducer throughout history. Cleopatra is said to have had the sails of her barge soaked in rose water before meeting Marc Anthony. Try to find a rhodochrosite crystal for this spell – it really is one of the best for increasing passion. If you can't find one, then a rose quartz will be suitable.

Timings: Full Moon, Friday, Midday

Find and Gather

+ a Red Tulip (*Tulipa*)
+ rose water
+ a rhodochrosite or rose quartz crystal
+ a pendant, which you will wear

The Spell

Outside, find a large flat stone. Alternatively, you could use a large flat bowl inside.

Earth Magick

Place your rhodochrosite or rose quartz crystal on the rock/in the bowl and place your pendant on it.

Hold your Red Tulip upright over the rock/bowl and slowly fill your tulip with the rose water, letting it run over and onto your crystal and your pendant. All the while, imagine what an increase in passion in your life would look like. Be very specific and really focus on how this energy might come into your life, how you would feel and what you would be doing.

What will you be doing?

What will you feel?

Who are you with?

Picture the scene completely.

Once complete, put the pendant on and keep wearing it until the increase you are searching for occurs in your life. Bury the tulip and the crystal in a place in your garden, or in nature nearby, which the sun shines on for the maximum amount of time each day.

Alternate Flowers

Red Chrysanthemum (*Chrysanthemum*), Passion Flower (*Passiflora incarnata*), Red Hibiscus (*Hibiscus rosa-sinensis*)

The black centre of Tulips is said to represent the heart of a lover, darkened by the intense heat of passion.

Tulips are not, as most believe, native to Holland, but from Central Asia. The name comes from the Turkish 'tuliband', which is the material turbans are made from.

Hibiscus and Cyclamen Separation Spell

Cyclamen flowers assist us to say goodbye and to leave a situation cleanly. All Hibiscuses will support your personal, long-term happiness, but White Hibiscus will also provide enlightenment, respect, female healing and, most importantly, help with progression. Cyclamen plants are poisonous, so please take care when using in this spell. Beware of the place you are planting the Cyclamen and keep the flowers out of the reach of young children and pets.

Timings: Waning Moon, Saturday, Midnight

Find and Gather

- a White Hibiscus flower (*Hibiscus*)
- a Cyclamen plant (*Cyclamen*)
- a plant pot and potting mix
- black peppercorns
- mortar and pestle

The Spell

This spell needs to be done in a place you and the person you wish to separate peacefully from have both been to, together.

Gently separate the petals of your White Hibiscus and place them in a circle around your pot. Carefully replant the Cyclamen in the new pot and say:

It is time for goodbye,
I wish us to part,
But peacefully go
and make a new start.

Leave the Cyclamen plant for seven nights and then gift it to the person you are parting with. If you cannot do that, place it at the back door, towards the back of your home, or in the rear yard.

Dry the Hibiscus petals and then grind them with the black peppercorns with the mortar and pestle. This powder is wonderful to use in places where memories of the two of you give rise to unwelcome emotions. Sprinkle a tiny bit of the powder on the ground.

Alternate Flowers

Hibiscus » White Daisy (*Bellis perennis*), White Carnation (*Dianthus caryophyllus*)
Cyclamen » Calendula (*Calendula officinalis*)

In Hawaii, wearing a Hibiscus behind your right ear indicates you are married; behind your left that you are available; both that you are married but seeking a lover.

Throughout Europe there are many instances of Cyclamen being used in gardens and homes to reverse the power of any spellcasting or witchcraft directed against the inhabitants.

Earth Magick

Golden Chrysanthemum Pet Protection Spell

All Chrysanthemums ensure the energy of longevity and happiness, but Yellow Chrysanthemums also provide a strong boundary against anything wishing harm. In China, the original place of the Chrysanthemum, mirrors are used as a magickal means of protection. I have combined both in this spell for your pets to provide a very powerful combination. For added protection and deflection of negative energies, grow Chrysanthemums near the entrance of your home.

Timings: Waning Moon, Saturday, Midday

Find and Gather

+ a Yellow Chrysanthemum (*Chrysanthemum*) for each pet
+ a small mirror

The Spell

You will need to repeat this spell separately for each pet. You can use the same mirror but select a new flower for each pet.

Holding the mirror and one Golden Chrysanthemum, walk around your home as close to the boundary as you can while keeping inside the perimeter. Then walk through your home, into each and every room, and as you do so say in each area:

Golden flower of sun,
Shine right and bright for (say your pet's name).
Silver mirror of light,
turn back the dark from (say your pet's name).

Place the mirror in a spot that faces the entrance to your home but one that will still catch the light.

Dry out the Golden Chrysanthemums and bury them near the entrance to your property.

Alternate Flowers

Chrysanthemums of other colours (*Chrysanthemum*)

Chrysanthemum tea originated thousands of years ago, in the Song Dynasty in China. It is said to be beneficial for the heart and to balance blood pressure. It also acts as a nerve relaxant and is favoured for its high levels of antioxidants.

In Japanese culture, the Chrysanthemum is considered to be symbolic of perfection because of the way the petals carefully unfold.

Baby's Breath Flower Family Harmony Spell

Baby's Breath works to bring harmonic energy into families. It embodies everlasting love and also reminds us to be present and treasure each moment together. As any family member knows, time goes by fast. This special flower helps us breathe, balance ourselves and enjoy the 'now'. The addition of a moonstone crystal brings peace and calm. These additions can be especially helpful for families experiencing discord or challenging times, and can offer protection. If you are anointing surfaces with the oil, please do a test somewhere inconspicuous first.

Timings: Full Moon, Monday, Morning

Find and Gather

- a sprig of Baby's Breath (*Gypsophila*)
- pure vegetable oil of your choice
- a moonstone crystal
- a clear glass/crystal bowl
- a yellow cloth
- a beautiful bottle
- organic cotton-wool pads or balls

The Spell

In the place in your home most used by your family, lay out your yellow cloth and place your clear glass/crystal bowl upon it. Place the moonstone into the bowl and then gently pour your pure vegetable oil into the bowl

Earth Magick

while breathing softly and deeply over the bowl. This will bring calming energy into the space.

Holding the sprig of Baby's Breath upside-down, use it to stir the oil slowly and trace out the first letter of each member of your family's names with it. Once completed say:

Oil of harmony,
Stone of moon,
Flower of lasting love.
Protect and breathe peace in our family home.

Set the stone aside and pour the oil into the beautiful bottle. You can now instil the energy of harmony by lightly anointing the doorways of each room with the oil or by placing a cotton pad/ball on a dish somewhere in each room of your home. Bury the flowers in your garden and place the moonstone near the place where you created your spell.

Alternate Flowers

Meadowsweet (*Filipendula ulmaria*)

Originally a Mediterranean plant, the botanical name *Gypsophila* indicates that it is 'gypsum-loving', meaning it prefers a gypsum (*chalk*)-rich soil.

Would you like to attract faeries to your garden? Plant Baby's Breath - it is one of their very favourite flowers.

Orchid Daily Self-Love Spell

Orchids live very differently to most plants, with many being epiphytes (living anchored on other plants) or occurring rarely and exclusively. All, it can be agreed, are anything but common in habit or appearance. These fascinating flowers are perfect for any spell that focuses on aspects of self-loving, self-esteem and acceptance. The water in this spell assists in calming emotions and opens the bonds between the energies of the Orchid and you. This is a spell you can use daily or when you feel your self-love slipping.

Timings: All Moon Phases, Every Day, Morning

Flower Spells ✦ 27

Find and Gather

◆ a small Orchid plant (*Orchidaceae*)
◆ a mirror
◆ a beautiful glass to be used only for this spell
◆ pure collected or bottled water

The Spell

My suggestion is that you find a place where you can keep your Orchid in front of a mirror, or that you have a plant small enough to place in front of a mirror. It does not matter if the Orchid is in flower or not – the energy of the flowers is still retained within the plant.

Have your orchid set so that its reflection can be seen along with yours in the mirror. Taking your glass of water, pour a little into the orchid's soil. (Be careful you do not overwater your plant – the tiniest drop will do if you are performing this spell every day.) As you do this, say:

Friend Orchid and I, how different are we,
Not perfect but right for what we may be.

Drink the rest of your water and say:

I celebrate and love,
all that we see.

Take a good moment to really study your Orchid each time you do this spell and see all of its differences from other traditional flowers. Really observe the leaves, the vines or stems and flowers if in bloom – different in many ways, in behaviour and form, and yet still serving as a perfect vessel for the spirit of the plant. Much like you.

Alternate Flowers

This spell really requires the energy of Orchids and so as suggested in the introduction to this book, if you really cannot obtain a fresh Orchid plant I would suggest using a beautifully framed painting or photograph of an Orchid, set before the mirror.

In the Middle East, Orchid tubers are used to create a healing drink called 'Salep', which is said to assist sore throats, digestive problems and gum disease.

Throughout the UK, Orchids have been used in witchcraft as a powerful addition to love potions and spells. They also have a reputation for being able to increase psychic abilities.

Love-in-a-Mist Heart-Healer Spell

Nigella flowers are also known as 'Love-in-a-Mist' and they are perfect for spells that support the healing of broken hearts, and will give you emotional clarity while doing so. In matters of the heart, they also add a touch of openness to a new tomorrow.

Timings: Full Moon, Friday, Midday

Find and Gather

- Love-in-a-Mist flowers (*Nigella damascena*)
- florist wire/wire coat hanger/length of wire
- florist tape/string
- electrical tape/strong tape
- a small hand mirror
- ribbon

The Spell

Find a place where you can see the sun – either outside or inside.

Place and angle your mirror on the ground so it catches the sun. (Be careful not to shine it into your eyes.) Sit and create a circle from your wire. It does not need to be large, but you will be adding your flowers to the centre so take into consideration their size and amount. Overlap each end of your wire circle and twist together. Cover the join with electrical/strong tape.

Place the circle over your heart and say:

Circle reformed,

Hold gently my heart.

Time will heal and wholeness will be.

Collect your flowers and add to the ring by laying stems on the wire circle and attaching with florist's tape or wire.

Once you have finished creating your flower circle, add a ribbon loop and hang it on your front door or in a window of a favourite room. Use your mirror to shine the sunlight through the centre and say:

Sunlight shine again.
Fill my heart with strength and joy,
Sparkling light to my hearth.
Again fill my heart.

When the flowers are spent, you can place them in a mojo bag and hang above your doorway or any window of your home, or you can bury in a sunny spot in the garden.

Alternate Flowers

Pink Gerbera Daisy (*Gerbera*), Wild Pansy (*Viola tricolor*)

Rich, black Nigella seeds are highly aromatic. This makes them popular in Middle Eastern, Turkish and Indian cuisine as well as for medicinal purposes.

Love-in-a-Mist gained its name from the story of the Emperor Frederick I (*1155-1190*). He was drowned after being seduced by a green-haired water spirit while on the Third Crusade in the Holy Land.

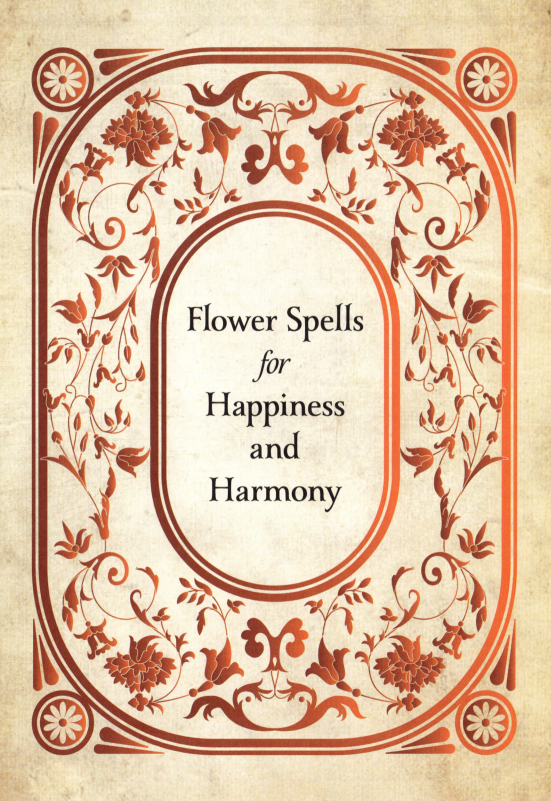

Flower Spells
for
Happiness and Harmony

Daisy Happiness Spell

How many of us have seen a bunch of daisies or a lawn sprinkled with their star-like joyfulness and not smiled? Daisies are the very best flowers of all to engage with should you be seeking happiness in challenging times. They offer protection and support. This spell creates a lovely, large amount of Daisy Happiness Bath Fizz. Keep it in lovely glass jars to use later on too, and to share!

Timings: Full Moon, Friday, Evening

Find and Gather

- 1 cup of organic dried Daises (*Bellis perennis*) - see page 15
- 1 cup of bath Himalayan/Dead Sea salt
- 2 cups of Epsom salts
- 2 cups of baking soda
- 1 cup of citric acid
- 1 tablespoon of coconut oil
- 20 drops of lemon essential oil
- a yellow candle
- a gold cloth
- a large bowl and wooden spoon
- a few beautiful airtight jars

The Spell

You can take your bath at any time to enjoy the energy of this spell but it will have added power if you observe the timings suggested, when you will ensure maximum happiness power.

Lay out your gold cloth and place all your ingredients upon it. Light your yellow candle and say:

With golden glow and golden light,
Here grows happiness and joyful delight.

With your wooden spoon, mix all of the ingredients together in your large bowl until roughly combined. As you do, repeat:

In mixes smiles, joy and delight,
  Love, laughter, happiness
  With radiant light.

Make sure in the last eight stirs you make the infinity sign as you turn the wooden spoon through the bowl. This will impart an infinite happiness blessing. Pot up the mix into your beautiful airtight jars. Use as needed. Half a cup is usually sufficient for a bath.

Alternate Flowers

There are no substitutions for Daisies for this particular spell.

'Daisy' comes from the old English term 'Day's Eye', referring to the way Daisies open with the rising sun and close when it sets.

Creating and wearing Daisy chains was seen as a way to protect you from being carried away by faeries.

Poppy Painful Memory Healing Spell

Poppies instil rest and peace while also connecting us with memories. They help us heal painful memories with their additional calming influences. Poppies also help us in our dream state; so if your memories are affecting your sleep, you may find this spell brings sweeter dreams. The addition of fresh rosemary will also assist with the cleansing of negative memories.

Timings: Waning Moon, Wednesday, Midday

Find and Gather

+ a bunch of Poppies (*Papaver*)
+ a length of orange ribbon
+ a large bowl
+ bubble wand or a wire coat hanger bent into a circle shape
+ a sprig of fresh rosemary/wooden spoon to stir

Flower Spells ✦ 33

To make the magickal Bubble Mix:

- ½ cup of dishwashing detergent
- ¼ cup of glycerin
- 1 cup of warm water

The Spell

Combine all the ingredients of the magickal Bubble Mix in the bowl and stir lightly with the sprig of rosemary/wooden spoon and say:

> *Memories which pain me,*
> *Swirl and away.*
> *With each drifting bubble,*
> *May they heal and fade today.*

With the orange ribbon, tie your poppies to a tree branch or in a high spot outside.

Dip your bubble wand or wire circle into the magickal Bubble Mix and blow bubbles around, through, over and under your Poppies. As you do, think of each memory and moment you want to ease as being inside the bubbles you are blowing. Capture them in a bubble and let them drift away.

The best way to release the Poppies you have used is to cast them upon moving water (the sea, a stream, river or creek). You can bottle your magickal Bubble Mix to use again.

Alternate Flowers

Zephyr Lily (*Zephyranthes*), Cherokee Rose (*Rosa laevigata*)

In the folklore of many cultures, it is believed that if one stares into the centre of a Poppy before bedtime a deep, peaceful sleep is assured.

It was the Battle of Waterloo, and the subsequent blooming of Poppies after the fighting, which began the belief that Poppies sprung from the blood of the fallen, as a token of remembrance.

Daffodil Hope Renewal Spell

Not only do Daffodils express hope for the future, they are also bringers of sunshine, inspiration, renewal and vitality. If you like, you can add crystals and items that have similar energies to this mist mixture. This is a very good spell to experiment with when writing your own spells. Find flowers that hold energies, via their meanings, that you wish to bring into your life and tailor the chants to suit. When the mist runs out, cast the spell again.

Timings: Waxing Moon, Sunday, Morning

Find and Gather

- 3 Daffodil flowers (*Narcissus pseudonarcissus*)
- a clear glass or crystal bowl (*it is preferable to obtain a bowl you will use only for making the essences*)
- 1 cup of pure water
- misting bottle
- a purple cloth

The Spell

Find a place, preferably outside, where you can leave your essence for an hour in the sunlight. Lay your purple cloth neatly and place your clear glass/crystal bowl upon it. Slowly pour your pure water into it and say:

Sparkle water,
Dance in the sun.
Take in the joy,
a new day begun.

Put your flowers into the water one by one. The flowers only need to have parts of their petals touching or in the water – they do not need to be fully immersed. As you place each flower into the water say each time:

I welcome sunshine.
I welcome happiness.
I embrace hope.

Flower Spells

Leave your essence water and flowers in the sunlight for an hour and then strain into your misting bottle. Use each morning in the air of your space (home/work) and repeat the above chant each time. The flowers should be buried in a spot that always has sunshine upon it.

Alternate Flowers

German Iris (*Iris germanica*), Petunia (*Petunia*)

In Wales, it is said that the person who finds the first Daffodil blossom in Spring will have 'more gold than silver over the next year'.

Never display a single Daffodil in your home. Whether it is a fresh flower or an image, ensure it is a bunch. It is very bad luck otherwise.

White Lily and Rose Truth Spell

If you are trying to cut through deception or hazy information and find the truth, then the pure White Lily and Rose will assist you. Both of these flowers are not only vessels of truth but they are also protective flowers that can help you on your quest.

Timings: New Moon, Wednesday, Night

Find and Gather

- 1 White Lily (*Lilium*)
- 1 White Rose (*Rosa*)
- white ribbon – about 60 cm/24" in length
- white sheet of paper – ensure it is completely clean, unmarked and without creases

The Spell

Snip the stems of both flowers so they are about 5 cm/2" long.

Lay the flowers next to each other – you can pop the Rose into the Lily if it is small enough and bind together by winding the white ribbon around the stems of the flowers. Tie three knots on top of each other at the end of the stems so you form almost a thick ball.

Hold this ribbon ball loosely between the thumb and forefinger of your dominant hand above the white paper.

Ask questions that you already know the answers to and have firm yes or no answers. For example, you can ask: 'Is my car blue?' or 'Is my dog's name Sundar?' or 'Do I have nine children?' Ask lots of questions and take close note of what happens to your Flower Pendulum. How does it move in relation to the answer? You should come to see that a 'no' answer will give you a different movement to a 'yes' answer. It could be a rocking movement in a certain direction or a circle in one direction or another.

Once you have deciphered how your flowers will answer, settle yourself by clearing your mind and grounding yourself again. Ask your Flower Pendulum to stop before you begin by saying:

Rest and be still.

You may like to say 'stop' as is popular with many who use pendulums.

After you obtain your answers, tie the Flower Pendulum to a tree branch and say:

Thank you for the truth.
I now set you free.

Alternate Flowers

It really is preferable that you do not substitute flowers in this spell. If you cannot obtain one of the flowers, then use two of the type you do have.

St Thomas did not believe that the Virgin Mary had ascended after her death so he ordered her tomb be opened. All that was within were Lilies and Roses, which has led to their connection, to this day, with her image in artworks.

Carrying fresh Lilies will ensure that any love spell cast upon you will be broken. This probably led to their popularity in bridal bouquets.

Frangipani Self-Confidence Spell

Using Frangipani in this spell will not only increase your self-confidence but will give you freedom to happily be your true self. Use the timings below in the creation of your Flower Spell Box as this will empower it. You can open it any time you need a boost in self-confidence.

Timings: Waxing Moon, Sunday, Midday

Find and Gather

+ a Frangipani (*Plumeria alba*)
+ a plain small wooden box with a lid
+ white fabric bag or cloth to place box in
+ a piece of rose quartz
+ a photo of yourself

The Spell

First dry your flower completely using one of the methods described on page 15.

Place your flower, rose quartz and photo into your box and say:

In you go, one by one.
Mix together.
You have work to do.

Close the box lid and say:

Magickal box,
Confidence build.
Each time you open, my spell will fulfil.

Put your Flower Spell Box in the white fabric bag/cloth and find a dark, quiet place to keep it.

When you would like the magick of your spell to assist in boosting your self-confidence, simply open the Flower Spell Box and say:

Magickal box,
Confidence build.
Now you are open, my spell will fulfil.

You can use this Flower Spell Box forever, but if you feel at any time that it is no longer working for you, bury it and create another.

Alternate Flowers

Yellow Hibiscus (*Hibiscus*), Poet's Narcissus (*Narcissus poeticus*)

It is believed in many cultures throughout Asia that Frangipani trees are home to ghosts. In Malaysia, the scent is said to accompany the appearance of the Pontianak - a female vampire.

To the Mayan Lacandon people, the gods were born from Frangipani flowers.

Hyacinth Tension-Relief Spell

Hyacinth flowers are all about playfulness, letting things go, games, sport and generally being free. In this spell we are getting a little arty/crafty, in order to connect with the energy of your flower and capture it in a gorgeous little charm bag to carry with you. If you have glitter pens, scented markers and the like, then use them – Hyacinths really do love a bit of fun. This spell is especially helpful for days when you feel general tension but can also be used when you know you are going into a high-stress situation.

Timings: Waning Moon, Friday, Evening

Find and Gather

- 1 Hyacinth (*Hyacinthus*)
- a vase
- a beautiful tiny bag
- a piece of paper to draw on
- a pencil
- colouring pens or pencils
- music that makes you happy

The Spell

Set your fresh Hyacinth before you in the vase.

Play your music – anything that makes you feel happy and carefree. Make sure it stays on for the entire spell. You might like to either put a song on a loop or play a selection of music.

Take out your paper and pens/pencils and draw your Hyacinth flower. Have fun and do not worry about the end result. In fact, the more loose, crazy, colourful and fun you can make your picture, the better. Do not judge what you are doing – just relax, scribble, doodle and get lost in creating, colouring and releasing lines on paper while your music plays.

Once you are finished and when your artwork is dry (if you used paint), hold it up to your Hyacinth flower and say:

Hop into my picture, sweet flower,
Now come dance around.
Please leave playfulness, tension release,
and your own magick sound.

Fold the artwork three times and place it into your beautiful little bag. Carry it with you to offer relief and protection in tense times. When needed, close your eyes and place the bag next to your ear for a few moments. Once your Hyacinth has spent, bury it in a cool dark place in the garden/Nature.

Alternate Flowers

Ginger (*Zingiber officinale*), German Chamomile (*Matricaria chamomilla*)

A growing Hyacinth in a pot or bulb vase will ease nightmares. The perfume will work to dissipate negative feelings.

Hyacinths are said to have made their way to Holland via a shipwreck off the coast of the Netherlands in the 18th century. Locals planted the expensive bulbs, which had originally been bound for medicinal use in European cities.

Gerbera Daisy Blues-Busting Spell

Feeling low? Especially if you cannot put your finger on exactly what is causing you to feel negative vibes, this spell with the inclusion of Gerberas will not only bring a burst of positivity, the onion will absorb negativity.

Timings: Waning Moon, Sunday, Midnight

Find and Gather

- 8 Gerbera Daisies (*Gerbera jamesonii*)
- an onion
- rubber gloves
- a knife
- a clear bowl of pure water
- 4 small vases

The Spell

Cut your onion into quarters, leaving the skin on, and place one quarter in each corner of your bedroom. Carefully lay a Gerbera Daisy in front of each onion quarter, with the stem close but not touching the onion and with the flower pointing towards the centre of the room. Leave overnight.

The Gerbera Daisies will attract all the negativity to the onion, where it will be absorbed.

Next morning collect all the onion quarters while wearing the rubber gloves – you do not wish to absorb back any energy yourself. Chop up the onion and bury in your garden/Nature in a sun-filled area.

Collect the Gerberas, still wearing the gloves, and immerse in the bowl of pure water. Leave in the sunlight for an hour and then, thanking them for their work, bury them in another sun-filled area away from the onion.

The next night, place each of the remaining Gerbera Daisies in a separate, small vase, and place in the areas you had the onion quarters the night before.

Leave them there until they are spent. They will emit all of their positive vibes into your space until they are spent. Once spent, bury in another sun-filled area of your garden/Nature.

Alternate Flowers

Buttercup (*Ranunculus acris*), Shasta Daisy (*Leucanthemum maximum*)

Gerbera Daisies originate from Transvaal, South Africa, near Barberton. They are mostly known in that country as Transvaal Daisies or Barberton Daisies.

Gerbera Daisies are now the fifth most popular cut flower in the world after Roses, Carnations, Chrysanthemums and Tulips.

Wild Rose and Geranium Stop Gossip Spell

Wild Rose makes up an important part of this spell because it is one of the great flowers of truth. It helps uncover the truth as well as any betrayal that has occurred. It also opens a new path for you to move on. Geranium is included in this spell because it offers comfort and helps you rise in elegance and grace above any gossip about you.

Timings: Waning Moon, Saturday, Dusk

Find and Gather

- 1 Wild Rose (*Rosa acicularis*)
- 1 Geranium (*Geranium*)
- 11 drops of rose geranium essential oil
- 1 cup of sea salt
- approximately ½ cup of sweet almond oil
- an airtight glass jar

The Spell

Use the timings above to create your spell, but you can use your magickal salt scrub ingredients (*above*) at any time.

Dry a handful of each flower using the methods shared on page 15.

Add the salt and flowers to the jar and stir well.

Pour the sweet almond oil into the jar in small amounts and mix as you go. Stop when you achieve the consistency you desire. You may like a wetter or drier mix and so may use more or less of the oil.

Add the rose geranium essential oil and stir through your mix.

When required: Before use, stir your mix with a wood spoon so the consistency is even.

You can either add a handful to a warm bath and soak, or use as a scrub in the shower.

If you are worried about gossip, then a warm bath is better as it will envelope you in a protective veil. However, if you are aware of particular gossip, then visualise it bouncing off you and disappearing down the drain while you use your scrub.

Alternate Flowers

Any type of Rose or Geranium can be used in this spell.

Faeries can become invisible by eating a Wild Rose hip and then turning counterclockwise three times. By eating another and turning clockwise, they become visible again.

Many Geraniums are beautifully scented. Layer sugar with the leaves in airtight jars for a few weeks. Discard the leaves and you will be left with delightfully scented sugar to use in drinks, teas and cooking.

Iris and Passion Flower Inspiration Spell

The Iris in this spell not only connects you with inspirational energies, it will strengthen faith and clear away negative feelings. Passion Flower holds exactly what its name suggests – passion! The flower also offers pathways to your higher consciousness that could assist you in seeking new inspiration.

Timings: Full Moon, Wednesday, Dusk

Find and Gather

- 1 Iris flower (*Iris versicolor*)
- 1 Passion Flower flower (*Passiflora incarnata*)
- a stone
- a clear glass/crystal bowl
- pure water

The Spell

Go for a walk in Nature – a park, a garden, the beach – on the day of a Full Moon, and wait until a smooth stone, which you know you can easily carry in your pocket or bag with you anywhere, appears in your path. Take the stone to running water. This could be the sea, a river or creek. Hold the stone under the water to cleanse it. The running water will release any negative emotions that can block inspiration. Pour your pure water in the clear glass/crystal bowl and then add your Iris and say:

And you are for inspiration,
The thoughts which excite,

Add your Passion Flower and say:

And you are for passion,
The fire that creates.

Add your stone and say:

Inspiration and passion,
A new touchstone fashioned.

Take out your stone, gently dry and leave it out in the moonlight for the evening.

In the morning, your Inspiration Touchstone will be ready for you. Take it with you whenever you wish and hold it and rub it between your fingers when you are seeking inspiration. Repeating the above spell can recharge your Touchstone if needed. Cast spent flowers upon running water.

Alternate Flowers

For either flower: Daffodil (*Narcissus pseudonarcissus*), Bee Orchid (*Ophrys apifera*), Red Tulip (*Tulipa*)

Iris flowers are named after the goddess Iris, of the rainbow. Her role was to guide women to the Elysian Fields and this is why planting Irises on women's graves has been popular throughout history.

Growing Passion Flower at the entrance to your house will ensure no harm enters.

Camellia and Freesia Calm Spell

You can use this spell at any time to bring calm to you or into a space. It is a very good spell to use after times of stress. Create it using the timings below, bottle it up and keep in your apothecary. Soft, blousy Camellias lend their calmness and promise of peace, while Freesia assures trust while showing you inner guidance so that you may feel more hopeful and balanced. Use a leaf to sprinkle the water to emulate the gentleness of calming rain. Collect your rainwater, preferably during a Full or Waning Moon. If you don't have any rainwater, use the purest water you can find.

Timings: Full Moon, Friday, Midnight

Find and Gather

- 3 Camellia flowers (*Camellia japonica*)
- 3 Freesia flowers (*Freesia*)
- a clear glass/crystal bowl
- rainwater
- a large leaf

The Spell

Half fill your glass/crystal bowl with rainwater.
    Place your Camellias in your bowl, one by one, and with each say:
        Calm and calmer.
    Now place each of your Freesias in your water and say:
        Balance and balanced.
    You can use this mixture straight away or bottle with 1/5 glycerin to preserve for use at any time. Spent flowers should be buried in a dark part of the garden/Nature.

To use, pour a little mixture into a clear glass bowl and dip a fresh leaf into it. Walk around the area you wish to bring calm to, and gently flick the leaf to sprinkle a tiny amount of the mixture into the air. You can also do this around yourself or another person for the same effect.

Alternate Flowers

Camellia » Flannel Flower (*Actinotus helianthi*), Rose Geranium (*Pelargonium graveolens*)

Freesia » Jasmine (*Jasminum officinale*), Daffodil (*Narcissus pseudonarcissus*)

Camellias can also attract money. Place with another plant near the entrance of your home or in a fresh bowl inside.

Freesias are the flower for seventh wedding anniversaries. With their energy of trust, hope and balance, they may be just the thing for avoiding the seven-year itch.

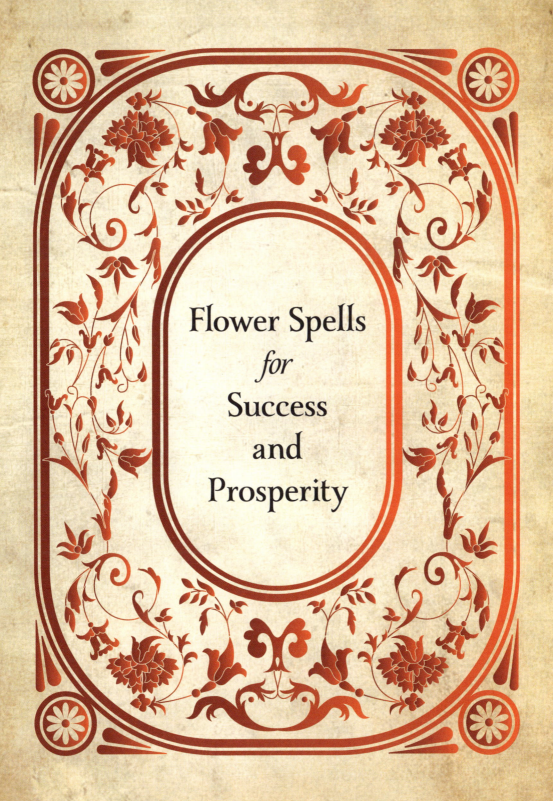

Flower Spells *for* Success and Prosperity

Nasturtium Goal-Setting Spell

This spell will help you set and strengthen new goals to ensure the maximum chances of success. If your belief in your ability to attain your goals is strong from the beginning, then you are more likely to stick with what is needed to succeed.

Timings: Waxing Moon, Thursday, Sunrise

Find and Gather

- a plant pot and potting mix (*or a place to plant in the garden*)
- a green candle in a holder
- Nasturtium (*Tropaeolum majus*) seedling or seeds
- white paper
- a green pen

The Spell

Using your preferred method, create protection for the space where you are planting your flower – the pot or area where your plant will reside.

Write your goal on the piece of paper and read out loud three times, then bury it in the soil, in the same place where you will plant your seed/s or plant.

Plant your seed/s or plant and, as you do, recite the following, three times:

Flower, hear my goals and grow.
Take them with you as you go.

Water your plant seed/s and then release energy, by clapping your hands three times and acknowledging that the spell is done. Ground yourself by placing your hands on the earth.

If possible, let the green candle burn down outside. Make sure you attend it at all times. If you cannot stay with it, bury it next to your plant or seed/s.

Make sure you look after your plant to encourage the success of your goals.

Alternate Flowers

Buttercup (*Ranunculus acris*), Pink Heath (*Epacris impressa*), Amaryllis (*Amaryllis*)

48 ♦ Earth Magick

Nasturtiums are edible. The leaves and flowers have a pepper-like flavour and can be used in salads and sandwiches as well as a flavouring for oils, dressings and butters. The immature seeds can be pickled and used in place of capers.

Common Nasturtiums are native to Peru. Their botanical name, 'Tropaeolum', comes from the Latin for 'shield', referring to the shape of their leaves.

Delphinium Make-Things-Happen Spell

Please note that all Delphiniums are poisonous to humans and animals. The ability of these flowers to make things possible, however, makes them a powerful ally in this spell. But you are advised to carefully use and release. You may wish to use gloves to handle these flowers as some people experience mild skin irritations.

For the 'bunch of flowers' used in this spell, go out and pick or purchase a bunch of flowers that you feel drawn to. You will be using their petals to make a mandala, so be mindful of their suitability for this task.

Timings: Waxing Moon, Tuesday, Daytime

Find and Gather

- a bunch of Delphinium flowers (*Delphinium*)
- another bunch of flowers that you are drawn to
- a picture or an object that describes what it is you wish to make happen
- a large purple cloth
- a smaller gold cloth
- 12 sunflower seeds
- 4 golden candles

The Spell

Lay your purple cloth out and place your smaller gold one upon it.

Place your golden candles in each corner of the gold cloth (North, South, East and West) and place three sunflower seeds in front of each candle. Place the picture or object that best describes what it is you wish to happen in the centre of the gold cloth. Arrange the Delphinium flowers closely on or around the picture or object.

Separate the petals of the flowers that you have collected and create a mandala around your Delphiniums and treasures. To do this, simply work in growing circles around your centre collection. Although you can be as creative as you wish, the energy to make this spell work comes from your focused concentration on the things you wish to happen, not on your artistic abilities. Once you are finished (take as long as you like), light your candles and say:

Circle of petals,
Dance into life.
These treasures you hold
With Delphinium tonight.

Let your candles burn down safely and leave your mandala for a day and night before putting away. Bury the flowers and petals under a tree you really love, with a small token that represents your desires. Plant the sunflower seeds.

Alternate Flowers

Delphinium » Hippeastrum (*Hippeastrum*), Crowea (*Crowea exalata*)

In many countries Delphinium are also know as Larkspur. This is because one of the petals of its flower points backwards like a spur.

Delphinium was used by Ancient Greek soldiers to help control body lice.

African Violet Study and Exam Spell

Although African Violets are traditionally connected with spiritual learning, they are also very helpful if you are studying – especially at exam time. African Violets also offer personal protection at these times so you are able to do your best work free from additional challenges. If you can, choose a yellow pot to plant your flower. Yellow is the colour of learning, intellect, memory and mental clarity. If you cannot find a yellow pot try painting one or tie a yellow ribbon around your pot. If you cannot find individual fluorite crystal beads, you can use a ready-made bracelet. Simply take the bracelet apart and then restring as the spell instructs.

50   ✦   Earth Magick

Timings: Waxing Moon, Wednesday, Morning

Find and Gather

- 1 African Violet plant (*Saintpaulia*)
- a yellow plant pot
- appropriate potting mix
- a collection of fluorite crystal beads, enough to circle your wrist
- beading elastic

The Spell

Make sure your plant is healthy. It does not need to be in flower, however – the energy of the flowers is always right through the plants they spring from.

Plant your African Violet into your yellow pot. As you complete the task say:

Wise violet sit with me,
From this day on.
Enhance my study and knowledge
So my mind remains strong.

'Plant' your fluorite beads around your African Violet. Count them and do not bury so deep that they are difficult to retrieve. Leave them overnight and 'harvest' the next morning.

Rinse the fluorite beads under running water and thread onto your beading elastic. I would suggest you thread onto two strands to ensure added strength. Wear when you are studying and when undertaking exams.

To recharge at any time, place on the soil next to the African Violet.

Alternate Flowers

There are no substitutes for this spell.

African Violet plants enhance spirituality while offering protection within a home.

New plants can be grown from a leaf of an African Violet plant. One 'mother' leaf will grow approximately 6-16 'babies'. Once the tiny plants have an established root system, you can repot.

Stargazer Lily Business Protection and Success Spell

This flower will open up new opportunities, invite abundance and prosperity and support ambition. Florida Water is a cologne made from flowers and herbs. It is traditionally used to magickally cleanse and protect either a person or space. For many communities, especially those connected with the practice of Vodou, it is a powerful spiritual protector and cleanser.

Do not drink this water – it is to be sprayed lightly as a personal fragrance, added to a bath or sprinkled around your place of business.

Timings: Waxing Moon, Thursday, Daytime

Find and Gather

- small handful of Pink Stargazer Lily petals (*Lilium orientalis*) dried as per instructions on page 15.
- 2 cups of vodka
- 2 tablespoons of orange-flower water
- 2 drops of jasmine essential oil
- 16 drops of bergamot essential oil
- 12 drops of lavender essential oil
- 3 drops of lemon essential oil
- 2 drops of rose attar essential oil
- a gorgeous bottle

The Spell

Make sure you use the timings to create your Business Protection and Success. Water to add a bigger boost when you are finding times particularly challenging.

Mix all ingredients together and bottle.

Sprinkle in the area where you work – such as your office – or dab a little on yourself. Use as needed to provide protection and to ensure success for your business endeavours.

You may find it useful to use the water at the beginning of your working week and again at times when you are attending important meetings, undertaking decision-making and working on anything especially challenging.

Before using as a fragrance on your skin, do a small patch test on your inner arm first and monitor for 24 hours.

Adding to a spray bottle can also make it easier to use.

Alternate Flowers

Stargazer Lily is the very best flower to use for this particular spell. If you really need to substitute, try Peruvian Lily (*Alstroemeria*).

Stargazer Lilies were bred by Leslie Woodriff, in California in 1974. He called the new cross 'Stargazer' because the blooms faced towards the sky.

Although many people adore the fragrance of Stargazer Lilies, a percentage find the scent completely repulsive.

Carnation Decision-Maker Spell

Carnations cannot make a decision for you but they can help by offering clarity to assist you find ways to progress, achieve positive outcomes and also support your life-force while doing so. By creating a spell bottle, you are emulating the cloudiness you may feel with your decision-making. The cloudiness when the bottle is shaken will be like all the pieces mixed up in your own personal puzzle. Watching the contents naturally settle will help you to become similarly aligned and see a balanced picture. This will help you to make your decision.

You can obtain tiny corked bottles easily from craft stores and online. Some come with pendant fittings already attached should you wish to wear your bottle.

Timings: Waxing Moon, Wednesday, Dusk

Find and Gather

+ ½ cup of dried Red Carnation petals (*Dianthus caryophyllus*)
+ 2 tablespoons of rose water

Flower Spells ✦ 53

- a piece of jade stone
- a beautiful clear bottle and seal
- water

The Spell

Divide the dried Red Carnation petals into two piles and set before your bottle.

Pick a few petals from each the pile – one for each hand. At the same time, say:

One hand for this way,
The other for that.

Add them to your bottle and say:

Together please help me
So I see where I'm at.

Add your rose water and say:

With love to guide me

Add your jade stone and say:

And clear sight ahead.

Seal your bottle and whenever you are seeking clarity to make a decision, simply shake your bottle and sit quietly and watch the contents completely settle. You should receive thoughts that will help you, or at least calm you, and clear your vision, to move forward.

Alternate Flowers

There are no alternatives for this spell.

Spell bottles are also known as witch bottles and have been in use since at least the early 17th century in the UK and USA.

The name 'Carnation' is thought to come from the word 'coronation' as the flowers were used as ceremonial headdresses in Ancient Greece.

Dandelion Wishing Spell

Dandelion flowers are the yellow tufted daisy-like blossoms that precede the dainty seed balls that we usually pluck from our lawns to make a wish. Dandelions have many health benefits and their use as such has been recorded since at least Ancient Persia. In this spell, we are connecting with the Dandelions' additional energies and reputation to make wishes come true. I would suggest you find a lovely vintage or new teapot and cup that you can use solely for this spell. Energetically cleanse it using one of the methods on pages 8–9 and empower it by leaving it filled with water under a Full Moon for a night.

Timings: Waxing Moon, Thursday, Daytime

Find and Gather

- 11 organic Dandelion flowers (*Taraxacum officinale*), fresh or dried
- boiling water
- honey (*optional*)
- lemon juice (*optional*)
- a beautiful teapot and cup

The Spell

Place your Dandelion flowers into your teapot and say:

> *Flowers of wishes,*
> *Flowers of light,*
> *Into the pot*
> *May my wishes be right.*

Pour in the boiling water and say:

> *Dance in the water,*
> *Dance with delight.*
> *The person who drinks you*
> *Has wishes in sight.*

Turn the teapot three times clockwise while saying your wish out loud and then pour your cup of tea and say:

Dandelion

Flower Spells ✦ 55

Now that I drink you,
My wishes come true.
Thank you sweet flower,
For all that you do.

Alternate Flowers

There are no alternatives for this spell.

Blowing the seeds from a Dandelion and making a wish is a long-lived English folk practice. Blowing the Dandelion helps the faeries to spread the seeds and, in doing so, granting our wish to us.

Dandelion root can be ground and used as a healthy substitute for coffee. This hot brew is also said to increase your psychic powers.

Water Lily Psychic Ability Spell

You will not necessarily need a fresh Water Lily for this spell – you can use one in dried form. With roots in the earth, stems and leaves weaving through the water, this flower sits aloft in the air under the gaze of the sun, connecting all elements – above to below – and everything between the worlds.

Water Lily reminds us that all is connected, no matter where we find ourselves or in what state. Use this spell at each New Moon to increase your psychic abilities. While you are using the spell for this purpose, you may receive messages.

Timings: New Moon, Monday, Late Night

Find and Gather

- 1 Water Lily (*Nymphaeaceae*) or a handful of dried Water Lily petals
- a beautiful purple cloth
- a deep, large bowl
- pure water
- a green candle
- a blue candle
- a red candle

- a yellow candle
- a pen and journal

The Spell

Place your purple cloth on a surface (such as a table). This represents 'spirit'. Rest your bowl on your cloth and half fill with water.

Place each of your candles around the bowl according to your hemisphere. The usual placement is: Earth – North (green), Fire – South (red), Air – East (yellow), Water – West (blue). You may like to reverse to suit the Southern Hemisphere or your geographic location, to correspond with the geography of the land. Light your candles. Float your Water Lily or cast your dried petals upon the water and say:

Above and below, from the East and the West,
Flower of all now come to rest.
Flower divine, from below to above,
Help me to see with truth and with love.

Ideally, you should stay with your spell until all candles burn down. Take notes of patterns, thoughts, visions and feelings. Once the candles have burned down, discard all spell items by burying them in a part of your garden in the direction of the next Full Moon.

Alternate Flowers

There are no alternative flowers for this spell.

The name of the plant genus 'Nymphaea' contains the word 'nymph', which describes those elemental beings who inhabit waterways.

The perfume of Water Lilies is said to be restorative and healing.

Gladiolus Creativity Success Spell

Gladiolus support those who are looking for success, particularly in the creative arts. They really are the very best flower to give to those enjoying an opening night, a book launch or an exhibition opening, for example. These flowers encourage people to never give up on their dreams; they encourage a healthy ego and support creative growth.

Timings: Full Moon, Friday, Daytime

Find and Gather

- 1 stem of Gladiolus (*Gladiolus*)
- an example of your creative work (*a painting/drawing or photograph of you dancing or performing in a play, some music or a sheet of music to play, for example*)
- a teaspoon
- a small and very beautiful container
- a tiny, silk copper- or gold-coloured drawstring bag

The Spell

Select nine petals from your Gladiolus and dry them according to the instructions on page 15.

You must do this spell on a Full Moon for it to work.

Take your creative work and sit on the ground and work on it or interact with it for as long as you like – you could draw, paint, write, play music, dance or act out a scene, whatever it is that you wish to increase success in. Make sure that whatever you do is your true passion and that you are comfortable and can enjoy yourself.

Collect a teaspoon of the earth from where you were creating. Mix it with your dry Gladiolus petals and crumble together.

Place this earth in your small container and put the container in your small silk bag.

To use, take out of the silk bag and sprinkle the mix on the spot you are performing or creating in.

To attract the success to your home/office/studio, repeat the spell above but collect ½ cup of earth and dry 27 petals to make your mix. Sprinkle the mixture from the road to your front door and hang some in a tiny silk bag in the centre of your studio space or your bedroom.

Alternate Flowers

Fairy Iris (*Dietes grandiflora*), Wisteria (*Wisteria sinensis*)

A 'gladius' is a sword of Ancient Roman Legionnaires, while a shorter sword was a 'gladiolus' and the word 'Gladiator' describes those who lived by the sword.

Most parts of Gladiolus plants are poisonous but they have been used throughout time in medicine, especially the corms in the extraction of splinters, thorns and drawing out infection.

Scotch Thistle Flower Find-What-Is-Lost Spell

A Scotch Thistle flower holds the energy of integrity, truth and pride, and so is a powerful ally to assist in ensuring what is rightfully yours is returned to you. Be very careful that what it is that you have lost is yours – Scotch Thistle has a nasty sting for those working with the energy of retaliation or dishonesty. Sunflower seeds offer light and strength for your quest.

In this spell you will be placing beeswax under your pillow so I would suggest that you not only place it into the cloth listed but encase the entire spell in something else to protect your bed linen from any staining.

Timings: New Moon, Monday, Midnight

Find and Gather

+ Scotch Thistle flower (*Onopordum acanthium*)
+ 6 sunflower seeds
+ a sheet of beeswax
+ a scribing tool
+ a thick piece of purple fabric

Flower Spells ✦ 59

The Spell

On a sheet of beeswax draw/write about what it is that you have lost. Be as descriptive as possible.

Place your Scotch Thistle flower in the centre of your beeswax sheet and say:

Flower of truth,

help return what is mine.

Place each of your sunflower seeds around the Scotch Thistle and with each say:

Seeds of the sun,

Light the place (say what it is you are looking for) *resides.*

Roll the beeswax up and wrap it in the purple cloth. Place it under your pillow.

You should hopefully dream of where your object is or what has become of it, or it will be revealed to you during the day.

Alternate Flowers

Snapdragon (*Antirrhinum majus*), Iris (*Iris*)

The Thistle has been a popular heraldic symbol throughout history and was first documented used by King James III of Scotland (*1452-1488*).

A Thistle worn in any form, either fresh or in textile design or jewellery, has long been considered a powerful protective symbol.

Yellow Rose New-Beginning Spell

Rose petal beads are traditionally created from either funeral flowers and called 'Memorial Beads' or from bridal flowers and called 'Memory Beads'. In this spell, you will be creating Rose petal beads and instilling them with hope and positivity for a new beginning. Wearing them will remind you of commitments made as you move forward in life and they will be very helpful to counter any challenges you face along the way. Yellow

Roses welcome and support new beginnings, hold promises of returns and are particularly powerful in any spellwork involving friends.

Timings: Waxing Moon, Sunday, Midday

Find and Gather

+ 9 Yellow Roses (*Rosa*) - old-fashioned ones are preferable
+ 3 Red Roses (*Rosa*) - old-fashioned are preferable
+ pure water
+ rose essential oil
+ mortar and pestle
+ baking paper and tray
+ nails or pins the thickness you wish the bead holes to be
+ a piece of Styrofoam

The Spell

Pluck the petals from the Roses and with the mortar and pestle grind them until they are broken down as much as possible. Spread your crushed Roses out on baking paper on trays to dry for a day.

Once dried, return the petals to your mortar and pestle and grind again, but add a small amount of water to help form a paste. Ideally you will want to work the mix as much as possible in order to make most of the small pieces in your mix 'disappear' into the dough. Make sure you end up with thick dough. If the mix is too thin, it won't set easily.

Next you will roll the beads. The size of your beads is totally up to you. Coat your fingers in rose oil and roll the petal dough mixture into the size and shape you wish your beads to be, and as you do say:

Yellow Rose, light my way,
A new beginning, starts today.

Thread each bead onto a nail/pin and push into the Styrofoam. Place in a sunny position to dry completely. This can take a few days. Once fully dried, thread your bead onto beading thread, elastic or ribbon. You can wear the beaded necklace

Flower Spells ✦ 61

whenever you wish, or hang in your home above a doorway or window near the front entrance to your home.

Alternate Flowers

White Rose (*Rosa*), Yellow Chrysanthemum (*Chrysanthemum*)

Up until the 18th century, no one outside the Middle East had ever seen a Yellow Rose. The Yellow Rose caused much excitement in Europe at the time of its discovery.

If you want to ask someone to give you another chance, give them a bunch of Yellow Roses.

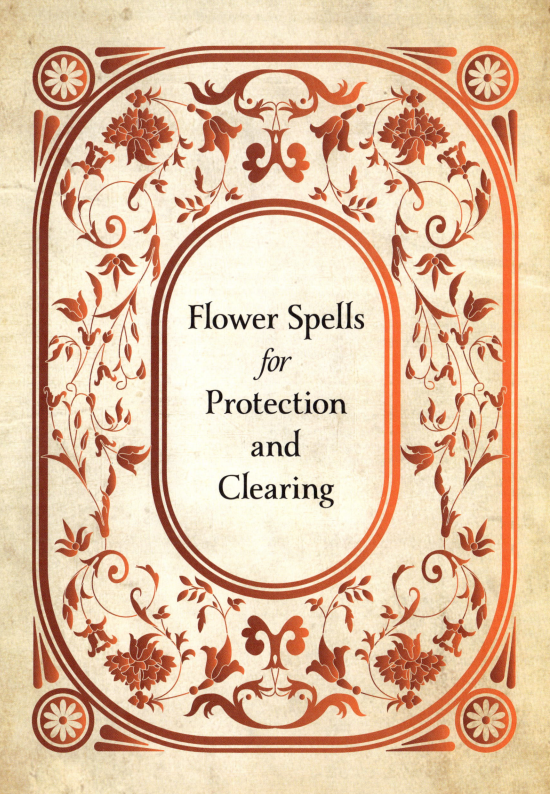

Flower Spells *for* Protection and Clearing

Triple Rose Smudging Spell

Smudge sticks work by collecting negativity in their smoke and whisking it away. While they do this, they leave behind their various properties depending on what they are made of. In this triple Rose flower smudge stick, I have used White Rose petals, because they offer protection and deep purification, and Pink Rose petals, which will lend a graceful energy to a space and help with healing. The addition of Rosemary also offers protection as well as lifting psychic awareness and clarity.

Timings: Waning Moon, Saturday, Midnight

Find and Gather

- Rosemary (*Rosemarinus officinalis*), preferably in flower
- 1 White Rose (*Rosa*)
- 1 Pink Rose (*Rosa*)
- cotton or hemp string

The Spell

Bunch together about 6–8 large fresh sprigs of Rosemary. Cut a piece of string at least four times the length of your bundle of Rosemary and tie your sprigs together very tightly at one end.

Loosen all the petals off both Roses.

As you wind your string in a spiral-type pattern to the end of the bundle of Rosemary, place your Rose petals under the string, against the Rosemary, to anchor them. You want to cover the Rosemary with the Rose petals, but they don't have to cover it completely.

Tie off at the end and cut off the string.

Tie the string again at the bottom and wind the string up the bundle, but this time crossing the previous string at an opposite angle. Again, lay the petals against the bundle and anchor with the string as you go. Make sure you end up with roughly an equal amount of pink and white petals on the bundle firmly held together in the string.

As you are anchoring the Rose petals say:

Triple Rose bundle, protection entwined,
Cleanse and release in the places you find.

Hang your smudge stick in a cool dry place to dry out completely. This could take up to two weeks. To use, carefully light and once it has 'caught', blow out to allow your smudge stick to smoulder. Use a large leaf to fan the smoke around the area you wish to cleanse and protect. Remember to start in the middle of your rooms and work your way out. Have windows and doors all open so that the smoke takes the negativity out with it.

Alternative Flowers

Any flowers that are safe to inhale when burning.

Many plants have the word 'officinalis' in their name, like the Rosemary suggested here. It means that the plant is an important herbal remedy.

To maintain youth, it has been suggested to bath daily in Rosemary water or sniff it daily.

Snapdragon Hex-Breaker Spell

This powerful hex-breaker relies on the energies of Snapdragon, a plant I grow and harvest every year in my own garden because it is the most reliable flower for such magick workings. Snapdragons break all types of hexes and curses and they do so gracefully and precisely.

You will be creating a small and very simple doll that is going to return the hex to the person who sent it to you.

Timings: Waning Moon, Wednesday, Midnight

Find and Gather

✦ a few tablespoons of dried Snapdragon flowers (*Antirrhinum majus*)
✦ 2 pieces of red fabric, 15 x 15 cm/6 x 6")
✦ sewing pins
✦ 2 tiny safety pins
✦ a needle

Flower Spells ✦ 65

- red thread
- scissors
- a black felt-tip pen
- a biro and paper
- a postage stamp

The Spell

Pin your fabric pieces together at their centre.

With the felt-tip pen, draw a simple person shape onto the fabric (around the pins). Cut out the shape of the person.

Sew the pieces together along the person shape, leaving a small opening at the top of the head. Fill the doll with Snapdragon flowers and say:

Snapping Dragons all, take this hex far away.
Break it in pieces and lose it today.

Sew up the opening.

With your biro write 'return to sender' on the piece of paper. Pin the paper to the front of the doll with one small safety pin. With the other safety pin add the postage stamp to the doll.

Take the doll to a place as far away from your home as possible and throw it in a bin.

Return home, but not directly. Take your time and take what you would think is a confusing route.

Alternate Flowers

There are no alternatives for this spell.

Need to quickly break a spell? Try stepping on a Snapdragon flower.

In Dutch folklore it is believed that if you want to make your love rivals disappear, then plant a large bed of Snapdragons.

Earth Magick

Lilac Space-Clearing Spell

Lilacs are the perfect flowers for a space-clearing spell because they help you remove energies you don't want. They will impart a new and positive vitality to a space and they will assist those connected with the space to move forward with safety, free from any hurtful or negative occurrences or feelings.

Timings: Waning Moon, Saturday, Midnight/Midday

Find and Gather

- Lilac flowers (*Syringa vulgaris*)
- a large white pillar candle
- an additional white taper candle
- a metal spoon
- wax paper

The Spell

Dry your flowers as flat as possible. Pressing would be best.

Lay out your wax paper to protect your work area. Light your taper candle and drip wax onto the side of your pillar candle. Now very quickly press your flowers into the melted wax on your pillar candle. Work in small areas, building up your design.

As you add each flower, say:

Lilac will call you and take you away.
Space to be cleared
When lit from this day.

Once you are happy with the result, drip more taper wax to cover your flowers to seal. You can use the metal spoon to gently spread and push down the wax.

When the wax is dry you can light the candle at any time in the area you wish to energetically clear.

Alternate Flowers

Lemon Blossom (*Citrus limon*)

Lilac's botanical name, 'Syringa', comes to us from the Greek word for 'pipe'. The stem of the flower looks like a pipe and there are references to Lilac being the plant that the 'Pipes of Pan' were formed from.

In Wales it is believed that if someone kills or pulls out an entire Lilac bush, the others in the area will not flower the following year in mourning for the lost plant.

Sweet Violet Deception Protection Spell

You will need to make very sure that the Violets you obtain for this spell are both organic and edible – some types are not. This is magickal cooking, so make sure your kitchen is clean and tidy and energetically clear. Also make sure you create with a magickal heart and mind on the task. These deception protection drops can be added to any drink, hot or cold, or as an additional garnish to foods as well.

Timings: Full Moon, Saturday, Late Night

Find and Gather

- 2 dozen organic, edible Sweet Violets (*Viola odorata*)
- 1 cup of regular sugar
- ½ cup of water
- ½ cup of castor sugar/super fine sugar
- baking paper
- flat baking tray
- tweezers
- flat bowl
- sweet/candy thermometer (*optional*)
- a small airtight container

The Spell

Place the regular sugar and water into a saucepan over a low heat and stir continuously until the liquid begins to boil. Cease stirring and wait until the mixture reaches

38°C/100°F or has become reduced to a clear syrup. You can use your thermometer to test the temperature.

Turn off the heat and let cool. Line your tray with the baking paper. Place your castor sugar in the bowl. Using your tweezers, dip each violet into the sugar syrup and then sprinkle castor sugar liberally over the flower. Shake off excess and place back on the baking tray.

After all are done, say:

Crystal sweet sugar,
From deception protect
Each lovely flower
As they magickally set.

Leave to dry for at least 24 hours and then store in a cool, dry place in an airtight container. Use these little flower drops in teas or other drinks when you want to protect yourself from deception.

Alternate Flowers

Other types of edible violets.

Violets were the favourite flower of Empress Josephine. Napoleon planted them on her grave. When he died he was found to have a locket containing a lock of Josephine's hair and a Violet.

In Ancient Greece people wore circlets of Violets to alleviate headaches and to induce a peaceful and deep sleep.

Red Clover Travel Protection Spell

This is, without fail, the very best travel-protection spell I have. Rinsing your hair in this special magick mixture will help to keep you safe on travels near and far. Red Clover is able to protect on a multitude of levels as well as bringing good luck. Rosemary is added for its powers to increase psychic awareness and White Rose petals provide protective energies as well as the ability to help people see the truth and remain honest.

Timings: Full Moon, Saturday, Daytime

Flower Spells ✦ 69

Find and Gather

- 1 cup of organic Red Clover flowers (*Trifolium pratense*)
- 1 cup of organic White Rose petals (*Rosa*)
- ¼ cup of organic fresh Rosemary (*Rosmarinus officinalis*) with flowers, if possible
- 2½ cups of water and a small pot
- ½ cup of apple cider vinegar
- ¼ cup of olive oil (*if you have dry hair*)
- a sterilised jar, to store

The Spell

Bring the water to a boil in the pot and then remove from the heat.

Gently stir in the Clover flowers, Rose petals and Rosemary and leave overnight.

Before you leave your brew say:

Sleep pretty flowers,
This night may your powers fill the water.

The next day, strain the mixture into the jar and add the apple cider vinegar and olive oil (if using).

Store in the fridge.

To use: Shake the bottle.

After washing your hair, massage 2 tablespoons of the travel-protection hair rinse through your hair and simply say:

Flower water, protect me wherever I wander.

You can wash the rinse out or leave it in. You can take the rinse with you on your travels – it will keep for a couple of weeks outside the fridge.

Alternate Flowers

Although there are many flowers that you could use to create a hair rinse, this particular magickal rinse works best with Red Clover flowers as the base.

Adding Red Clover to your bath the day before you need to attend to financial dealings and negotiations will help outcomes go your way.

Red Clover is one of the world's oldest crops and is used primarily as animal fodder. It was also the model for the suit of Clubs in playing cards.

Azalea and Chrysanthemum Personal Protection Spell

Azaleas can assist in self-care and help you stay true to yourself. Azaleas will make sure you do not let negative energies into your personal sphere. Yellow Chrysanthemums are excellent boundary protectors.

This spell is another type of spell bottle like the one described on page 53 in the Carnation Decision-Maker spell. You can obtain tiny corked bottles easily from craft stores and online. Some come with pendant fittings already attached should you wish to wear your bottle. Be aware that Azaleas are highly toxic if consumed.

Timings: Full Moon, Saturday, Dusk

Find and Gather

- a dark-coloured Azalea flower (*Rhododendron*)
- a Yellow Chrysanthemum (*Chrysanthemum*)
- a tiny glass corked bottle you can carry with you
- water
- glycerin
- sealing wax
- a piece of black flannel or thick soft cloth to wrap the bottle in
- a thin black ribbon

The Spell

Dry the Azalea and Chrysanthemum flowers using one of the methods on page 15. You will only need a petal from each for this spell.

Crush your petals and add to the glass bottle. Fill the bottle halfway at most and say:

Flower Spells ✦ 71

Flower of dark,
Flower of light,
Bind together now
and make all things right.

Add a few drops of glycerin and then fill the rest of the bottle with water.

Seal by adding the cork and dipping the entire top in sealing wax.

To store, wrap in the black cloth and tie the thin black ribbon around it.

Whenever you need added personal protection, carry your personal protection spell bottle with you. To keep it safe in a bag or pocket you can leave the cloth and ribbon on. When you need to add an extra boost to your personal space, shake the bottle and repeat the chant above.

Alternate Flowers

Azalea » Lily (*Lilium*)

Yellow Chrysanthemum (*Chrysanthemum*) » Red Clover (*Trifolium pratense*)

It is thought that if you wear Chrysanthemums you will be protected from the wrath of the gods.

Honey created from the nectar of Azaleas is known as 'mad honey' and usually causes confusion, vomiting, convulsions and, ultimately, death.

Cornflower Home Protection Spell

Cornflowers can provide a natural dye and we are going to use this attribute to create a little flag to hang at your front door to offer you protection. You may wish to make bunting or a larger flag. This mixture should dye up to about a shirt's worth of fabric. If you wish to dye more fabric, adjust the measurements accordingly.

Timings: Full Moon, Monday, Evening

Find and Gather

+ 2 cups of fresh, finely chopped Cornflowers (*Centaurea cyanus*)
+ a 30 x 30 cm/12 x 12" piece of natural fabric (*cotton, silk, linen*)

- 4 cups of cold water
- 1 cup of white vinegar
- a bowl for this purpose only
- a glass or stainless-steel pot for this purpose only
- 4 cups of room-temperature water
- protective covering for work areas (*plastic sheet is best*)
- gloves

The Spell

Before beginning to chop your Cornflowers, say:

Powerful flowers of protection and knowledge
I thank you for sharing your wisdom and care.

Wash the fabric, rinse very well and leave damp.

Mix together the cold water and vinegar in your bowl and add the fabric. Leave for an hour.

Add the Cornflowers to the stainless-steel pot and add the room-temperature water and then simmer for at least an hour until you obtain the colour you desire.

Put on your gloves. Strain the coloured water back into the bowl, discarding the flowers as you do so (bury in the garden near your front door). Be careful with straining as this mixture will dye anything it touches. You may wish to purchase a cheap strainer just for this purpose, or use a piece of cheesecloth.

Return the liquid to the pot. Put on the heat again and add the fabric. Simmer for another hour and turn off the heat. Leave the fabric in this mixture until it is the depth of colour you would like.

When happy, take out the cloth and rinse really well.

Cut into a flag shape, hem the edges, hang near your front door and say three times:

All within are safe,
Under the flag of Cornflower grace.

Alternate Flowers

There are no alternatives for this particular spell.

The botanical name of Cornflower is 'Centaurea' and refers to Chiron, the centaur who Achilles gained herbal medical skills from.

Cornflowers are also known as 'Bachelor's Buttons'. Men would wear them to indicate they were available and interested in courtship.

Lemon Blossom Freeze-and-Banish Spell

Lemon Blossom is a wonderful flower to call on when you need to remove something from your life. Not only are these flowers very good at clearing unwanted energies, they are wonderful deep space clearers and they banish negativity completely.

Timings: Waning Moon, Tuesday, Midnight

Find and Gather

- 3 Lemon Blossom flowers (*Citrus limon*)
- pure water
- a small plastic container
- a small piece of paper
- a pen

The Spell

Sit and write down on your paper the thing that you want removed from your life.

Fold the paper, place it in your plastic container and say:

In you go,
Your energy flows.

Place the three Lemon Blossom flowers on top of the paper and say:

One for cleansing,
Your light now fades.
One for closing,

74 ✦ Earth Magick

Your memory done.
One for leaving me,
Your power now gone.

Now pour the water to fill the container and place in the freezer. As you do, say:

Frozen you are,
No longer you move.
Be gone from my life,
And never return.

Alternate Flowers

Any Citrus blossom.

Lemon juice diluted in water is an excellent purifier of magickal tools. Be careful you only use a little as it does have bleaching properties. Eating lemons also increases your psychic and magickal powers.

We now know, thanks to DNA, that lemons are most likely to be a hybrid of Bitter Orange (*Citrus aurantium*) and Citron (*Citrus medica*).

Heather Danger-Shielding Spell

Heather flowers, both lavender-coloured and white, hold valuable properties that assist in the creation of this blessing water. You can use this water to cleanse magickal objects, and to impart protection blessing upon objects and also people.

White Heather can protect from danger and grant wishes, courage and faith.

Lavender Heather assists with the removal of negative energies, instils good luck and can also assist those seeking a peaceful sleep if suffering nightmares.

Timings: Full Moon, Sunday, Night

Find and Gather

+ a handful of White Heather (*Calluna vulgaris*)
+ a handful of Lavender Heather (*Calluna vulgaris*)

Flower Spells + 75

- a large pinch of salt
- 3 drops of rose essential oil
- a white candle
- 1 cup of pure water
- a glass/crystal bowl
- a glass misting bottle

The Spell

Make sure that you work under the light of the Moon.

Light your white candle.

Pour your pure water and rose essential oil into your bowl and say:

Water of crystal light,

May the light of candle and moon bless you.

Sprinkle the salt over the water and say:

Salt of the earth,

Balance and ground.

Add your Lavender Heather flowers and say:

Heather flowers,

Remove all the darkness you find.

Add your White Heather flowers and say:

Heather flowers,

Protect all the light you find.

Bottle your water in your misting bottle.

Blow out your candle and say:

I thank light for the blessings.

Alternate Flowers

Roses of different colours are suitable, White Rose (*Rosa*) in particular.

Heather stalks provide food for faeries. If you find a field of Heather, you may very well stumble upon a faerie portal to their world.

It is said in English folklore that you can make it rain by burning Heather and a Fern sprig together outdoors.

Lavender Ultimate Protection Spell

This spell is best used when you know exactly what you need protection from. You will need rather long stalks of Lavender in order to achieve a good result. French Lavender is best. Lavender also cleanses. The inherent qualities of grace and trust in Lavender also assist in strengthening your spell vessel, and the energies you weave into it. Make sure you are completely focused on this task.

Timings: Waning Moon, Saturday, Midday

Find and Gather

✦ 33 long stems of fresh Lavender (*Lavandula*)
✦ 200 cm/90" of lavender-coloured ribbon

The Spell

Carefully strip all the foliage from each stem of Lavender from below the flower head. You can do this by slowly pulling it off in a downward motion.

Hold the bunch together and tie one end of the ribbon firmly under the flowers to keep them together.

Turn the bunch upside down and then fold each stem back over the bunch of flowers.

Begin weaving the ribbon through the bent stems, up and over each stem to ensure a checkerboard pattern emerges. Keep your weaving firm so that you are enclosing the flowers within.

While you are weaving, say:

Over and under,
Above and below,
Weaving protection
Wherever I go.

Once you have woven enough to encase the flowers, keep going a little more to neaten up, pulling the weaving tight to completely enclose the flowers. Then tie off with a knot and bow at the top of the bundle around all of the stems.

Flower Spells ✦ 77

This spell vessel can be hung in an area you would like to protect, or shake it three times before you set out to do whatever it is that you are seeking additional protection for.

Alternate Flowers

There are no alternatives for this spell.

Lavender is thought to be a very attractive scent to men and so has a long history as an aphrodisiac. Cleopatra wore it as a perfume. Victorian woman bathed in Lavender water before meeting their love interests. and in England it was an extremely popular bed linen scent for centuries.

Carrying or wearing Lavender will avert the evil eye.

Flower Spells *for* Health and Healing

Peony Vitality and Good Health Spell

This spell involves creating a classic Pot Pourri using a traditional method. It is particularly good for times when you are seeking physical immunity or recuperating from illness. It does take about two months to create, so make it as flowers are in season and store for use throughout the year. Peony and Pink Roses are the main flowers in this Pot Pourri spell because of their strong healing powers. The addition of Marigold imparts strength and vitality.

Timings: Full Moon, Thursday, Midday

Find and Gather

- 1 cup of Peony petals (*Paeonia officinalis*)
- 3 cups of Pink Rose petals (*Rosa*)
- 1 cup of Marigold petals (*Tagetes evecta*)
- 1 cup of Rose leaves
- ¼ cup of orris root powder
- 3 drops of rose essential oil
- 3 drops of lemon oil
- 3 cups of cooking salt
- a large airtight container and lid
- a beautiful open bowl or container
- a pink cloth
- a peridot stone

The Spell

Mix all of your fresh flower petals and leaves together. Place a layer into your airtight container and then sprinkle with a layer of the salt.

Keep layering fresh flowers, leaves and salt until you use up all your flowers and leaves and finish off with a layer of salt. Seal and wrap the container in pink cloth and store in a cool, dry place for two weeks.

After two weeks, open and break up the hardened mixture and mix in the essential oils and orris root powder and the peridot. Place back into container, seal and wrap in pink cloth again and leave in a cool, dry place for six weeks.

To use, place into a beautiful bowl and leave in places near to you to impart the healing and strengthening energy of these flowers.

You can refresh the fragrance and boost the energy of the mix by adding a few drops of essential oils from time to time.

Alternate Flowers

Peony » a cup of Pink Rose petals (*Rosa*)
Marigold » Sunflower (*Helianthus annuus*)

Peony is named after Paeon, who studied the usage of plants for healing and who was a student of Aesculapius, the Greek god of medicine.

Peony roots were once carved to create 'piney beads'. These beads formed a necklace that would protect the wearer from faeries and evil.

Elderflower Rejuvenation Spell

This spell involves the creation of a rejuvenating beauty oil, which is not only beneficial for your skin but also boosts confidence, lifts negative attitudes, boosts self-esteem and helps promote vigour and resilience via the Elderflower.

Timings: Full Moon, Sunday, Morning

Find and Gather

- 1 cup of Elderflowers (*Sambucus nigra*)
- 1 cup of Chamomile flowers (*Matricaria recutita*)
- 1 cup of Rose petals (*Rosa*)
- ½ cup of almond oil
- ½ cup of apricot oil
- ½ cup of avocado oil
- ¼ cup of rosehip oil
- ¼ cup of olive oil
- 1 teaspoon of vitamin E oil
- muslin cloth

- ✦ large sealable glass jar
- ✦ sterilised jar/s to keep
- ✦ yellow cloth, large enough to wrap around your jar
- ✦ yellow ribbon, approximately 30 cm/12" in length
- ✦ rose essential oil

The Spell

Add the flowers and the oils (except the rose essential oil) to the large glass jar and say:

Flowers gather together and rest in the oil.

Now is your time to rest for a while.

Seal the jar and wrap in yellow cloth and keep in a warm place. Every morning for nine days knock on the jar gently and say:

Wake up, wake up now flowers and oil.

On the ninth day strain the oil through muslin cloth into sterilised jar/s to store. Add as much rose essential oil as you like to each mix. Go lightly at first – you can always add more at a later time. Tie the yellow ribbon around the neck of the jar. Store in the fridge and bury the strained flowers in a sunlit area. Do a patch test of the oil first by putting a small dab on your inner arm for 48 hours.

To experience the rejuvenating magick of this oil, each morning place a few dabs on your face and massage in. As you do, say:

Renewed and refreshed, in body and mind.

Alternate Flowers

Any flower that is safe for topical use can be substituted except the Elderflowers.

In Russian folklore, placing Elderflower branches around windows and doorways protects against vampires and the devil, who would be too busy counting the blossoms or berries.

82 ✦ Earth Magick

Sunflower Strength and Courage Spell

Bring the strength of sunshine in to help speed up recuperation. Marigold imparts vitality and vigour, and supports renewal as well as having strong connections with life-force energies. Sunflower is a physical healer and supports strength and courage.

Timings: Full Moon, Sunday, Midday

Find and Gather

+ a Sunflower (*Helianthus annuus*)
+ a few Marigolds (*Tagetes evecta*)
+ wax paper, 30 x 30 cm/12" x 12")
+ newspaper
+ washi or pretty masking tape
+ an electric iron
+ golden ribbon, long enough to hang your suncatcher with

The Spell

Pluck the petals from your flowers and dry thoroughly according to the directions on page 15. It would be preferable to use a method that presses them.

You can make these suncatchers in any size and use any number; in fact, a collection hanging in the window of someone facing health challenges would not only be helpful, but rather beautiful.

Cut your wax paper into two identical shapes. You may like to start with circles but any shape including diamonds, triangles, squares would be suitable.

Lay one piece of wax paper on some newspaper. Arrange your Sunflower and Marigold petals on the wax paper in patterns that please you. Recreating the symbol of the sun or a star is very helpful for this spell.

Lay the other piece of wax paper on top and lay a piece of newspaper over the lot.

Using your iron on a medium heat, press your creation carefully until the wax melts and fuses the wax papers together.

As you press, say:

Flowers of sun, may you shine health, courage and strength over all.

Flower Spells + 83

Finish off the edges with your washi/decorative tape or you may like to sew a decorative edge around your suncatcher. Hang in windows to catch the sunlight and empower the flowers within. Share with everyone who is near.

Alternate Flowers

There are no alternatives for this spell.

Sunflowers (*Helianthus annuus*) are native to the Americas, so most references to 'Sunflowers' throughout the rest of the world, in literature and folklore prior to external discovery of these countries, refer to Marigolds and other flowers which appear to track the sun. If you wish to know the truth about something, sleep with a single Sunflower seed under your bed. The truth will be revealed within a week.

Dahlia Detox Spell

These drops help those who are undergoing a detox or experiencing a withdrawal from something. The drops are created with the help of Dahlia flowers, which impart incredibly supportive energy: they boost inner strength and confidence and instil greater faith and resiliency while constantly being encouraging.

Timings: Waning Moon, Thursday, Midday

Find and Gather

- a Dahlia flower (*Dahlia*)
- pure water
- a glass/crystal bowl
- a glass storage bottle
- small dropper bottles (*optional*)

The Spell

You will be creating a flower essence in this spell, so you will need a sunny day with preferably an hour of clear sunlight.

Set your bowl up in the sunlight in a place where it will be safe.

84 ✦ Earth Magick

Pour your water into the bowl and say:

Pure water, ready to hold the energy of Dahlia.

Encouragement, confidence, vitality, inner strength, faith and resiliency keep.

Place your Dahlia flower upon the water and say:

Stay a while and leave behind,

The gifts I seek, flower beautiful and wise.

Sit with your flower spell for exactly an hour. Do not touch it or move it.

Relax and focus on your commitment to your detox. After the hour, remove the flower and thank it. Place it in the shade of a tree.

Pour the water into the storage bottle. You can also pour into smaller dropper bottles to carry around with you. The water will keep in the fridge for a month, but if you wish to extend its life and store it outside refrigeration add 1 part glycerin to 4 parts flower-essence water.

To use, add three drops to a glass of water three times a day and drink.

Alternate Flowers

Pink Carnation (*Dianthus caryophyllus*)

Dahlia, which originated in Mexico, was cultivated and prized by the Aztecs for its various medicinal properties.

Empress Josephine adored Dahlias and had an impressive collection in her gardens. She loved to think she was the only person in Europe to grow them, so when some were stolen she had the rest destroyed. Being tubers, however, they grew back.

Hibiscus Stress Release Spell

This spell creates a beautiful, calming magickal lip balm, which not only ensures calmness and stress relief, but will give you lovely soft lips. By using as a lip balm, what you say and do as you go about your day will not be tainted with any stress you have had to endure.

Hibiscus is used as the primary flower in this spell due to its ability to connect us to happiness and instil a stronger belief in our abilities.

Flower Spells   ✦   85

Timings: Waning Moon, Saturday, Midday

Find and Gather

- ½ cup of organic Hibiscus petals (*Hibiscus*)
- 3 drops of lavender essential oil
- 1 cup of organic olive oil
- 2 tablespoons of vitamin E oil
- 1 tablespoon of honey
- 40 gm/1.5 oz beeswax
- small, sterilised containers to keep lip balm in

The Spell

Over a low heat, slowly warm the Hibiscus flower petals in the oil for 30 minutes and say:

> *Hibiscus lovely,*
> *happy and true,*
> *When next I wear*
> *Let me be more like you.*

Strain oil, discard petals by burying in garden and then return oil to very low heat. Stir in vitamin E oil, honey and beeswax and keep stirring until beeswax has melted. Remove from heat and beat until mixture is smooth.

As you are whipping your lip balm, say:

> *Air take all thoughts,*
> *Tainted, tangled and heavy.*

Pour into containers and allow to cool before use.

Alternate Flowers

Pink or White Roses (*Rosa*)

In many nations the Hibiscus is known as the Queen of the Tropics as well as a symbol of happiness and peace.

A popular thirst-quenching herbal iced tea known as 'karkade' is created from Red Hibiscus, in North Africa. Thought to be an aphrodisiac, women are often prohibited from drinking it.

86 ✦ Earth Magick

Moonflower Stop Nightmares Spell

This is not the easiest flower to obtain, but because this spell uses the imagery of Moonflower an image on an oracle card, artwork or photo which you are really drawn to will do.

There are many plants that share the common name of Moonflower, but all look over the dream state and ensure peaceful dreams as well as increasing power over negative dreams.

Timings: Waning Moon, Saturday, Evening

Find and Gather

- 1 Moonflower (*Ipomoea alba*) or an image of one
- a small easel or frame
- pens/pencils
- sketch pad
- silver paint
- small paintbrush
- 2 blue candles
- 2 candleholders
- a white cloth
- a candlesnuffer

The Spell

Lay out your white cloth on your nightstand or a surface close to your bed. Place your candles in candleholders on either side of the cloth. Place your Moonflower/oracle card or image in frame or on easel between the two candles.

Light the candles and say:

Light fills the dark,
With your brilliant clean spark.
Moonflower of power
Hold the light with your flower.

Sit before your Moonflower or Moonflower image and draw your flower. This is not an art test and the artistic merit is not important at all; in fact, it will be more powerful if you draw your flower without looking at the paper. Gaze at the

Moonflower and focus on its line and shape. When you have finished, take the silver paint and paintbrush and lightly colour your creation. When completed, say:

Silver healing light, take hold of my flower.
Bring healing light while shielding my dreams from negativity.

Place your picture in place of the Moonflower or oracle card/image and snuff the candles out.

Leave your image and spell for a few nights. Relight the candles for a while each night until they have burned down.

Alternate Flowers

There are no alternatives for this spell.

The Moonflower's fragrance is beautiful, but not all of us can smell it – you need to have a certain gene to detect the scent.

Morning Glory Habit-Breaker Spell

Grids help focus energy and hold it for a period of time. Grids are therefore very helpful in spells that provide you with a little more time. Habits are usually formed over time and so it makes sense to use magick that is of a longer duration to ensure they are broken completely.

Using Morning Glory as a habit breaker supports commitment to change. As each day dawns these flowers impart vitality, which can help with personal energies as you go through withdrawal from any habit.

Timings: Waning Moon, Saturday, Early Morning

Find and Gather

- 4 Morning Glory flowers (*Ipomoea purpurea*)
- 4 small vases
- pure water
- a flat stone

Earth Magick

- ✦ 4 white feathers
- ✦ black fine marker

The Spell

Find a place where you can set up this spell and leave it for up to a week or more.

The space should be big enough to contain your spell grid as described below and not be disturbed.

On your flat stone write down what the habit is that you wish to break.

Place it in the centre of your space and say:

Lay here habit, you are not going to leave.
Your power over me will break this week.

Place each vase around the stone. Add water to the vases and say:

Pure sweet water, life you sustain.
But only good things from now on remain.

Add a Morning Glory flower to each vase and say:

This is the last morning my habit will hold.
Flowers of dawn take it away.

Between each vase, in a pattern, place a white feather and say:

Light as the breeze, fly my habit away.
Never return, not even a day.

Stand back and say:

A flower grid with feather and stone.

Once the blooms have left, habit leave me alone.

Your habit will be broken once the flowers are spent. Once they are spent, take them, the feathers and stone to a place far away from your home and bury in a dark place. Return home in a non-direct route so your habit won't follow you.

Alternate Flowers

Common Thistle (*Cirsium vulgare*)

Although it is considered a noxious weed in many countries, if Morning Glory grows well in your garden, peace and happiness is assured.

Morning Glory flowers were used by the Aztecs and other South American peoples as a way to communicate with the gods.

Flower Spells ✦ 89

White Chrysanthemum Health Commitment Spell

White Chrysanthemums help you stay committed to promises made. In this spell you will be creating a rather lovely mirror to help you stay committed to a promise made each day.

Timings: Full Moon, Wednesday, Morning

Find and Gather

- a bunch of dried White Chrysanthemums (*Chrysanthemum*) with stems of at least 6 cm/2".
- a mirror with a flat, plain frame
- raffia
- glue gun
- wire
- a pen and paper

The Spell

Write out a list of things you could do to improve your health.

Raffia Plait Frame: Work out how thick you would like your plait to be. You may like it as thick as the mirror frame, or thinner. Lay out your raffia in a thickness to suit. Neatly wrap 15 cm/6" of wire around one end of the raffia to secure it. Divide the raffia into three equal sections and plait. Keep going until you have a length that will go right around your mirror. Bind the end as you did the beginning. If your raffia runs out before the length you need is achieved, simply make more plaits until you have enough. As you plait, envision yourself as healthy as possible and what you might need to do to achieve that health. Picture yourself happily eating, living and thinking positively. Any time a negative thought comes into your head, say:

Over and under, through darkness and light,
Healthy and happy, with all of my might.

Using the glue gun, attach your plaits to your mirror so that they frame it. This is the most secure way of affixing your raffia to a flat surface, but for the sake of magick, never use such a method for securing your flowers.

Hang your mirror in a place where you will see it first thing in the morning. Stand before your mirror and thread your White Chrysanthemums into the plait frame.

With each flower set in the plait, read out a different commitment you will make to ensure better health. Extra flowers can be saved and added at a later date for additional commitments or re-commitments you wish to add.

Each day look into the mirror and say:

I remain committed today to each flower I see.

Alternate Flowers

There are no alternatives for this spell.

Originating in China, Chrysanthemums were noted by Confucius in his writings 500 years before the birth of Christ.

Drinking from a glass with a single Chrysanthemum petal in the bottom will ensure health and longevity.

Madonna Lily and Pink Rose Healing Spell

Together, Madonna Lily and Pink Rose form a powerful bond perfect for healing. Madonna Lily will also help to uncover reasons for illness, pathways for recovery, protection and encouragement to heal. Pink Roses offer strong healing energies and stand by as a friend to offer support.

Timings: Full Moon, Thursday, Midnight

Find and Gather

- ✦ a Madonna Lily (*Lilium candidum*)
- ✦ a Pink Rosa (*Rosa*)
- ✦ either a piece of rose quartz crystal or rose quartz set in a piece of jewellery
- ✦ a pink candle

Flower Spells ✦ 91

- a darning needle, awl or blunt pen to inscribe the candle
- a glass or crystal bowl
- pure water

The Spell

Pour water into your bowl until it is half full.

Add your rose quartz crystal or jewellery to the water and say:

Cleanse in the water,
Clear and clear.

Place your Madonna Lily in the water and say:

Lady of flowers, show me the way.
Protect and encourage me each of my days.

Place your Pink Rose in the water and say:

Rose of great friendship,
Stand with me here with your comfort and cheer.

Take your candle and inscribe a spiral sun. This will look like a small spiral circle with rays coming out around it to look like a sun. This symbol is one that will encourage healing.

Light the candle so that the reflection of the flame is caught in the water.

Let the candle burn down while you attend it. Take out your crystal/jewellery.

It is now ready to carry or wear as a powerful healing tool.

Dry the flowers and add to a small bag and carry with you should you wish to boost healing.

Alternate Flowers

Madonna Lily » other White Lily (*Lilium*)
Pink Rose » White Rose (*Rosa*)

The Ancient Greeks associated Lily with Hera, the goddess of home, motherhood and marriage. In Rome, a similar goddess, Juno, represented these qualities.

It is said in many folklores that Lilies will always grow best for a good woman and, in some instances, fail completely if she has been in any way dishonest.

Everlasting Daisy Immunity Spell

This spell involves creating a pillow sachet, which can be added to an everyday pillow or cushion slip. You could make this pillow any size you like, however, and not attach it to another pillow at all. Smaller pillows make wonderful gifts for others. Fabrics will also add their meanings to your spellcrafting. The use of flannel in this spell is to impart the energies of protection and also comfort.

Timings: Waxing Moon, Sunday, Midday

Find and Gather

- 1 cup of Everlasting Daisies (*Rhodanthe chlorocephala*) or (*Helichrysum*)
- 1 x 15 cm/6" square piece of beautiful fabric
- 2 x 15 cm/6" square pieces of soft flannel or similar fabric
- sewing pins
- sewing machine or needle and gold thread
- 3 drops of tea-tree essential oil
- 3 drops of rosemary essential oil
- 3 drops of lemon essential oil
- large glass bowl

The Spell

Dry Everlasting Daisies completely according to the instructions on page 15.

In your bowl, mix dried flowers with essential oils and set aside.

With your needle and gold thread, sew together your piece of beautiful fabric and a piece of flannel. Your beautiful fabric will be on the top of your pillow to ensure it is comfortable against your skin, so make sure you find a fabric that won't scratch you.

Pin your completed pillow to the remaining flannel square and sew together, leaving a small opening.

Fill your pillow with your Everlasting Daisies and take outside into the sunshine. Sitting in the warmth of the sun, try to catch some sunlight in the opening you have left on your pillow and say:

In you go, sunshine.
Stay brilliant and long.
May those who lay upon this pillow
stay healthy and strong.

Then carefully close up the opening by sewing the pillow closed. Sew this onto a pillow or cushion slip or use alone.

Alternate Flowers

Other types of Everlasting Daisies.

Everlasting Daisies are also known as Strawflowers and Paper Daisies. Both Everlasting Daisies are found throughout the world. while Rhodanthe is an Australian wildflower and a popular international florist flower.

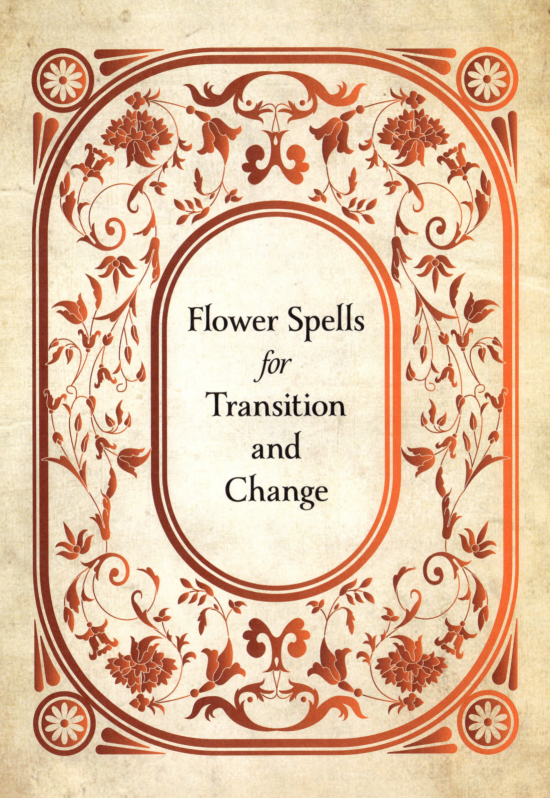

Flower Spells *for* Transition and Change

Gardenia Divination Spell

I love using Gardenia in spells – it has a wonderful way of reaching out and connecting with us and directing us to divine messages. Next time you are drawn to a Gardenia, pay attention to what you are doing and what is around you. One of the aims of this spell is to enrich your spell box with Gardenia's strong powers to receive messages.

Timings: Full Moon, Wednesday, Late Night

Find and Gather

- a dried Gardenia flower (*Gardenia jasminoides*)
- a beautiful wooden box
- a piece of lavender-coloured silk, at least the size of a handkerchief
- 9 small clear quartz crystals
- a small mirror that will fit in the bottom of the box

The Spell

On the evening of the Full Moon, take your mirror and capture the image of the Full Moon in it. Place your lavender cloth loosely into your box and then place your mirror on top and say:

Light has come, from above to below.
Hold it tight, to help me know.

Place your Gardenia into the box and say:

Listen, flower, day and night.
When I open the box, bring messages to light.

Place the crystals around the Gardenia and, as you add each, say:

Protect and empower.

You can use your divination spell box on its own or to assist you when using other forms of divination such as tarot or oracle cards, runes, pendulum work and so on.

Set the box before you and simply open it and look inside. You may experience certain feelings that will guide you, or hear/see/feel actual messages. Leave open while you are working with divination and then close when complete. You should simply thank your spell box before putting it away.

Alternate Flowers

Gardenia really is the preferred flower but you could use a White Rose (*Rosa*).

Gardenias are members of the coffee family, Rubiaceae. The name 'Gardenia' means 'garden flower'.

Wearing Gardenia either fresh, in artistic form or in a perfume will attract new friends and love. It will also ensure that you are protected from the negative influences of others.

Stephanotis Planning Spell

Stephanotis supports us while we plan, usually major things, in our lives. This spell works really well for those planning travel, events such as weddings and business plans. You will be able to keep this shaker tool to help 'shake things up' down the track or to make needed adjustments.

Timings: Waxing Moon, Sunday, Morning

Find and Gather

- a handful of Stephanotis flowers (*Stephanotis floribunda*)
- a few drops of orange essential oil
- a cardboard tube
- a marker
- an A4 sheet of sturdy cardboard (*you can recycle a used mailing tube with caps for this and the cardboard tube*)
- orange paint
- a paintbrush
- a handful of dry rice
- packing tape
- an awl or sharp-pointed tool to make holes in the tube

The Spell

Dry flowers well according to the instructions on page 15. Paint your cardboard tube and A4 cardboard sheet with the orange paint. You may wish to be a little more creative and paint a design. Just make sure that the overall colours are oranges, which boost planning energies.

When your tube is completely dry, pierce it a few times all around. Make sure the holes are much smaller than the rice grains.

Stand your cardboard tube upright on your A4 cardboard sheet and trace out two circles. These will serve as the ends of your shaker. Cut both out and, using the packing tape, seal a circle to one end of your cardboard tube. Make sure it is well sealed so your spell doesn't fall out. Now fill your tube with your flowers and rice. Sprinkle in a few drops of the orange essential oil. Seal the tube with the other circle.

To use:

When you are settling down to undertake any activity connected to planning, shake your Stephanotis flower planning shaker and say:

Stir up the energies, come now my way,
For I have decided that today is the day.
Clear all the muddling, untangle the mess,
Planning (insert what you are planning)
and doing my best.

Alternate Flowers

There are no alternative flowers for this spell.

The flower name 'Stephanotis' comes from the Greek words 'stephanos', which means crown, and 'otis', which means ear (*the stamens are ear-shaped*).

Sacred Blue Water Lily Second-Chance Spell

Tablets with magickal symbols, pictures, numbers and words on them have been used since ancient times to import their energy upon all in their space. This tablet will be embedded with Sacred Blue Lily, so will hold the promise of rebirth, second chances and understanding, to repair a relationship, take advantage of an opportunity or try something again. The size of the tablet is completely up to you but you will find directions below to create a tablet of approximately 10 cm/4" x 14 cm/5".

Timings: New Moon, Sunday, Morning

Find and Gather

+ 2 tablespoons of Sacred Blue Water Lily (*Nymphaea caerulea*), dried
+ air-dry clay
+ rolling pin
+ wax paper/baking paper
+ knife
+ thick white ribbon
+ thin yellow ribbons
+ an earth-coloured cloth
+ 3 tiny bells

The Spell

Prepare your air-dry clay as per the directions it came with. For the size mentioned below, use a piece roughly the size of your palm. Sprinkle Sacred Blue Water Lily over the clay and then knead it in well. Place on the waxed/baking paper and roll out to 1.5 cm/1" in thickness.

Create a hole in the top big enough to thread your thick ribbon through. Create eleven smaller holes along the bottom large enough for the thinner ribbons to thread through. When creating these holes, take into consideration any shrinkage that may occur with your clay.

Place your clay on your earth-coloured cloth and leave to dry. Once completely dry, thread through the thick ribbon, to hang. Tie your yellow ribbons to the bottom

Flower Spells ✦ 99

of the tablet. Make them long enough so that when the tablet is hanging from a doorway you can reach up and touch the ribbons as you walk under them. Tie your tiny bells on to some of the ribbons.

Hang the tablet in a doorway and say:

Empowered with chances, tablet of clay,
Hold them close and then release when I say.

Each day as you leave the bedroom or house, reach up and lightly touch your ribbons to make the bells sound.

Alternate Flowers

Bee Balm (*Monarda*)

Often mistaken for a Lotus, *Nymphaea caerulea* is also known as Egyptian Lotus. It has been used in perfumery, rituals and medicinally since Ancient Egyptian times.

Sacred Blue Water Lily open sky-blue petals to reveal a golden, sun-coloured centre, which represents the Sun god and life itself in Ancient Egypt.

Sweet Alyssum Clarity Spell

Mists can be used to fill spaces around us with magickal energy. In this spell, the properties of Sweet Alyssum flowers — mental release, understanding and clarity — are obtained via a traditional flower essence creation method. This mixture is then placed in a misting bottle that can be used where clarity is required.

Timings: New Moon, Sunday, Morning

Find and Gather

- 11 Sweet Alyssum flowers, preferably white (*Lobularia maritime*)
- pure water
- a glass or crystal bowl
- glycerin
- misting bottle

Earth Magick

The Spell

Place your glass/crystal bowl on the ground in a sunny spot, which will remain so for at least an hour. Make sure it is on the earth or grass so that it becomes 'grounded'.

Half fill your glass/crystal bowl with the pure water and say:

Water pure, ready to hold,
Flower energy and the power from light gold.

Gently float the Sweet Alyssum flowers upon the water and say:

Eleven flowers, clear and bright,
Bring me clarity and full, clear sight.

Leave out in the full sun for an hour. Take the flowers out and bury with thanks under a large, healthy tree. Bottle the water in a misting bottle with four parts water to one part glycerin. Spray into the space around you when you are seeking clarity.

Alternate Flowers

Boronia (*Boronia ledifolia*), Dandelion (*Taraxacum officinale*)

To calm someone angry, simply place Sweet Alyssum in their hands or on their body. You could try shaking their hand with some of the flowers in yours.

Sweet Alyssum is well known as a spell-, hex- and curse-breaker. To ensure protection from any enchantments being cast on you, hang above your bed/main living area of your home.

Magnolia New Home Search-and-Protect Spell

Magnolia is a flower denoting strength, wisdom and longevity. It is a very supportive flower through times of change, which makes it a really good choice for spells involving the search for a new home.

In this spell we are creating a spell bottle and filling it with items that contain energies that, when shaken together, stir up and release a magickal boost.

When you have found your new home, burying it in the front yard will seal protection for the house and also for those within.

Timings: Waxing Moon, Monday, Evening

Find and Gather

- 1 Magnolia flower (*Magnolia*)
- a beautiful, sealable jar
- 3 bay leaves
- 3 sage leaves
- 1 tablespoon of salt
- 3 cloves of garlic
- 1 tablespoon of black peppercorns
- a small magnifying glass (*a child's toy will work*)
- a brown ribbon and a blue ribbon
- pure water
- 3 nails

The Spell

Add all your botanicals, except the Magnolia, to the jar and say:

Plants of the land,
A new home seek and find.

Add your Magnolia. You may need to fold it to fit. Then say:

Magnolia sweet and wise, protect and abide.

Fill the jar with your pure water and close the lid. Using both ribbons, tie the magnifying glass to the jar. Shake the bottle each morning before you set out to look for your new home and say:

Show me the house, soon to be home.

Once you have found your new home, take the magnifying glass off the bottle. Open the jar and place the three nails inside it. These will 'nail' protection to your home. Bury the jar in your front yard.

Alternate Flowers

Cornflower (*Centaurea cyanus*)

With fossils of the plant dating back over 95 million years, Magnolias are one of the oldest flowers still in their original form in existence.

Magnolias have been used in Chinese medicine for centuries. Currently there are more than 200 patented Chinese medicine drugs based on the Magnolia plant.

Wild Rose New Beginning Spell

An old tradition to clear away the past and welcome the new is to energetically sweep an area of your home, or your entire home. This broom is created using Wild Rose, which is known to help open up new paths. If your way ahead involves contracts, then this flower offers protection for your part in them and assures promises are kept. Lavender also ensures trusts are kept and that you can find a way ahead whilst under protection; it also cleans away anything from the past that may hinder your progress to move forward.

You do not have to create a full-sized broom – the energy will still be the same with a smaller broom as long as it is created in the same manner.

Timings: Waxing Moon, Saturday, Morning

Find and Gather

- Wild Rose (*Rosa acicularis*) with long stems
- Lavender (*Lavandula stoechas*) with long stems
- a small branch to use as a broom handle
- finer sticks to form a brush head
- thick white ribbon
- thinner white ribbon

The Spell

Go for a walk and find a suitable small branch/stick and some smaller sticks to create your broom. Thank the area where you found your gifts.

Using your thick white ribbon, tie your smaller sticks around your large branch to form a broom.

Tie your flowers into the broom by threading them into the sticks and tying with the thinner white ribbon. The flowers can be fresh or dried. Leave them in the broom and store it in a cool, dry place. Hanging your broom will let the flowers dry out.

To usher in your new beginning:

Holding the broom, start in the middle of your home/office/space and use a sweeping motion. You do not have to touch the ground because you are sweeping the energy.

Move from the centre to the outside, and say:
>   I am making way for the new to come in.
>   A new beginning awaits.
>   Clear away what now impedes,
>   And leave all the things that I need.

Alternate Flowers

Wild Rose » Lupin (*Lupinus perennis*)
Lavender » no substitution.

It has been discovered that Wild Roses existed more than 35 million years ago.

The buttonhole in men's jacket lapels was always there to hold flowers, usually a Rose. It was thought that men who wore a Rose would be afforded luck with the women they met.

Tuberose Obstacle Remover Spell

This spell involves creating a magickal eraser to release obstacles. Tuberose will assist you in getting what it is you desire. This flower also offers protection and strength, which are important while you are focused on your goal.

Timings: Waning Moon, Thursday, Dusk

Find and Gather

- 1 single Tuberose flower (*Polianthes tuberosa*)
- a slice of white bread with crusts
- a 6H pencil
- a piece of white paper
- a knife
- a wooden chopping board
- a glass of warm water

Earth Magick

The Spell

Write down your obstacle/s as faintly as possible but so you can still read it/them on the piece of white paper.

Place your piece of white bread on your chopping board, with the crusts lying parallel to the cardinal directions. Slice off the North crust and say:

Free to the North.

Repeat for each direction as you slice your crusts away. Chop each crust up finely and scatter over the earth.

Finely chop up the Tuberose flower and then sprinkle it over the crustless piece of white bread. Start kneading the bread and flower pieces together until you form a putty-like ball. Roll the ball between your palms until it firms up.

Use this ball to erase your obstacles from the paper and say:

Open the borders,
Let the air flow.
May what I desire,
Be free to now go.

Tear up your paper and your magickal eraser into tiny pieces and mix with water. Pour this over the earth and say:

Free now to roam.

Alternate Flowers

Red Tulip (*Tulipa*), Althea (*Hibiscus syriacus*)

....

Traditional Hawaiian brides wear a headdress called a 'haku', which is made of Tuberose and Pikaki flowers.

....

Tuberoses have a beautiful fragrance, but this scent also stimulates creativity in the brain and can increase a person's emotions, instilling a feeling of blissful serenity.

Flower Spells ✦ 105

Jasmine New Opportunity Spell

Jasmine flowers not only herald spring with their flowers, they share the gifts of abundance, victory and hope with their energy. This spell requires an egg and I would suggest that you make sure you use the egg, not waste it, to ensure that new opportunities coming to you will also not be wasted.

Timings: Waxing Moon, Sunday, Daytime

Find and Gather

- a sprig of Jasmine (*Jasminum officinale*)
- an egg
- sticky tape
- water

The Spell

Under a very old and healthy tree, dig a hole big enough to bury your egg.

Crack your egg and retain the yolk and white for another use. Be very careful and try to crack your egg so that you have two eggshell halves.

Place your Jasmine into one half of your shell and then close it as best as you can with the other half, sealing together with clear tape, and say:

> *Sweet flower of abundance,*
> *New chances and success.*
> *Help grow them right here,*
> *In the earth I like best.*

Bury your magickal egg in the hole you dug under the tree.

For the next nine nights you must return to the place where you buried your egg and sprinkle a little water on the earth covering it, and say:

> *Grow my hopes little flower,*
> *Make them see light of day.*

I ask you tonight,
Send new opportunities my way.

Alternate Flowers

Delphinium (*Delphinium*)

Jasmine flowers are a powerful aphrodisiac and they have many therapeutic benefits. In herbal medicine, they are reputed to regulate blood sugar, improve digestion, improve blood circulation, boost the immune system and act as a calmative.

The Duke of Tuscany introduced Jasmine to Europe in 1699. He refused to share it with anyone, but his gardener gave a sprig to his girlfriend, who grew it. The gardener and his girlfriend then became rather comfortable from selling the flowers.

Snowdrop Career and Lasting Change Spell

This spell works well if you are looking for a new job or a change in position or career. Importantly, it makes the change last. Snowdrops help bring new beginnings your way and light up the path to find ways to obtain what you are looking for. Jonquils help us define our desires and attain them.

Timings: Waxing Moon, Thursday, Daytime

Find and Gather

- 1 Snowdrop (*Galanthus nivalis*)
- 1 Jonquil (*Narcissus jonquilla*)
- 2 small magnets
- 2 small pieces of green felt, 11 x 11 cm/4.5 x 4.5"
- glue
- needle and gold thread
- a pen and paper

Flower Spells ✦ 107

The Spell

Divide your paper into two pieces no bigger than 6 cm/2.5" square. On one write down what it is you desire; for example, what the job or position is. This will be your 'desire' paper.

On the other piece of paper, write down how you think you may achieve this; for example, answering an advertisement, winning a contract. This will be your 'path' paper.

Trim your flowers of most of their stems, leaving about 6 cm/2.5". Leaving a small space on the top, anchor each flower to a piece of the green felt, using the needle and gold thread, by stitching over the stem. Glue a magnet on each piece of felt, on the opposite side to the flower, making sure that the attracting sides face out so when the two pieces of felt are brought together they stick.

Place your two pieces of paper together and then place your Jonquil behind your 'desire' paper and your Snowdrop behind your 'path' paper so that the magnets stick the papers together. The papers will be caught between the pieces of felt when the magnets connect.

Sew a loop through the papers and felt and hang in a front window of your home, and say:

> *Attract my desires,*
> *And open the path.*
> *The beginning before me,*
> *A place for my heart.*

Alternate Flowers

Snowdrops » Daffodils (*Narcissus pseudonarcissus*)
Jonquils » Red Tulip (*Tulipa*)

To dream of Snowdrops means that it is time to share the secret or news you may be withholding from others.

Is it a Daffodil or Jonquil? An easy way to identify each is to remember that Jonquils display multiple flowers on each stem.

Sweet-Pea Change Spell

Sweet Peas are a comforting flower but they also share good luck, protection, and ensure harmony. White Roses offer purification and protection. In this spell you will be making a flower confetti box, which became popular in larger houses in England in the 19th century. These boxes were given to overnight visitors; each would receive a different-coloured flower petal inside. Sprinkling the petals from their room to where dinner was served would ensure, later on, when retiring or wandering around the great halls at night, they would find their way back to the right bed.

Timings: Full Moon, Sunday, Midday

Find and Gather

✦ a large bunch of Sweet Pea flowers (*Lathyrus odoratus*)
✦ 6 White Roses (*Rosa*)
✦ 1 teaspoon of earth from a place you feel attuned to
✦ a beautiful box

The Spell

Carefully detach and gather all the flower petals. Dry them completely, then crush them with your fingers until they are small, confetti-like pieces.

Place the petals in the box.

The earth you need should be from a place you feel very connected to: a place where you feel comfortable, safe and welcome.

Add the teaspoon of earth to your box, close the lid and shake gently, making the shape of the infinity symbol, while saying:

Things must change, but I go on.
Things must change but gently I go.
Things must change and I change, too.
Gently I bend but on I go.

When you are at the place of change, take some of your flower confetti with you and sprinkle it in a circle around you. This will help you feel at ease with the changes going on and support you as you adapt to the new path ahead.

Flower Spells ✦ 109

Alternate Flowers

Bee Balm (*Monarda*), Mayflower (*Epigaea repens*)

Carrying a Sweet Pea in your hand will ensure whoever you speak with will only tell the truth.

Most gardeners have favourite secrets to ensure a wonderful crop of Sweet Peas. You could try soaking the seeds in milk overnight or making sure you sow the seeds before sunrise on St Patrick's Day.

Hydrangea Problem-Solving Spell

Dedicating a particular bowl to flower scrying is something you might find very useful. A beautiful flat clay bowl is perfect, but any bowl that you feel an affinity with will work.

Hydrangeas are very good at helping you understand a situation and assisting you to keep going until you find solutions. They are also a flower of great interconnectedness between all energies, so are very helpful for problem solving.

Timings: New Moon, Monday, Late Night

Find and Gather

- Hydrangea flower heads (*Hydrangea*)
- a beautiful, large flat bowl
- pure water
- a clear quartz crystal
- a violet-coloured cloth
- a pencil and sketch pad

The Spell

Lay your cloth out and set your bowl upon it. Pour the pure water into the bowl, filling it about halfway.

Place your quartz crystal into the centre of the bowl.

Carefully remove the Hydrangea flowers and bracts from their stems until you have a lovely pile. The pink or blue petals are actually bracts. The flowers are the tiny centres.

Sit and focus on your problem. Put your fingers in the water and swirl it around in the shape of infinity and say:

All possibilities to solve my problems come to me now.

Set your pencil and sketch pad up.

Cast flowers upon the moving water a few at a time.

Let the water settle between each addition and check in to see what patterns appear. You may like to jot down notes/sketch the images that the petals create, for later study. Perhaps there are letters or images that may be descriptive and indicate direct answers, or the patterns could be symbolic and lead the way to solutions.

Once you have completed your session, bury your flowers in a sunlit place and pour the water over it.

Alternate Flowers

Any flowers can be used for this spell, but Hydrangeas are best.

Never plant a Hydrangea along the walls of your home. especially near the front door. if you are single and wish to one day marry. Doing so ensures a lifetime of being alone.

Hydrangea colours are very susceptible to the pH level of soil. Lower than 6.0 and you will see blue tones. Between 6.0 and 7.0 offers purple. and over 7.0 will have your flowers turning pink.

Introduction

In this section I have shared 60 spells that focus on herbs and their energies.

So what exactly are herbs? They are plants that, through their aromatic or savoury properties, present usage in medicinal, culinary or spiritual application. In these herbal spells, we will explore the magickal qualities of herbs and learn along the way the history and the botanical lore that will bring us again a little closer to Nature. In doing so we may instigate change, support and inspiration when needed.

Herbs for Spells

I will indicate in which state (*fresh or dried*) the herbs can be used, but most of these spells use dried herbs. Select herbs that look and feel energetically positive and make sure you take fresh herbs home swiftly and look after them. Remove excess foliage that may turn water brown. Use the excess immediately, or dry for later use. Snip stems at an angle to remove any dried ends and immediately place in water to enable them to take a good long fresh drink. Change water completely every two to three days and snip stems if the herbs appear to be drying or collapsing.

You can easily dry most herbs by tying in loose bundles and hanging in a cool, dry space. Single stems can also be dried on racks or pressed, and for those particularly dedicated there are various food dehydrators on the market that work very well. Another popular herb-drying method is the use of silica gel. Herbs are placed in containers layered with the gel in bead form and dry out over a number of weeks.

Once dry, keep your herbs in a cool, dry place out of direct sunlight in airtight jars. Label by herb type. You may also like to add the place, time or season in which the herb was harvested. Ensure that your herbs are completely dry before bottling or they will grow mould.

How to Harvest Herbs

Correct plant identification is crucial as many plants are toxic and can even cause death. So while wildcrafting (*harvesting plant material in the wild*) is a wonderful way to collect your herbs, you must ensure that you have correctly identified the plants. There are many field guides on the market but contacting local experts would be the safest option if you have no, or limited, experience.

The key to using plant material for spellwork is in how you harvest the herbs, whether they are your own herbs or wild herbs. Do so with care and respect, never take more than half of any plant and never use iron metal in any of your harvesting tools as it will destroy the spirit of a herb. It is generally believed that herbs destined for medicinal and magickal work should be collected at sunrise or, better still, during a New Moon. They are stronger from the energy of the Sun during sunrise and boosted by the New Moon phase.

Giving thanks to the herbs also ensures a balance of energies. This can be done with simple words or by giving something back in the way of an offering. Traditionally this can be a copper coin, bread, sweets or cake, beer or grain.

Herb Spells ✦ 115

Herb Spells *for* Love, Relationships and Friendship

Motherwort and Lemon Verbena Dispute Spell

Motherwort is included in this spell because it promotes trust, protection and motivation. This herb will ensure that everyone involved in a dispute is able to be open to a resolution or compromise. Lemon Verbena will help open the heart chakra of all those involved in the dispute. It will also lift negative behaviour patterns that may be getting in the way of constructive negotiations.

Timings: Waning Moon, Wednesday, Sunset

Find and Gather

- ¼ cup of dried Motherwort (*Leonurus cardiaca*)
- ¼ cup of dried Lemon Verbena (*Lippia citriodora*)
- 4 drops of lemon essential oil
- a small heart-shaped rose quartz crystal
- a beautiful bowl, preferably orange in colour
- a piece of paper, pen and envelope

The Spell

You do not have to take notice of all the suggested timings for the additional energy boost, but you do need to ensure you create the spell on a morning and complete it by the following morning. Have all the items for the spell ready. Write down what your dispute is on the piece of paper and tuck it into the envelope.

Place the rose quartz crystal in your bowl and over it say:

Quietly now, be still and listen,
May everyone calm and now want a new mission.

Add your herbs and essential oil and mix well. Place the bowl next to a window and put your envelope with your written dispute in it under the bowl. Note the time. Exactly 24 hours later take the envelope outside, burn it and say:

Dispute, you listened all day and night,
May you take our quarrels away with the light.

Herb Spells ✦ 117

Resolution, welcome, here and now,
Let us all be open to knowing how.

Leave the bowl where it is and top-up the essential oil when you wish.

Alternate Herbs

Basil (*Ocimum basilicum*) can be used to substitute either or both herbs.

Culpepper, a revered 17th-century English herbalist, stated of Motherwort: 'There is no better herb to take melancholy from the heart.'

In Morocco, Lemon Verbena is referred to as the friendship herb and is shared to celebrate and express all forms of friendship.

Slippery Elm Release-Anger Spell

Slippery Elm is derived from the inner bark of Red Elm, an American species of Elm tree. It is included in this spell for its ability to release anger and to soothe. An alternate herb, dried Vervain, can be used as a substitute. By adding almonds and Lavender flowers, additional cleansing and calming is imparted to your magickal powder.

Timings: Waning Moon, Tuesday, Midday

Find and Gather

+ 3 tablespoons of dried and crushed Slippery Elm (*Ulmus fulva*)
+ 3 almonds
+ 1 tablespoon of dried Lavender flowers (*Lavandula*)
+ a yellow cotton bag
+ a mortar and pestle

The Spell

Grind the almonds and Lavender together and then mix with the Slippery Elm.
    As you do, say over and over:

118   ✦   Earth Magick

Calm and calm,
soothe and soothe.

Place the mixture in your yellow bag and store.

Sprinkle it on the ground between you and the person who has, or is, displaying anger towards you. You can also sprinkle it across the threshold of your home to prevent angry energy entering your home.

To soothe the anger of a person remotely, write their name on a sheet of paper, place it in a white cotton bag and sprinkle the spell powder into the bag. Shake and say:

Calm and calm,
soothe and soothe.
May you see things more gently, wisely and cool.

Additionally, if you feel that anger is hard to let go of, sprinkle a circle on the ground outside around you in an anti-clockwise direction and say:

Anger stay here, right in this spot.

Then hop out.

Alternate Herbs

Vervain (*Verbena officinalis*)

You can stop gossip directed at you by tying a length of yellow thread around a large piece of Slippery Elm and tossing it into a fire.

If a child wears a necklace created from the bark of the Slippery Elm tree they will grow up to be eloquent and even possess a very persuasive tongue.

Parsley and Mint Attraction Spell

Although Parsley is very entwined with folklore and historical usages as a herb associated with death, it is also very much a plant of attraction and celebration. The inclusion of Parsley in this spell will increase your powers of attraction and invite the energies of future celebration. Mint helps stimulate, and its addition will remove blocks between you and the one you desire or towards a relationship you would like. The Rose bud will help

Herb Spells ✦ 119

add protection and courage, and the rose quartz crystal another element of love as well as a boost in your ability to love and believe in yourself.

Timings: Waxing Moon, Friday, Morning

Find and Gather

- 1 tablespoon of dried Parsley (*Petroselinum crispum*)
- 1 tablespoon of dried Mint (*Mentha*)
- a tiny Red Rose (*Rosa*) bud
- a square of red cloth
- a rose quartz crystal
- a pink ribbon

The Spell

Mix your Parsley and Mint, place in the middle of your red cloth and say:
> *Lift away the clouds, so others may see,*
> *What is attractive and lovely in me.*

Place the rose quartz crystal on the Parsley and Mint and say:
> *For love that is true.*

Place the Rose bud on the collection and say:
> *Unfurl and protect.*

Lift up the corners of the cloth and then twist to contain everything inside. Tie with the pink ribbon.

Use when you feel you need to boost your attraction by tying to the tap over a bath so water runs over your magickal bath tea. Immerse yourself in the water and focus on your positive attributes. This bath helps bring these attributes to the fore.

Alternate Herbs

Parsley » Bay Leaf (*Laurus nobilis*)
Mint » Rosemary (*Rosmarinus officinalis*)

Mint is also associated with concentration and mental stimulation. Pliny the Elder (*AD 23-79*) a Roman author, naturalist and military commander, advised scholars to wear wreaths of mint to stimulate their minds.

Earth Magick

It is believed that parsley needs to go down to the devil and back nine times before it can grow well, so you need to sow nine times more than what you actually need so the devil gets his share.

Lemon Balm and Dill Get-Closer Spell

This magickal, warm drink is an earthy, herbal honey water, which will be particularly good for those who feel they have drifted apart from one another. This could be because of a disagreement, but the spell will also be very effective for those who just want to take a relationship to the next level or invite a warmer, closer bond. Lemon Balm is included for its power to bring people together, inspire success and to mend. Dill will enable people to see the attributes that attract them to another. Cinnamon will ease communication and, for those using this spell for romantic relationships, increase libido.

Timings: Waxing Moon, Tuesday, Daytime

Find and Gather

✦ 6 fresh leaves of Lemon Balm (*Melissa officinalis*)
✦ 1 fresh sprig of Dill (*Anethum graveolens*)
✦ 1 tablespoon of organic honey
✦ 2 cinnamon sticks
✦ 2 cups of water
✦ 2 beautiful glasses

The Spell

Heat the Lemon Balm in the water in a saucepan. Simmer for a few minutes, but do not boil. Remove from the heat. Chop up the Dill, add to the water and let cool a little. Use the water only in this spell. Place ½ tablespoon of honey into each of your glasses and say:

Sweet golden glow,
warm and heal.

Pour a tablespoon of the Lemon Balm-and-Dill water into each of the glasses and say:

Bring us together, closer and closer.

Top up the glasses with plain water.

Put a cinnamon stick in each glass and, holding one in each hand, stir in a clockwise direction. If you wish a friendship to be closer, say:

Bring us together, held fast in warmth,
Closer in friendship.

If you wish a romantic relationship to be closer, say:

Bring us together, held fast in warmth,
Closer in love.

Drink together. You may also wish to make a toast or express a commitment to each other.

Alternate Herbs

There are no alternates for this spell, but you can use 1 tablespoon each of dried Dill and Lemon Balm in place of fresh plants.

Lemon Balm is said to help end disputes and lighten thoughts. It can also attract love, success and healing.

Placing a sprig of Dill and a pinch of salt in each shoe on your wedding day is said to ensure a good marriage.

Damiana and Cardamom New-Lover Spell

Cardamom has the ability to draw in a new lover and make you more attractive to others. Damiana is included because it is a powerful aphrodisiac and assists with psychic abilities, which can help sharpen your intuition and make you more alert to any opportunities that will help you find your new lover.

Timings: Full Moon, Friday, Evening

Find and Gather

- 2 leaves or 2 pinches of dried Damiana (*Turnera aphrodisiaca*)
- 2 pinches of Cardamom seeds (*Elettaria cardamomum*)
- a mojo bag - a small red bag that you can carry with you
- 2 dried Red Rose (*Rosa*) petals
- a rose quartz crystal
- a malachite crystal
- a rhodonite crystal

The Spell

Hang your mojo bag outside your bedroom window before you go to bed and say:

> *Dance in the moonlight,*
> *Sing in the air.*
> *Welcome a lover,*
> *Who is good, right and fair.*

The next night place your Red Rose petals and Damiana leaves in the bag and place it under your pillow. You may find you dream of your new lover or receive a message about how to meet them.

The next night add your malachite and say:

> *Let nothing from my past get in my way.*

Add your rose quartz and rhodonite and say:

> *I welcome new love from this day.*

Sprinkle the Cardamon into your mojo bag and close.

Wear it upon your person to attract a new lover.

Alternate Herbs

There are no alternatives for this spell.

Damiana is originally from Mexico and has been used as a powerful aphrodisiac in South American countries since the Mayan culture. It is also found in many modern herbal preparations for this use.

Chewing Cardamom seeds before going out in the evening will increase your sexuality and ensure you find a new lover, too!

Basil and Red Clover Fidelity Spell

Not only will Basil ensure the fidelity of a partner, it will protect against quarrels and even help mend those that have occurred. Red Clover will also ensure fidelity as well as lust between those who use it. Storing the mix over a few weeks will impart the energies of the Basil and Red Clover into the oil.

Timings: Full Moon, Friday, Evening

Find and Gather

- 4 fresh Basil leaves (*Ocimum basilicum*)
- 4 fresh Red Clover flowers (*Trifolium pretense*)
- sweet almond oil or coconut oil
- a beautiful airtight bottle that can hold at least 1 cup of oil

The Spell

Sterilise your bottle. This can be done by placing it in a pot of water and bringing it to the boil for five minutes.

Wash and dry the Basil leaves and Red Clover flowers completely.

Add both to your bottle and say:

Stay true to me with this flower and leaf.

Gently pour the oil into the bottle and say:

Hold all together,
Mix in the dark.
Next time you are open,
Release irresistible sparks.

Store for at least two weeks in a cool, dark, dry place.

To use, offer your partner a massage. Sprinkle the oil on them and massage lovingly.

If you are worried about being unfaithful, massage a little oil into your arms before going out or being in a situation in which you do not fully trust yourself, and say:

These arms will hold no other.

Massage onto your feet and say:

These feet will never walk away.

Alternate Herbs

Basil » no alternative.

Red Clover » Yerba Maté (*Ilex paraguariensis*) – use just a very small amount.
A little pinch of dried Yerba Maté will work well.

In many European gardening folklores, you must curse the ground as you plant Basil to ensure it grows well. This is because it is generally believed that this plant belongs to Satan.

Red Clover is used in many ways for purification. It makes a really good addition to smudge sticks. You can also add a flower to your purse or wallet to attract abundance and financial luck.

Meadowsweet Relationship-Ending Spell

Ending a relationship is never an easy task and so this spell is one that helps ease the transition period. This is a very good spell for those who wish to break up with someone, but it also supports those who have been told their relationship is over. You can use the butter each day on a simple piece of toast or treat yourself to something lovely like a muffin, scone or fruitcake slice. Meadowsweet will support you through the termination of the relationship and help you transition to a new chapter of your life, and St Mary's Thistle eliminates negative energies surrounding the breakup. You can use other edible substitutions for the butter, such as oils and vegetable spreads.

Timings: Waning Moon, Saturday, Midday

Find and Gather

+ ¼ teaspoon of dried Meadowsweet (*Filipendula ulmaria*)
+ ¼ teaspoon of dried St Mary's Thistle (*Silybum marianum*)
+ 1 cup of organic butter
+ a small white ceramic bowl
+ a wooden spoon
+ a small wooden knife/spreader

Herb Spells + 125

The Spell

Beat the butter with the wooden spoon until it is fluffy, and say:

Light come in,
Welcome and bright.
Let a new day begin.

Sprinkle in the Meadowsweet and St Mary's Thistle and say:

Herbs supportive,
Join with me now.

Keep this butter covered in the fridge. Use for seven days straight. It is best eaten first thing each morning to ensure a smooth transition period after the breakup.

At the end of the seven days, bury whatever is left of the butter under a large and strong tree and say:

Take what is left.
I am now free.

Alternate Herbs

There are no alternatives for this spell.

Meadowsweet is one of the three herbs most sacred to the Druids and was used to flavour mead and wine. It contains Salicin, which is the ancient equivalent of aspirin, although meadowsweet is a much safer and natural pain reliever and anti-inflammatory and fever reducer.

Milk Thistle, also known as St Mary's Thistle, has been used for centuries for liver ailments. It is believed that the milky marks on the leaves are the result of milk that fell from the breast of the Virgin Mary while she was breastfeeding Jesus.

Marjoram Communication Spell

Dedicate one plant solely for communication spells. Do not use the plant for any other purpose other than nourishment. Marjoram is used in this spell because it brings swift awareness to those in its presence or under its focus. It can bring people back into consciousness and, in fact, can be used for those who have fainted (in place of smelling salts). If you are unable to find a blue plant pot, purchase a plain terracotta one and paint it blue or tie a large blue ribbon around it.

Timings: Full Moon, Wednesday, Dusk

Find and Gather

- a small Marjoram plant (*Origanum majorana*)
- a portable yet good-sized blue plant pot
- good-quality potting mix
- a small chrysocolla crystal
- pure water

The Spell

Take your Marjoram plant, blue plant pot, potting mix and crystal to a very sunny spot outside. Half fill your pot with the potting mix and then place the chrysocolla crystal in the centre and say:

> *Crystal of communication, power and knowledge,*
> *Open the paths.*

Sprinkle a little water on the crystal.

Fill the rest of the pot and then plant your Marjoram plant and say:

> *Magickal plant,*
> *Open the way.*
> *Let communication flow,*
> *Each day and each way.*

Herb Spells ✦ 127

Take care of the plant in a way that suits your climate. You may need to grow it inside or in a particular spot in your garden. Seek local advice when you obtain your plant or find information in a gardening guide or on the internet.

When you need to improve the communication between you and another, simply position the plant near the place where you are expecting communication to come from. This could be the mailbox, your computer or your phone.

Alternate Herbs

Oregano (*Origanum vulgare*)

Marjoram was believed to have been created by the Greek goddess Aphrodite and so can strengthen love between two people. Young lovers in both Ancient Greece and Rome would wear wreaths of Marjoram on their heads to induce happiness and love.

The Ancient Romans believed that Marjoram grew on the graves of the departed who were happy in the afterlife.

Chicory Obstacle-Remover Spell

Chicory is considered the most powerful obstacle remover. You should dedicate this candle spell to just one person, institution or entity. Although there are a few ways to add dried flowers and botanicals to candles, I find the method below the easiest and most effective. Harvesting Chicory must be undertaken with additional energetic care. It is best to collect at either Midday or Midnight, and you must do so in complete silence.

Timings: Full Moon, Saturday, Midday

Find and Gather

- Chicory flowers and leaves (*Cichorium intybus*)
- a thick white pillar candle
- a tea light candle
- a metal spoon
- a heat-safe surface to work on
- a flower press
- a black cloth

128 ✦ Earth Magick

The Spell

Chicory leaves are optional. You will first need to dry the Chicory flowers and leaves and you will need to use a method that ensures they are flat, so either use a flower press or an old book and tissue paper with weights.

Once the flowers and leaves are ready, set yourself up to create your pillar candle by laying the candle on its side on the heat-safe surface.

Light the tea light and use this to heat the back of the metal spoon.

Place the first flower or leaf on the pillar candle and lightly work the spoon over it so it presses down into the candle. The heat will transfer through the flower or leaf and melt the wax. Work gently and patiently.

As each flower or leaf is set, say:

Our troubles pressed into wax (say the person's or thing's name)
Held softly there.
But I know the light will release into air.

Once the candle is decorated to your satisfaction, use it whenever you feel there are obstacles between you and the person or thing you created the candle for. Light it and watch the melting wax while envisioning the obstacles dissolving. When not in use, store the candle in the black cloth and only ever use it for this person or thing that you need to communicate with, and for this magickal purpose.

Alternate Herbs

Yarrow (*Achillea millefolium*)

Chicory is said to be capable of opening locks and can even expose people to various entrances to the Underworld.

Carrying Chicory will ensure good luck to travellers, especially those exploring new lands, seeking a new life or even prospecting. It was a very popular herbal talisman during the North American gold rush.

Herb Spells ✦ 129

Marshmallow and Chamomile Grief-Support Spell

Marshmallow is one of the great medical herbs and has been used extensively throughout history. The entire plant can be utilised and its addition to this spell takes advantage of its soothing properties. Marshmallow encourages good and supportive spiritual energies and banishes malevolent energies that can be attracted to us when we are in a low state of energy, which may be due to grief. Marshmallow was added to wine in Ancient Greek times to act as a cough suppressant as well as a soothing tonic.

If you would rather create a non-alcoholic spell, I have included instructions on making this spell without the traditional wine. You will end up with the same results in a lovely tea.

Timings: Full Moon, Sunday, Midnight

Find and Gather

- 1 tablespoon of Marshmallow root (*Althaea officinalis*)
- 1 tablespoon of dried Chamomile (*Matricaria chamomilla*)
- 1 cup of white organic wine, or 1 cup of pure water
- a screw-top glass jar

The Spell

Gently warm the wine or water, without boiling. Pour into the glass jar.

Sprinkle the Marshmallow root into the jar and say:

> *Energies soft and subtle relieve,*
> *Calm and support this time that I grieve.*

Sprinkle in the Chamomile and say again:

Energies soft and subtle relieve,

Calm and support this time that I grieve.

Swirl the mixture in a clockwise pattern and then place it in the fridge.

The next day, strain into a glass and sip as you will. You can have it cool or you can warm it slightly and sweeten with a little honey, if desired.

Alternate Herbs

There are no alternatives for this spell.

Marshmallow sweets, which today are created from a mixture of water, gelatin and sugar, were originally made from the roots of this plant, which has gelatinous properties. It was often used in cough drops.

Marshmallow bears the botanical name of *Althaea officinalis*. Plants which have the word *'officinalis'* in their name are recognised as being of importance, usually medicinally. *'Althaea'* comes from the Greek word 'altho', meaning 'to heal'.

Herb Spells + 131

Herb Spells
for
Home, Family and Pets

Skullcap and Oregano Settle Pet Spell

Historically, Skullcap has been used to remedy canine rabies. It is used in this spell as a calmative. Oregano helps bring awareness and clarity and opens channels of communication, all vital when settling pets down after a difficult event that has caused them anxiety.

You will be creating a type of flower mist in this spell, and although the addition of glycerin will extend the mist's shelf life I would suggest you keep it in the fridge.

Timings: Full Moon, Monday, Midday

Find and Gather

- a few Skullcap leaves (*Scutellaria lateriflora*)
- a few Oregano leaves (*Origanum*)
- some pure water
- a glass or crystal bowl
- glycerin
- a glass misting bottle

The Spell

Find a very sunny spot that will remain sunlit for at least an hour.

Place your glass/crystal bowl on the ground. Make sure it is on the earth or grass so that it becomes 'grounded'.

Half fill your glass/crystal bowl with the pure water and say:

Water pure, ready to hold,
the energies of plants and their gifts from gold.

NOTE: 'gifts from gold' refers to this method of transferring the Sun's energy through the plants.

Gently place your Skullcap leaves upon the water and say:

For (say your pet/s names/s).
Settling herb, your gifts to share.

Herb Spells ✦ 133

Then place the Oregano upon the water gently and say:

For (say your pet/s names/s).

Clarity herb, your gifts to share.

Leave your bowl out in the full sun for an hour. Take the herbs out and bury them, with thanks, under a large, healthy tree. Bottle the water in misting bottles: four parts water to one part glycerin. Spray around the areas your pet/s live in. The mist can also be sprayed, sparingly, directly on pets.

Alternate Herbs

Oregano » Marjoram (*Origanum majorana*)

A North American native, Skullcap's botanical name (*lateriflora*) describes the interesting way the flowers and seedpods only grow on one side of the stem.

Native Americans called the plant 'Mad Dog' due to its reputation for curing rabies.

Hop Neighbour-Boundary Spell

The inclusion of Hops in this spell instils the energy of peace. Although there are Hops in the beer you will be using, more are needed to secure the boundary of your home or neighbourhood. Black tourmaline crystal will offer protection from negativity, as will the length of black ribbon. Although this spell will make friendships between neighbours easier, it will protect your privacy as well, making you and your life appear uninteresting to others unless you step forward. It will also make neighbours with negative energy want to move on.

Timings: Waning Moon, Wednesday, Evening

Find and Gather

+ a large cup of dried Hops (*Humulus lupulus*)
+ a bottle of hop-based organic, home- or craft-brewed beer
+ a clear glass/crystal dish/plate/bowl
+ 2 long black tourmaline crystals
+ a length of black ribbon (*approximately 70 cm/27.5" long*)

134 ✦ Earth Magick

✦ a blank invitation card
✦ a pen

The Spell

Define an area between you and the neighbours and focus on this area. This could be near your fence line that your neighbours look over or a wall that you can hear them through, or the front door if they constantly visit, unwelcomed.

Tie a black tourmaline crystal to each end of the black ribbon and lay it on the ground or floor at your defined point, as a barrier between you and your neighbours.

Fill in the invitation with your neighbour's name and yours.

If you do not know their name/s, then describe them.

For the 'event', write: 'To share this space in peace.'

Set the invitation down on your side of the ribbon.

Place the dish on the ground on their side of the ribbon and place the beer, opened, in the centre. Sprinkle the Hops onto the dish, around the beer, and pick up the invitation, prop it up in front of the beer on their side of the ribbon and say:

I invite you to now share this space in peace,

Let what has occurred before now cease.

Leave in place for at least an hour and, if possible, bury the invitation, Hops, ribbon and crystal in this place. Pour the beer over the top. If it's not possible to bury then place all items in a box (except the beer) and keep as close as possible to your boundary with them.

Alternate Herbs

You could leave out the additional Hops. There are no alternatives for this spell.

For those suffering insomnia, you can make a very effective sleep pillow by loosely stuffing a small cushion or bag with dried female Hop flowers and Lavender.

Not always favoured as an ingredient in beer. Hops were actually banned from use by some authorities in England in the 1530s due to their inferior taste and quality.

Herb Spells ✦ 135

Ginkgo, Lavender and Sage Family-Blessing Spell

A blessing box can be used in a variety of ways; this one is created with herbs, intentions and magick, and is opened to release blessings when a family is in need of additional support. Wishes, prayers, rituals and offerings can be made over and to the blessing box

Ginkgo is included in this spell because it facilitates flow and because it has remained fairly unchanged since prehistoric times. The plant can live for over 1,000 years and is said to hold the energy of life – perhaps even the 'Tree of Life' itself. Lavender is included for its calming, protective and cleansing energies and Sage for its wisdom, protection and negativity-clearing abilities.

Timings: Full Moon, Monday, Sunrise

Find and Gather

- ¼ cup of dried Ginkgo (*Ginkgo biloba*)
- ¼ cup of dried Lavender (*Lavandula*)
- ¼ cup of dried Sage (*Salvia officinalis*)
- a small wooden box with a lid
- photo/s of your family
- paper, pens and pencils
- a white tablecloth

The Spell

Gather all family members to sit down at a table, if possible. Lay the white tablecloth out on the table and place the wooden box in the centre. Give each person pens, pencils and paper. Ask them to draw something that makes them feel happy. If any family member is distant or unable to do this, then you can do it for them.

Place the dried herbs into the box and say:

Plants of protection,
love and of earth,
Live now together
and blessings impart.

Put your photo/s in the box.

Add the drawings one by one and say each time:

A blessing of happiness upon us.

Store the box somewhere central in your home. The blessings and magick will always be imparted on you all, but in times of additional need open the box and say a prayer, make a wish, blessing or place a request over it. When you do, be sure to thank the box with a little additional sprinkling of any of the herbs.

Alternate Herbs

There are no alternates for this spell.

Women who comb their hair while seated beneath a male Ginkgo tree will have their wishes granted.

To ensure Sage grows well, someone else must buy it or give it to you, and you must plant it.

Echinacea and Bay Home-Protection Spell

This little bag will provide protection for your home while you are away. It can be used continuously in a special place, but for an added boost when you wish to go away for an extended period you should give your mojo bag a little energetic boost by repeating the chant below, over it, and adding a little more Echinacea. Make sure you thank your bag when you return from longer trips. Echinacea will protect your home and draw good energies to it, especially if needed for a particular reason. For example, if there is a natural disaster in your area, your mojo bag can attract support to protect your home. Bay leaves are always a good addition to spells when you are looking to stop outside influences or negative actions.

Timings: Full Moon, Monday, Midday

Find and Gather

- ✦ 1 tablespoon of dried Echinacea leaves/flowers (*Echinacea purpurea*)
- ✦ 3 dried Bay leaves (*Laurus nobilis*)
- ✦ small black bag
- ✦ a teaspoon of salt

Herb Spells ✦ 137

- black ribbon 30 cm/12" long)
- a black obsidian crystal

The Spell

Place the obsidian into the black bag and say:
> *Protect this home from within and without.*
> *Absorb and dispel energies of doubt.*

Sprinkle in the salt and say:
> *Protect and ground,*
> *Within and without.*

Put the Echinacea into bag, and say:
> *Protect and hold,*
> *Within and without.*

Add the three Bay leaves and say:
> *Together you three,*
> *No one cross over.*

Decide where it is you wish to keep your mojo bag. The best place is the most central area in your home, preferably hung from the ceiling with the black ribbon. For an energetic boost, plait the ribbon first.

Alternate Herbs

Cloves (*Syzygium aromaticum*), Basil (*Ocimum basilicum*), Sage (*Salvia officinalis*)

Echinacea, which originated in North America, is used by the Native American Plains Nations, in healing, more than any other plant.

Bay Laurel is thought by many cultures throughout history to be one of the strongest protective plants, especially when used in the home. Burning the leaves has traditionally been part of exorcisms.

Chive Garden-Guardian Spell

This spell allows you to dedicate a rock as your Garden Guardian, if you do not currently have one. Chives are used for their powerful energy-offering protection, in general, but particularly against disease. Chives boost the vitality of the space around them and those within it. Plant your Chives next to a rock that you decide will be your Garden Guardian and use the Chives to create your blessings and protection oil now and again in the future.

Timings: Full Moon, Monday, Morning

Find and Gather

- a seedling plant of Chives (*Allium schoenoprasum*)
- olive oil
- a glass bottle with stopper
- a pen and paper

The Spell

You will need to dedicate a particular rock as your Garden Guardian. This can be a magnificent standing stone already in place or one you move there yourself, or it can simply be a smaller stone, even tiny, that you dedicate. The size is not important: it is the energy, intention, love and care with which you regard this rock.

Once such a rock is identified, set aside a good hour to dedicate yourself to your rock. Sit with it, in a sunny place in your garden, and write down on the paper all that you wish for in your garden. Include your hopes, the things you wish to do with the produce, what you hope to gain, learn and share with this space. Fold the paper twice and bury it deep next to your rock. Next, plant your Chive seedling onto the paper and say:

Protector of rock,
Live here now.

Pick three Chive leaves and place them into the glass bottle. Fill with olive oil.

Leave in the sunshine, next to the Chive plants and rock, for an hour.

You may wish to use the oil to anoint your Garden Guardian.

Simply trickle a little of the oil on your fingers and then rub them on the rock while saying something special to mark the occasion. As an example:

Awake my Garden Guardian.
Watch over all who live and grow here
With love, guidance and protection.

Use your Garden Guardian oil in tiny amounts to add additional protection around plants, boundaries, on tools and even on yourself, for protection and blessings of good fortune.

Alternate Herbs

Garlic (*Allium sativum*), Leek (*Allium ampeloprasum*)

To give your Chives a boost, feed them your coffee grounds. They add much-needed minerals to ensure good growth.

Chives come to us from Asia, where they have long been prized as a respiratory illness remedy. They are also known to chase away evil energies, especially those energies ready to prey on the sick.

Garlic House-and-Contents Selling Spell

Garlic helps with breakthroughs and so it is perfect for anyone trying to sell – anything! – but is particularly good for people who sell online from home. It can even be used for selling the house itself! Rosemary is used to protect your financial transaction and to ensure the value of the item you are selling is appreciated. Gold is the colour of abundance, so you are going to use it liberally.

Timings: Waxing Moon, Thursday, Daytime

Find and Gather

- a clove of Garlic (*Allium sativum*)
- a sprig of Rosemary (*Salvia rosmarinus*)
- a white pillar candle
- 4 gold coins
- a gold permanent marker
- a gold candleholder/plate
- a compass

The Spell

Place your golden candle onto your holder/plate.

Sprinkle rosemary leaves onto it and say:

Today I begin a spell to sell.
Today I will find a buyer.
They will love the item I have to sell,
in fact it is all they desire.

With your gold pen, draw the object you want to sell on your candle. Cut the garlic clove in half and rub it over your candle holder/plate. Place the candle in the middle of the sprinkled Rosemary leaves on the plate and place it in a window that faces the street or close to the main entrance to your home. Place the gold coins around the candle at North, South, East and West. Use the compass to be sure if you do not know North. When you are ready to invite the selling energy, light the candle and say:

From all directions,
Let them come.
Buy my (say whatever it is you are wanting to sell)
Before the setting of the Sun.

The time that you do this could be during the 'open for inspection', if selling a house, or when you have someone negotiating the sale of an item with you either in person or via the phone or even via email. You can cut the flame and relight it at any time (this boosts the energy), but leave it in your window/near your front entrance until you sell your item.

Alternate Herbs

There are no alternates for this spell.

Rosemary has been used as a magickal ingredient, usually a wash, to promote longevity and beauty, for centuries. It ensures that people, and objects, are appealing.

Garlic has been used in healing for well over 3,000 years. Ancient Egyptians revered it so much they believed that onions and garlic were equally powerful and deities themselves.

Passion Flower Sweet-Family Spell

Passion Flower will not only bring balance to a situation and between people, it will calm everyone down. This spell is very effective between sparring siblings and could be called a school-holiday magick potion.

Timings: Waning Moon, Wednesday, Dusk

Find and Gather

- 1 tablespoon of dried Passion Flower flowers (*Passiflora incarnata*)
- 1 cup of fresh lemon juice
- ¾ cup of castor/fine sugar
- 1 cup of boiling water
- 2 cups of cold water
- ½ cup of additional water
- a large glass jug to store lemonade in fridge

The Spell

Mix together the boiling water and the sugar and stir until dissolved. Let cool completely.

Bring to the boil the Passion Flower flowers and additional water. Remove from heat and let cool completely.

Add lemon juice and cold water to the sugar mix and say:

Sweet and sour,

Mix and mingle.

Add the Passion Flower mix and say:

Balanced and calm,

Waters flow.

Bring happier times,

Wherever you go.

Store in the fridge and serve in tumblers full of ice cubes.

This drink is particularly good to serve if siblings are not getting on or they are about to go on a trip together or share an activity.

Alternate Herbs

You can use commercially prepared organic Passion Flower tea.

NOTE: Passion Flower should only be consumed in small amounts and occasionally.

Passion Flower is a mild sedative and is used extensively in herbal remedies for insomnia, anxiety and stress.

Christian missionaries in Spain during the 15th century integrated the flowers of Passion Flower within their teachings: the ten petals represent the ten apostles; the radial filaments represent the crown of thorns; the three stigmata, three nails; the five anthers, five wounds; the tendrils, the whips used against Christ; and the blue and white colours represent Heaven and purity.

Feverfew and Comfrey Travel Spell

This talisman can be easily slipped into a cotton crochet crystal holder or tiny mojo bag. You might like to craft a loop out of air-dry clay to thread a necklace chain or cord through. You can also tuck the talisman into your bag or suitcase. Walnut shells are perfect natural lockets as they are natural guardians of magick.

The addition of Feverfew will offer you protection from accidents and Comfrey will ensure safe and trouble-free travels. The crystal malachite is used in this spell for its ability to offer protection to travellers, to ward off the evil eye and for the additional gift of helping those who fear flying.

Timings: Full Moon, Thursday, Midday

Find and Gather

+ ¼ teaspoon of dried Feverfew (*Tanacetum parthenium*)
+ ¼ teaspoon of dried Comfrey (*Symphytum officinale*)
+ two clean and dry walnut shell halves
+ a very small malachite crystal
+ strong glue
+ optional: crochet crystal holder or tiny mojo bag

The Spell

Mix together the Feverfew and Comfrey and place into one half of a walnut shell.

Place the malachite crystal on top of herb mix and say:

> *Travel well,*
> *Within this shell.*
> *Take me with you,*
> *Travel well.*

Glue the two walnut shells together and leave to dry as per the glue manufacturer's instructions.

You may like to decorate the closed walnut shells or cover them in air-dry clay.

Wear when travelling.

You can give this talisman to another, but ensure that you ask their permission to cast a spell over it for their protection.

Alternate Herbs

There are no alternates for this spell.

In many Italian fairytales, walnuts are depicted as containing something very precious.

Feverfew has been used to protect against accidents and as a medicinal aid for the injured. During the construction of the Greek Parthenon in 5 BC, a workman's life was saved after being treated with Feverfew. Such was the regard for the incident that the plant still today bears reference to it with the name *parthenium*.

Lemongrass and White Sage Argument-Release Spell

The use of smoke in magickal work assists in spreading the energies you wish to impart into a space and also releasing those you do not want, which the smoke takes away when it dissipates. For this reason, it is vitally important that you open all windows and doors when wanting to release certain energies. This helps them waft away with the smoke.

The addition of Lemongrass in this spell helps improve communication and refresh the atmosphere, which will probably be rather heavy after a disagreement. Sage is a favourite for smudging because it offers protection and very effectively clears away negative energies.

Timings: Waning Moon, Wednesday, Evening

Find and Gather

- a small bunch of Lemongrass leaves (*Cymbopogon*)
- a small bunch of Sage leaves (*Salvia officinalis*)
- organic cotton or hemp string
- a feather or firm leaf
- a bowl
- sand

The Spell

Bunch together your Lemongrass and Sage leaves.

Ensure that they are dry (*not fully dried, though*). Cut a piece of string at least four times the length of your bundle.

Tie your bundle together very tightly at one end, at the top of the leaves.

Wind your string to the end of the bundle in a spiral-type pattern. Tie off at the end and cut off the string. Tie the string again at the bottom and wind the string up the bundle but this time try and crisscross across the previous string. You should end up with the bundle firmly held together with the string.

As you are winding the string, say:

Around I circle you, around and within.
The blessings you share with me.
The blessings I send.

Hang to dry out completely for a few weeks in a cool, dry place.

To use, ensure that all windows and doors are open. Light the end (with the leaves) with a flame. Once it has caught, gently blow out so it is left smouldering. Use the feather or leaf to help waft the smoke around the space you wish to cleanse and empower. Put out embers on your smudge stick by pushing it into a sand-filled bowl.

Alternate Herbs

Lavender (*Lavandula*), Cedar (*Cedrus*)

Growing Lemongrass around the garden is said to keep snakes away from your home.

Write a wish on a Sage leaf and place it under your pillow for three consecutive nights. If you dream of what you wish for, you will receive it. If you do not, then make sure you bury the leaf in the garden. To not do so can cause bad luck.

Gotu Kola Dog-Training Spell

Liquid Gotu Kola drops are relatively easy to obtain from health-food shops, but should you be lucky enough to have access to the plant, simply boil up a cup of water and a handful of leaves, strain and use ¼ cup of the liquid in this recipe.

Gotu Kola helps with memory and to ensure the mind stays focused, but most importantly it imparts calm. This spell is best done when giving your dog a bath, but you can also place the Gotu Kola into a misting bottle and top up with water and spray lightly over your dog's coat before a training session.

Timings: Waxing Moon, Wednesday, Midday

Find and Gather

- 10 drops of liquid Gotu Kola (*Centella asiatica*)
- 4 cups of pure water
- 1 cup of baby shampoo
- 1 cup of apple cider vinegar
- ⅓ cup of glycerin
- large glass bowl
- wooden spoon
- glass bottle to store

The Spell

Place all the ingredients together into the glass bowl.

Slowly stir in a clockwise direction to mix well and say:

Magickal mix, created with care.

Calming and learning the things that we share.

You may also like to add a few drops of lavender essential oil for fragrance. Lavender will also impart an additional calming influence should your dog be highly excitable.

The addition of 2 tablespoons of pure Aloe Vera gel will assist dogs who may have sensitive skin or be experiencing heat rash or any other mild skin irritation.

Pour into the glass bottle, seal and keep in a cool, dry place.

To use, shake well and use about a tablespoon for a medium-sized short-haired dog. Adjust the quantity to suit the size and coat of your dog. Lather up well and, as you do, speak calmly to your dog about training and your hopes and goals for it, which you will both benefit from.

Rinse your dog very well.

Alternate Herbs

Brahmi (*Bacopa monnieri*), Rosemary (*Rosmarinus officinalis*)

....

Gotu Kola is also known as Pennywort and has been used for hundreds of years for many health issues including arthritis and other age-related problems. A popular saying testifies to this: 'Two leaves a day keeps old age away.'

....

A traditional Sri Lankan breakfast dish, 'Kola kanda', is created from Gotu Kola, boiled rice and coconut.

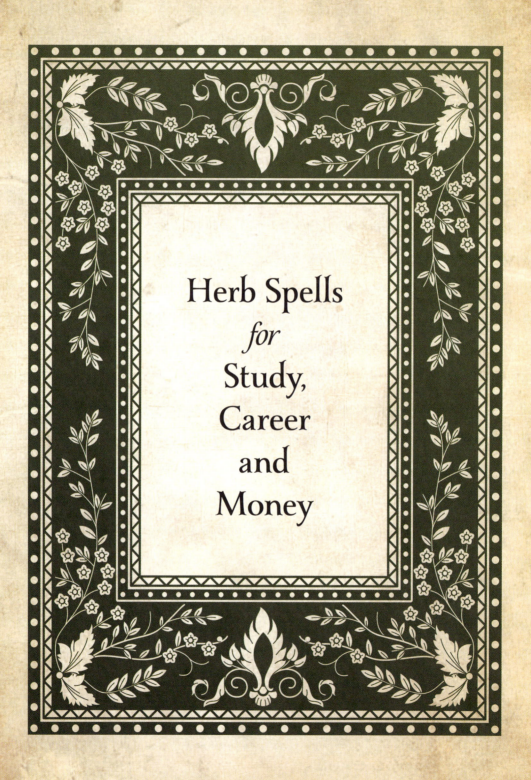

Herb Spells
for
Study,
Career
and
Money

Hawthorn Work-Harmony Spell

Hawthorn imparts harmony, happiness and fertility. It makes a very good herb to use in workplace spells, ensuring that everyone is working productively, getting on and being happy.

You should obtain permission before tapping into anything in their personal space and I have given suggestions for alternative places to position your spell boxes.

The option of black tourmaline could be considered if there have been very stressful/negative workplace dramas – it will clear the energy and offer support against the negativity returning.

Timings: Full Moon, Wednesday, Sunrise

Find and Gather

+ dried leaves/flowers of Hawthorn (*Crataegus laevigata*)
+ a small matchbox for each work station or desk
+ strong tape
+ optional: a tiny piece of black tourmaline for each box

The Spell

Place all matchboxes in a circle.

Add a small pinch of Hawthorn into each box, working in a clockwise direction, and say with each:

Harmony, happiness, working together.

Happiness, harmony, no matter the weather.

If you would like to add an additional energetic boost, particularly if there is a lot of tension in the workplace, add a tiny piece of black tourmaline.

Tape a box under each desk/workstation. As you do say:

Harmony, happiness, working together.

Happiness, harmony, no matter the weather.

Herb Spells ✦ 149

If obtaining permission for those you work with is not possible, you can either bury a box at each corner of your workplace building or tape one in each inner corner of the workplace.

If tensions rise in the office, try tapping three times gently on your box and say:

Calmly now,
Settle low.
Work together as we go.

Alternate Herbs

Hops (*Humulus lupulus*)

Hawthorn, Oak and Ash trees growing together indicate places where you may see faeries.

Maypoles are often created from, and decorated with, Hawthorn branches. Because Hawthorn symbolises fertility, love and marriage, it is a good choice for May Day fertility-connected rites and rituals.

Thyme New-Place Spell

The addition of Thyme in this spell helps to make the wearer of the oil more attractive to others, but it also gives the wearer courage and a boost in energy. This support can help when settling into a new job, a new place of study or even undertaking a new pastime, hobby or sport.

Only a very small amount needs to be used, but still, make sure that you use carrier oil that suits your skin. Roll or place a drop on your inner wrist when needed. Empty roller bottles can be sourced online. You can use a small dropper bottle as well.

Timings: Waxing Moon, Sunday, Sunrise

Find and Gather

+ 11 fresh Thyme leaves (*Thymus vulgaris*)
+ sweet almond oil or other skin-safe pure oil
+ a glass/crystal bowl
+ a gold cloth
+ a picture of the place of your new beginning
+ a small glass roller bottle or dropper bottle

The Spell

Set this spell up in a sunny place – one you feel really safe and happy in because you want this energy to blend with the oil.

Lay down the gold cloth and set the bowl and picture upon it.

Pour the oil into the bowl.

Place the Thyme leaves into the bowl and say:

> *Starting now,*
> *With things all anew.*
> *Thyme guide me there*
> *With the things that you do.*

Leave the bowl in the sun for a good hour to absorb the positive energies of your chosen place as well as the power of the Sun.

After an hour, stir the Thyme-infused oil in a clockwise direction and then pour into your bottle and seal.

To use, roll or drop a tiny amount on your inner wrist or your inner arm and rub in.

Use before you go to your new place and any time you feel uneasy and can no longer detect the scent of Thyme.

Alternate Herbs

There are no alternatives for this spell.

Thyme will help you see fairies. Wearing it in your hair, in a locket or pinned to your clothing will allow you vision into their world.

A popular herb with the Ancient Greeks. Thyme was used to purify sacred places such as temples as well as being burned for magickal rituals. You could do the same today.

Catnip Change-at-Work Spell

With its mint-like and refreshing properties, Catnip will help invigorate any situation. Apply after washing and conditioning your hair, especially on the first day of your working week, to see energies move in your favour. Catnip also attracts happiness and friendship. An added benefit of this rinse is that it promotes a healthy scalp, and removes dandruff and build-up of residue.

Don't make this rinse too far ahead; it should be created no more than 24 hours before you wish to use it. The perfect time would be the night before the first day of your working week.

Timings: Full Moon, Late Night

Find and Gather

+ 2 tablespoons of Catnip leaves (*Nepeta cataria*)
+ 2 cups of pure water
+ a glass jar

The Spell

Boil the water and then remove from the heat.

Add the Catnip and stir well.

Cover and leave for a few hours to steep and cool, then strain into a glass jar or other glass container.

Wash your hair as usual and then pour the Catnip rinse over your hair. Massage through your hair and focus on exactly how your day will look when your changes happen. Be very specific.

Say the things you want to occur, out loud, then rinse out.

Don't use this rinse too often if you have dry hair as it can be a little harsh.

The effects will last a very long time so you really do not need to anyway.

Alternate Herbs

There are no alternatives for this spell.

Shake hands with a person you wish to be long-time friends with while holding a catnip leaf. Keep the leaf somewhere safe and the bond will last forever.

Catnip is entwined strongly with magick, possibly because cats, which are a witch's familiar, love this herb. It is said that if you provide it for your cat, a strong psychic bond will develop between you both. A dried larger leaf is believed to be the very best bookmark for any magickal texts.

Goldenseal New-Skills Spell

Awaken yourself to being receptive to learning new skills with the properties of Goldenseal. As well as bringing a calm and cooling effect, this herb helps open up the magickal energies of possibility. Herbalists often use Goldenseal in conjunction with other herbs to boost their effectiveness. For this spell you will need something connected with your new skill. This can be a textbook, a tool or other materials.

Timings: Waxing Moon, Wednesday, Late Night

Find and Gather

- 1 tablespoon of dried Goldenseal (*Hydrastis canadensis*)
- 1 cup of pure water
- a fluorite crystal bracelet, pendant or tumblestone
- a glass/crystal bowl
- something connected with your new skill
- a piece of paper (*larger than your bowl*)
- a pen
- an orange cloth

The Spell

Bring the water to the boil and add the Goldenseal.

Simmer for a few minutes, then take off the heat and let cool completely.

Place your paper on a table and put the bowl upon it. Set up the thing you selected to represent your new skills above your bowl (above means the side furthest from you on the opposite side of the bowl to you).

Pour the Goldenseal water into the bowl.

Take your fluorite crystal and lower it into the water and say:

Sealed with gold,

New skills be mine.

Using the pen, write down all the things you will need to learn in order to gain your skill. Don't worry if you cannot think of all of them. Write as many as you can and then say:

May I learn all that I need

to be all that I want to be.

Take out your fluorite and dry it on the orange cloth. Wear or carry it with you when you undertake study or training for your new skill. Fold the paper and bury it under a large tree. Pour Goldenseal water over it.

Alternate Herbs

Ginkgo (*Ginkgo biloba*)

Goldenseal was an important medicine for the North American Indians. It was used for a vast amount of ailments and as an antibiotic and antiseptic.

You can also use Goldenseal in spells to promote abundance and to increase your finances.

Allspice and Patchouli Luck Spell

Patchouli is included in this spell because it helps things to grow and attracts money. Allspice is a naturally lucky herb and is also a good friend of money. The use of a citrine crystal will help with prosperity. Aventurine is also included because it supports those seeking luck.

Timings: Full Moon, Thursday, Morning

Find and Gather

✦ ½ cup of dried Allspice (*Pimenta dioica*)
✦ ½ cup of dried Patchouli (*Pogostemon cablin*)

154 ✦ Earth Magick

- 2 green candles
- 2 candleholders
- a beautiful box with a lid
- a green cloth
- a citrine crystal
- an aventurine crystal

The Spell

Place a green candle in a holder on either side of your box

Place the green cloth into the box. Add the citrine crystal and say:

> *Brilliant crystal,*
> *Glow and my luck grow.*

Place the aventurine crystal in the box and say:

> *Lucky crystal,*
> *Share your charms my way.*

Sprinkle in the Allspice and say:

> *Herb of Earth,*
> *Herb of Money and Luck,*
> *Grow.*

Sprinkle in the Patchouli and say:

> *Herb of Earth,*
> *Herb of Money and Abundance,*
> *Grow.*

Light the candles and leave them until they burn out. Place the candle stubs inside the box. When you wish to boost your luck, open the box and ask for it.

Alternate Herbs

Patchouli » Bergamot (*Citrus bergamia*)
Allspice » Basil (*Ocimum basilicum*)

Sprinkling Patchouli into your purse or wallet will attract money. Sprinkling Patchouli directly onto the money you plan to use for investment or gambling is supposed to add luck.

Allspice is made from the dried, unripe berries of a Pimenta tree.

Ginseng and Guarana Study Spell

Ginseng has been used for centuries in herbal medicine and magick to increase and maintain stamina as well as cure just about anything. Guarana is a natural stimulant which contains caffeine, but also other compounds, which seem to prolong its effect. The inclusion of Ginseng and Guarana in this spell harnesses those attributes to create a small mojo bag that you can carry on your person to give you a mental and physical boost while studying.

Timings: Waxing Moon, Wednesday, Late Night

Find and Gather

- 1 teaspoon of dried Ginseng (*Panax pseudoginseng*)
- 1 teaspoon of dried Guarana (*Paullinia cupana*)
- a small gold bag
- a tiny piece of paper
- a pen
- a tiny magnifying glass or piece of glass with smooth edges

The Spell

Place all the ingredients for your spell before you.

Take your piece of paper and write the following words on it:

Study hard and study well.

Focus strong and focus well.

Place the tiny magnifying glass or piece of glass on the centre of the paper. Fold the paper up around the glass, then pop the bundle into the gold bag.

Sprinkle the Ginseng into the bag and say:

All that I need is provided.

All that I need to do I can.

Sprinkle in the Guarana and say:

Study long, study well.

Close the bag and carry it with you whenever you are studying.

Alternate Herbs

None are suitable, though you can create this spell with just one of the herbs. Be mindful that although either is good for study, you will miss the additional attributes each brings.

The Latin name of Ginseng affirms its reputation as a cure-all. 'Panax' is broken down to 'pan', which means 'all', and 'ax', which comes to us via the word 'akos', meaning remedy. Ginseng has been in use in China for over 5,000 years.

Guarana is an Amazonian plant, which has been used for centuries by local Amazonian cultures. Most myths about the herb relate to its appearance - the peeled seeds that look very much like human eyes. All myths seem to tell of an unfortunate incident and the gods gifting the Guarana to the tribe to somehow make things right.

Elecampane Legal-Success Spell

Elecampane is used in this spell because it has a very strong influence on progress and so can help you move legal matters along and to your favour. Bay leaves bring victory.

Timings: Full Moon, Thursday, Morning

Find and Gather

- ✦ dried or fresh Elecampane flowers (*Inula helenium*)
- ✦ 1 Bay leaf (*Laurus nobilis*)
- ✦ an orange cloth
- ✦ an orange candle
- ✦ a candleholder
- ✦ a knife, scalpel, awl or something to carve candle with

The Spell

Lay out the orange cloth.

Carve the candle with the date that is important to your legal matter. This should probably be the court or arbitration date.

Herb Spells ✦ 157

With both hands, hold the candle before you and say:

On (say the date) *my time will come.*

(Say the outcome you desire)

Will be done.

Place the candle in its holder in the middle of the orange cloth.

Beginning at another corner of the cloth, first place the Bay leaf pointing to the left, then place your Elecampane flowers in a row which gradually spirals around the candle until you circle around and around and end up at the candle. You can intersperse the spiral with small white flowers if you have not found enough Elecampane flowers.

Once you reach the candle, light it and say:

We meet at the middle,

Balance shall be.

Now light my way forward,

A win for me.

Once the candle has burned down, bury the flowers and candle stub in the earth. If your legal matter involves you wanting to receive something, then bury on your property. Should a win mean that you are released from something, then you must bury as far away from your property as you can manage.

Alternate Herbs

If you do not have many Elecampane flowers, you can fill out your spiral mandala with simple white flowers such as Daisies.

The flowers of Elecampane often smell like chocolate and the roots, when dried, of sweet Violet. The plant is used to flavour absinthe along with other liqueurs, beers and confectionery.

Elecampane was a very treasured medicinal herb in monasteries throughout Europe. Its properties for healing respiratory diseases are well documented, particularly for whooping cough (*when all else has failed*).

Wild Yam and Potato Money Spell

Wild Yam is native to North America and is included in this spell because it has properties that attract abundance. Potatoes ensure prosperity and comfort, and the action of planting this spell encourages growth. Be sure that you look after your 'Money Plant' well.

Timings: Waxing Moon, Thursday, Daytime

Find and Gather

- 1 tablespoon of dried Wild Yam root (*Dioscorea villosa*)
- a gold coin
- a large potato
- a patch of sunny earth (*from the garden*)
- a knife
- a spoon
- a length of gold ribbon 30 cm/12"

The Spell

Cut the potato in half and, using the spoon, scoop out a hole in one half big enough to fit your gold coin and Wild Yam root into.

Place your coin into the hole and say:

> *Seed of gold,*
> *Time to grow.*

Sprinkle Wild Yam root onto the gold coin and say:

> *Fertilised and fed,*
> *Awake from your bed.*

Put the potato back together and tie the ribbon around it to hold the halves together.

Bury near the front entrance of your home, in a sunny spot, preferably on your land.

Water and care for your Money Garden as you would any garden.

Water, weed and watch over it.

You may like to decorate the area. If you are having money problems in the future, fertilise again by sprinkling Wild Yam root over the earth.

Alternate Herbs

There are no alternatives for this spell.

Wild Yam was also known as Devil's Bone and can be used for other magickal purposes including carrying a piece in a red cloth so you might attract a suitable new lover.

Soak Wild Yam in rainwater overnight and then use it to wash your hands before performing magickal work. It will increase your power.

Valerian Make-the-Best-of-Things Spell

Valerian is used in this spell because it helps us to accept the way things are but to still make the best of them. It is also a herb for protection and purification, which may support you when you find life a little difficult.

Kyanite crystal is said to boost our determination and stimulate creativity.

Timings: Waxing Moon, Saturday, Daytime

Find and Gather

Plate XLVIII.

- a small chunk of Valerian root (Valeriana officinalis)
- a teaspoon of dried, chopped Valerian root)
- a small dome-type hand-rung bell
- a small square of white cloth
- a tiny Kyanite crystal
- some string

The Spell

Take the ringer out of the bell.

Place the chopped or crushed Valerian root into the middle of the small piece of cloth and place the Kyanite crystal in the centre.

Tie it into a ball to replicate a bell ringer. You might need to trim excess fabric.

Tie a piece of string to the original anchor point inside the bell and then the ball of Valerian root to the other end of the string. It may hang a little lower than the original ringer.

Keep the bell in a sunlit spot, preferably a windowsill, so it can absorb the positive and optimistic energies of the Sun each day.

When things are not going your way and you are looking to make the best of your situation or to encourage ideas and inspiration to find your way forward, 'ring' the bell three times and say:

May I find that I can do as I please,
With what I've been given.

Alternate Herbs

Frankincense (*Boswellia*)

The Pied Pier used a piece of Valerian root as well as a flute to encourage the rats of Hamelin to leave. It was this myth that lead rat poison manufacturers to include it in their formulas.

The Ancient Greeks would hang Valerian under their windows to ensure evil would not enter the house.

Sandalwood and Cinnamon Better-Business Spell

Sandalwood inspires and keeps optimism fresh. Cinnamon is a herb that attracts luck in business, as well as money. In this spell you will be leaving the 'dreamcatcher-like' circle completely open so you may catch more business. Using ribbons, threads and yarns in red, yellow and orange will encourage success, creativity and boost workers' and customers' passion for your business.

You can make this catcher as large or small (even very tiny) as you desire. It will not affect the power of the spell.

Timings: Waxing Moon, Thursday, Daytime

Find and Gather

- pieces of dried Sandalwood (*Santalum*)
- pieces of dried Cinnamon (*Cinnamomum verum*)
- wire or a wire coat hanger
- wire cutters
- pliers
- scissors
- strong electrical tape
- ribbons, threads and yarns in various shades of red, yellow and orange

The Spell

Cut a length of wire from your coat hanger or cut the wire you have to the desired length (*enough to create a circle large or small enough to your liking*).

Bring the two ends together and connect by overlapping the ends of the wire and twisting them together with the pliers, then cover the join with the electrical tape.

Tie your collection of ribbons, yarns and threads to the bottom third of the circle so that they hang down from the circle. Make them random lengths and mix them up.

Next, tie pieces of Cinnamon and Sandalwood to some of the hanging ribbons.

Make sure you end up with an even number of pieces of the two herbs.

Once you have completed your catcher, hang it in a place that faces the door to your business, or if you have a home/online business, hang it facing either the front door or your main working area and visualise your business increasing and becoming very successful and say:

Welcome, business,
Old and new.
Let's grow together,
Me and you.

Alternate Herbs

You can create this circle by using just one of the herbs.

The fragrance of Sandalwood comes from its heartwood. The tree was recognised as having been saved from extinction after Tippu, Sultan of Mysore, India declared it a 'Royal Tree' in 1792.

Cinnamon oil was used by the Ancient Egyptians in their embalming process.

Herb Spells *for* Protection, Clearing and Banishment

Agrimony and Coltsfoot Bad Vibe Clearing Spell

Agrimony has a long history of being a very good home protector. It is also a general protective herb against evil. Coltsfoot is included in this spell because it has the ability to cleanse an area and add tranquillity in its wake. It is a spreading plant, much like mint, and it is this as well as the other mentioned qualities that make it a great floor-wash herb. Orange blossom water will effectively and positively lift the energy.

Timings: Waning Moon, Monday, Late Night/Midnight

Find and Gather

+ ½ cup of dried Agrimony (*Agrimonia eupatoria*)
+ ½ cup of dried Coltsfoot (*Tussilago farfara*)
+ ¼ cup of orange blossom water
+ ½ bucket water

The Spell

Open all the windows and doors of the space you wish to cleanse of bad vibes.

Mix together all the ingredients in the clean bucket.

Place a mop in and mix in a clockwise direction and say:

> *Herbs of happiness,*
> *Herbs of light,*
> *Dark vibes now leave,*
> *Good vibes in sight.*

Wash over the floor and, as you do, visualise the bad and negative vibes leaving via the doors and windows while the good vibes are welcomed in. Pour the remaining water into the ground under a good, big tree.

164 + Earth Magick

Alternate Herbs

You can substitute the orange blossom water with rose water. Coltsfoot can be a little difficult to obtain, so a good substitute is Lavender (*Lavandula*).

Agrimony has a solid reputation for being a multi-faceted healer of nearly all human adverse conditions. Its name suggests it has benefits for eye problems - 'agremone' means 'white spec on the cornea'.

Coltsfoot is used to create a UK confectionery product named Coltsfoot Rock. It is from Lancashire, England and is a hardened stick of brittle rock candy flavoured with Coltsfoot.

Tansy and Mugwort Protection Spell

A Seguro, created by South American Sharmans, is a magickal bottle filled with herbs. Seguros are believed to hold the shadow side of the Sharman and the spirit of the herbs. Shaking the bottle awakens the magickal energy. In this Seguro spell, we are harnessing the energy of the Sun and the Moon to create a powerful guardian.

Tansy is added to represent the Sun and offer you longevity and life, while Mugwort is there to represent the Moon and will gift you strength and protection.

Timings: Full Moon, Wednesday, Dusk

Find and Gather

- 1 tablespoon of dried Tansy (*Tanacetum vulgare*)
- 1 tablespoon of dried Mugwort (*Artemisia vulgaris*)
- a beautiful bottle with seal/lid
- pure water
- 1 teaspoon of tiny pebbles or crystals

The Spell

Put the Tansy and Mugwort into your bottle and say:
> *Herb of Sun,*
> *Herb of Moon,*
> *Together watch over me*
> *Day and night.*

Herb Spells ✦ 165

Put the pebbles or crystals into your bottle and say:

Grounded in Earth

The Spirits hold true.

Top up the bottle with water.

Blow into the bottle three times and then quickly seal.

Blowing into the bottle adds your energy to the Seguro and the spirits of the herbs so that they will know you, to take care of you and protect you.

Place your Seguro where you feel you need protection.

If you need additional help, shake the Seguro bottle three times and simply ask for its help.

Alternate Herbs

Tansy » St John's Wort (*Hypericum perforatum*)

Tansy is thought to prolong life. This belief is said to have come from the story of Ganymede, who was given Tansy so he could become immortal. Ganymede was a Trojan prince who was turned into an eagle and then carried off to Heaven by the god Zeus, where he became the cup-bearer of the gods.

Folklore states that if you put Mugwort into your shoes you will be able to walk all day. Roman soldiers did this so they could march for prolonged periods.

Yerba Maté Barrier-Breaker Spell

Yerba Maté is a stimulant and will assist you in breaking through any obstacles you are currently facing. It will activate things that have been dormant or have not been working. There are many spells that prescribe freezing objects in order to hold their energy, but in this spell we are meeting the 'frozen' barrier and then bursting through it.

Timings: Waxing Moon, Tuesday, Midday

Find and Gather

- about a teaspoon of Yerba Maté (*Ilex paraguariensis*) in any form
- a piece of paper
- a pen
- a ziplock bag or similar
- pure water
- a hammer
- a thick towel

The Spell

Write your obstacle on the piece of paper.

    Put the paper in the ziplock bag.

    Half-fill the ziplock bag with the water.

    Place the Yerba Maté into the bag and seal.

    Shake well to mix.

    Put in the freezer and leave for seven days.

    Each morning take out the bag, breath over it and say:

    Slowly you melt, walls soon to fall.

    Soon to be down and I'll have it all.

    On the seventh day, take the bag outside.

    Place it on the towel and smash up the ice as much as possible.

    You must be thinking of your obstacle as you do this.

    Visualise the obstacle disappearing with the ice.

    Collect all the remains of the spell and bury far from your property.

Alternate Herbs

Agrimony (*Agrimonia*)

Yerba Maté is a traditional South American herb used for medicines and in ritual. It is said to have been gifted to the tribes by a 'white-bearded God'.

The stimulating effect of Yerba Maté makes it a milder and, some think, healthier alternate to coffee because it does not interfere with sleep.

Foxglove and Dragon's Blood Complete-Protection Spell

The creation of witch bottles goes back hundreds of years and, still today, occasional bottles from years ago have been dug up. Witch bottles were popular throughout the UK and Europe and even North America. They were traditionally buried in the front garden of a home to protect the house, garden and all who lived within.

You will need a selection of sharp objects for this spell. These can include: pins, needles, broken glass, broken mirror, razor blades, metal pieces, nails and thorns.

Foxglove is included for its powers to protect the home – especially the gardens and borders of properties. Dragon's Blood is a resin obtained from the trees of the Dracaena *genus of plants and it is included here for its exceptionally good reputation for providing protection and exorcising demonic and evil entities.*

Timings: New Moon, Saturday, Midnight

Find and Gather

+ 1 teaspoon of Dragon's Blood resin (*Dracaena*)
+ 9 fresh or dried Foxglove flowers (*Digitalis*)
+ a selection of sharp objects
+ a glass bottle with a lid
+ urine or vinegar
+ 1 tablespoon of coarse-ground salt
+ a candle
+ newspapers

The Spell

Fill the bottle to about halfway with all the dry ingredients and then add the urine or vinegar until the dry ingredients are covered.

Secure the lid and then seal it with wax. To do this, hold bottle on its side over a newspaper, light the candle and drip wax over the bottle's lid until it is fully covered.

Bury the bottle approximately 30 cm/12" deep in your front yard.

The protection will last a year and you should create a new witch bottle each year. You do not need to dig up the old bottles, nor should you.

Alternate Herbs

Traditionally, all witch bottles are made with urine but white vinegar is a good substitute.

If you add a tiny pinch of Dragon's Blood resin to any other incense, you will increase its potency. This is also true for herbs in spells. If you feel you need a magickal boost, try a tiny sprinkle.

In Wales, a dye was made from Foxglove and painted on the floors of homes, in crossed lines, to stop evil from entering.

Juniper Berry Personal-Boundary Spell

Sometimes it can be very hard to set personal boundaries. If you are feeling that yours are not being respected or that setting them is a challenge, then this spell will help you focus good and clear energy to not only set boundaries but keep them strong.

Juniper will provide personal protection from accidents, sickness and negative spiritual activity like malevolent ghosts, and break any magickal work directed towards you.

Timings: Full Moon, Sunday, Dusk

Find and Gather

✦ a dozen dried Juniper berries (*Juniperus communis*)
✦ a large sheet of paper
✦ a pen/pencil
✦ a white candle
✦ 4 black candles
✦ a heatproof dish/incense burner
✦ a block of incense/charcoal
✦ matches

The Spell

Draw a compass on your paper like the one pictured.

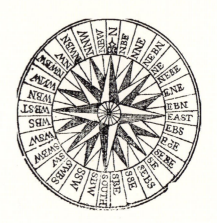

Place a black candle next to each of the Cardinal Points: North, South, East and West. Light the candles and say:

Power of light from the dark,
Hold my space and protect.

Place three Juniper berries between each candle on the curve of the compass.

Place the white candle in the middle of the compass. Light it and say:

Filled with purity,
Filled with light.

Let the candles burn down (almost to their ends) and then light the incense/charcoal as per the manufacturer's directions. Place the incense/charcoal in the heatproof dish/incense burner and drop the Juniper berries into it. The smoke will further purify and strengthen your personal boundaries.

Bury all remains of your spell under a tree on your property.

Alternate Herbs

Rose Geranium flowers (*Pelargonium graveolens*) can be used in place of the Juniper berries. If you wish to burn these flowers you will need to dry them first and then crush them.

It is believed, particularly in Wales in the United Kingdom, that anyone cutting down a Juniper tree will bring death to themselves or to a family member within a year.

In the Scottish Highlands, the New Year has been marked with the burning of Juniper incense to ensure good fortune for the coming year.

Garlic Psychic-Attack Protection Spell

Garlic is one of the most powerful protectors against evil, negativity and misfortune. In this spell, you will be weaving strands of hemp or cotton with dried garlic leaves to make a simple bracelet that is very effective in stopping psychic attack or intrusion. People are often unaware that they are intruding upon others with their psychic energy. This is very common at larger gatherings. You may wish to weave some crystal beads or light charms into your bracelet.

Timings: Full Moon, Sunday, Late Night

Find and Gather

- dried stem of Garlic (*Allium sativum*)
- hemp or thick cotton string
- a black candle
- a white cloth
- a black cloth
- a bowl of water
- 9 drops of lavender essential oil
- a thick hand towel

The Spell

Select a quiet corner of your home or garden to create this spell. Smudge the area well with your choice of an energy-clearing and protecting smudge. You could also use a Lavender or Sage misting spray. Drop the lavender essential oil into the bowl of water. Soak the hand towel in the water and then wring out and lie flat. Separate a long but thin piece of garlic stem and wrap it in the washcloth. This will help it absorb the lavender oil and also soften it to make it easier to work with. Set out your white cloth with all of your ingredients for this spell, then cover with the black cloth and say:

> *Quietly rest, pure in dark.*
> *Nothing to find.*

Leave for one hour.

When you return, take off the black cloth, light the black candle and say three times:

> *Dark light, fill the night.*

Herb Spells

Take the garlic stem and the hemp or cotton string and create a simple plait to a length that will fit your wrist. Tie off each end with a knot. Extinguish the candle flame once you have finished. This bracelet works better if used for only one occasion, event or trip. After use, bury in a place far from your home.

Alternate Herbs

Larger dried Society Garlic leaves (*Tulbaghia violacea*)

Garlic has been used since ancient times to ward off evil. The Sanskrit name of Garlic, 'lasunum', means 'slayer of monsters'.

Garlic harvested on Good Friday is said to hold the strongest medicinal qualities.

Angelica and Honeysuckle Release, Ground and Balance Spell

Using the root of one plant and the flower of another will bring balance and power by combining what is above with what is below. This spell requires the two halves of an eggshell. I recommend that you use the egg white and yolk to ensure that new opportunities know that you will not waste them.

Angelica will offer protection and guard over the balance of your energy, while Honeysuckle will inspire generosity, luck and peacefulness as well as dispel negativity.

Timings: Full Moon, Saturday, Dusk

Find and Gather

- a small piece of Angelica root (*Angelica archangelica*)
- 3 fresh or dried Honeysuckle flowers (*Lonicera*)
- an egg
- a piece of paper
- a pen
- clear tape
- pure water

172 ✦ Earth Magick

The Spell

Dig a hole big enough to bury your eggshell in the ground in a dark area on your property.

Crack your egg and retain the egg white and yolk for another use. Be very careful and try to crack your egg so that you have two halves.

Write your hopes on the piece of paper.

Place your Angelica, Honeysuckle and your written hopes into one half of your shell and then close it as best as you can with the other half, sealing together with clear tape.

Bury your magickal egg in the hole you dug.

For the next seven nights sprinkle a little water on it and say:

Grow my hopes, little flowers,
From above and below.
May balance return to all that I know.

Alternate Herbs

This spell could still work with a combination of a root and flower from any two plants.

Angelica is named after the Archangel Michael and is said to have been his gift to humans as a cure of the plague. Its seeds were often chewed as a form of protection against all contagious diseases.

The root of Angelica is a very popular talisman with the Native Americans when carried on the person. It is believed to promote luck, particularly when gambling.

Nettle and Meadowsweet Reverse Negative-Action Spell

This spell salt can be used in a variety of ways, including as a bath salt and an addition to other spells. You can sprinkle it in a circle around you to contain the negativity you may have caused and then hop out of the circle, or you could add the salt to a water-misting bottle and spray an object or place which has caused, or is connected with, negative action.

Nettle is very good at reversing actions, from curses to bad luck, and can help reverse any negative actions you may have made or those you experience around you.

Meadowsweet will help bring peace to all those connected with the action and lift spirits in order to feel positive about moving on from the negativity.

Timings: Waning Moon, Saturday, Dusk

Find and Gather

- 2 tablespoons of dried Nettle leaves (*Urtica dioica*)
- 2 tablespoons of dried Meadowsweet (*Filipendula ulmaria*)
- 1 cup of rock salt
- a mortar and pestle
- a glass storage jar

The Spell

Place the rock salt, Nettle and Meadowsweet into the mortar and grind together well. While you grind move the pestle in an anti-clockwise direction – this is a spell in which you want to put the energy of 'undoing' something.

You need the mix to be fairly fine. When you are happy with the mix, turn the bowl three times anti-clockwise and say with each turn:

All that was done,
Turn around and undo.
Unravel, go back,
All that was done.

Store the dry ingredients in the glass jar and use as required.

Alternate Herbs

None are suitable for this spell, although the Meadowsweet could be substituted with Meadowsweet flower essence.

Nettle is considered a 'Plant Doctor' and can ensure the good health of all other plants growing near it. Nettle is also believed to have been brought to Earth, from Heaven, by the Angel of Mercy.

If you would like to see fairies and chat with them, inhale fresh Meadowsweet flowers. Doing so gives you the gift of second sight.

Fennel and Cloves Paranormal-Banishment Spell

In this spell you will be making a pair of maracas from two very powerful banishing herbs, Fennel and Cloves. Shaking these herbs will send all types of unwanted paranormal entities out of the area you are cleansing. Rhythmic sounds have been used throughout time in this way, to clear energies and to welcome new ones in.

Fennel will offer healing, protection and purification to your spell while Cloves will offer their own form of protection and, if necessary, will help exorcise any entities found.

You may wish to decorate your maracas. Doing so will lift the energy and help expel unwanted paranormal activity.

Timings: Waning Moon, Tuesday, Midnight

Find and Gather

- 2 tablespoons of Fennel seeds (*Foeniculum vulgare*)
- 2 tablespoons of Cloves (*Syzygium aromaticum*)
- uncooked rice
- 2 cardboard tubes
- an A4 sheet of sturdy cardboard (*or you can recycle 2 x used mailing tubes with caps for the previous 2 items*)
- a marker
- packing tape
- decorative paints and embellishments

The Spell

Decorate your cardboard tubes or A4 cardboard sheet as you like. You may wish to be a little more creative and paint a design. Stand your cardboard tubes upright on your A4 cardboard sheet and trace out two circles for each tube. These will serve as the ends of your maracas. Cut all circles out and with packing tape seal one circle to one end of each of your cardboard tubes. Now fill your tubes with the Fennel seeds

Herb Spells ✦ 175

and Cloves and enough rice to fill the tubes to about a third. Seal the tubes with the other circles and packing tape.

To use, simply shake both maracas in a rhythmic way around areas you feel are experiencing unwanted paranormal activity. The maracas can also be used in combination with other methods and spellcastings focused on banishment of paranormal acitivity.

Alternate Herbs

One of the herbs can be omitted as they have similar energies. Double the quantity if you need to do this.

Fennel was commonly used on Midsummer's Eve in mediaeval times to protect against enchantment.

Cloves are very good at masking odours, which is probably why, in folklore, they have a reputation of making those who carry them on their person more attractive to the opposite sex.

Hyssop and Honey Purification Spell

It is good practice to set aside teacups that are dedicated to singular magickal purposes. In this spell, for example, the purpose is purification and so a white teacup is best. The cup could feature a white flower or design, which will not only attract energies associated with the particular colour and design but also remind us not to use it for any other purpose.

Timings: Full Moon, Sunday, Evening or Morning

Find and Gather

- dried Hyssop (*Hyssopus officinalis*)
- organic honey
- pure water, preferably Full Moon rainwater
- a beautiful teapot
- a white, or predominantly white, teacup
- a white candle
- a candleholder
- a white cloth
- a tray

The Spell

Use 1 teaspoon of Hyssop for each cup of boiling water in your teapot.

Sweeten tea with honey. Sit quietly somewhere in the sunlight to drink your tea.

Create a purification ritual to surround the occasion. Here is one which you may enjoy.

Set a tray with a white cloth and say:

Covered in purity.

Set the candle in its holder on the tray, light it and say:

Filled with light.

Place the teapot, teacup/s and honey pot and spoons on the tray and take to where you will be drinking the tea. You might like to add a White Rose and perhaps a clear quartz crystal to the setting.

Raise the cup before the first sip and say:

Fill me with good, with light and with love.
Leave me/us anew with blessings from above.

Alternate Herbs

There are no alternatives for this spell.

Hyssop has been used since ancient times as a strewing herb, to purify temples and homes; branches of Hyssop were dipped in blood to paint doorways at Jewish Passover.

The liqueur Chartreuse is one of many liqueurs flavoured with Hyssop - the herb was very popular in European monasteries where brewing experiments with many medicinal and sacred herbs were conducted.

Herb Spells ✦ 177

Herb Spells
for
Health,
Self-Care
and
Happiness

Ginger and Peppermint Creativity-Boost Spell

Smelling salts have been used for centuries to revive one who has fainted. In this spell you will be creating a magickal mix to revive and boost dormant or sluggish creativity. This spell is perfect for writer's and artist's block and includes Ginger, to stir passion, and Peppermint, for its ability to raise energetic vibrations.

This smelling-salt mixture can be added to a tiny bottle to be carried and opened when needed, or you may wish to create a tiny fabric sachet to hold the ingredients. Do not hold too close to your nose while inhaling, or breathe over-vigorously. Simply wafting the herbs gently under your nose will do the trick.

Timings: Waxing Moon, Friday, Morning

Find and Gather

- a small piece of fresh Ginger root (*Zingiber officinale*)
- 3 drops of peppermint essential oil
- ¼ cup of rock salt
- a mortar and pestle
- a glass jar to store
- a tiny bottle or a small fabric sachet
- artwork of, or book about, someone you admire
- an orange ribbon

The Spell

Place the rock salt into the mortar and pestle.

Grate the Ginger finely until you have about ½ teaspoon and add to the salt.

Drop in the peppermint essential oil.

While mixing well say:

Awaken my passions
Of book and of brush.
Move blocks in my way,
To inspire my day.

Store in the larger jar, tie the orange ribbon around the neck and leave for seven nights on top of the artwork or the book about the person who inspires you. After seven days, decant the herbs into the smaller bottle or sachet to carry and use as needed.

Alternate Herbs

Any mint oil can be used in place of peppermint.

The Pacific Islanders of Dobu chew Ginger and then spit it onto the site of illness to cure it. They also do this towards oncoming storms to keep them at bay.

Peppermint's medicinal use dates back well over 10,000 years, which has earned it the reputation of perhaps being our oldest medicine. It is generally used as a vascular stimulant, disinfectant and an anaesthetic.

Burdock and Onion Illness-Absorption Spell

Burdock is a herbal folklore favourite when blood cleansing, purifying and health rejuvenation is sought, making it perfect for a general illness spell. The added properties of Burdock's magickal energies help draw out illnesses and carry them away.

Onions are a negative-energy vacuum cleaner and will help boost the power of Burdock in pulling out the illness you are targeting.

Black tourmaline will help protect you while you are opening up to withdraw the illness.

Timings: Waning Moon, Thursday, Midnight

Find and Gather

- 1 teaspoon of dried Burdock (*Arctium lappa*)
- 1 large white onion
- a knife
- a chopping board
- 3 pieces of black tourmaline crystal
- a small red candle
- a small black candle
- a large plate

Earth Magick

The Spell

Set the plate near the ill person.

On either side of the plate, place the candles in holders – the black on the left and the red on the right.

Peel the onion and slice off the top and the bottom so that it sits flat on the plate and you have a flat area on its top, then centre it in the middle of the plate.

Place the black tourmaline crystal pieces evenly around the onion.

Light the candles.

Place the Burdock on the top of the onion and say:

Draw down to onion,

Draw down and hold.

Illness come here and in onion behold.

A new place to live,

a new place to see.

Leave where you are and to onion now be.

When the candles have burned down, take all remains of the spell (except the plate) and onion to a place as far away as you can manage and bury. Come back via a confusing path so that the illness cannot follow you.

Alternate Herbs

You can use a potato in place of the onion, Marigold (*Tagetes*) in place of Burdock.

Burdock collected during a Waning Moon can be made into a very powerful amulet to protect against evil. To make the amulet, dry the root and string it onto a necklace.

Burdock is also used to cure gout. It can be eaten as a vegetable, or its leaves can be placed in shoes or bound to suffering feet.

Yarrow and Calendula Self-Confidence Spell

Yarrow gives courage to those who lack self-confidence. This herb dissipates fears connected with anything that hinders self-expression. It also releases negativity. Calendula will actually draw admiration and respect from others while also helping you realise your potential.

Timings: Full Moon, Wednesday, Midday

Find and Gather

- 1 tablespoon of dried Yarrow (*Achillea millefolium*)
- 1 tablespoon of dried Calendula (*Calendula officinalis*)
- a small purple candle
- a candle holder
- 20 drops of ginger essential oil
- 1 cup of pure water
- a heat-proof glass bowl
- ½ tablespoon of coconut oil
- a bottle to store

The Spell

Boil the water and pour into the glass bowl.

Stir in the Yarrow and the Calendula and say:

Herbs of sun, herbs of powers,
I'm leaving you now to brew for some hours.

Set the candle in the holder and next to the bowl and light it.

Leave the brew to steep until the candle has spent. This will ensure that the energies and attributes of the herbs are imparted into the water.

When ready, strain the water into the bottle and add the coconut oil and ginger essential oil.

Shake well to mix and, as you do say:

Confidence, courage, and belief I now know.
Each time my hair is washed,
These things I will grow.

Make sure you shake this shampoo very well each time you use it.

The strained herbs and candle remains can be buried in a sunny section of your garden.

Alternate Herbs

This spell can be made with other herbs, but to remain faithful to the magickal energies you must use at least one of the listed herbs.

The Greek mythological hero Achilles was dipped head first by his mother into a bath of Yarrow tea, for protection. Because she held him by his heels, this area of his body was unfortunately unprotected.

Since ancient times Calendula has been strung into garlands to celebrate weddings and religious rituals.

Herb Robert and Ginseng Ultimate-Healing Spell

This spell can support those suffering any illness and injury and help them regain their constitution. Herb Robert has a long association with healing and is highly regarded by the herbal medicine community for the breakthroughs it appears to be making in the treatment of certain cancers and terminal illnesses. In this spell we will be focusing on the powerful energies of this herb to support a return to good health.

Ginseng offers endurance so that one can keep their strength in their fight with illness.

You must hand-sew this little spell pillow so that you can 'sew in' the healing energy as you go. This spell pillow can be created for someone else, with their permission, or for yourself.

Timings: Full Moon, Thursday, Midday

Find and Gather

- 1 teaspoon of dried Herb Robert (*Geranium robertianum*)
- 1 teaspoon of dried Ginseng (*Panax ginseng*)
- 1 dried organic flower
- a clear quartz crystal
- 2 squares of red flannel cloth about 15 x 15 cm/6 x 6"
- red thread
- needle

The Spell

Go for a walk and pick the very first non-toxic flower you see. Suitable flowers would be Daisies or Roses. Dry the flower using one of the methods described on page 114. Once your flower is completely dry, choose your day to create your spell and make sure you have everything ready.

On one square of cloth place the dried herbs, with your crystal in the centre. Then lay your flower on top. If your flower is too big, a petal will be enough. Then say:

> *Herbs of healing*
> *Crystal of same.*
> *I gift this precious flower –*
> *Please return health again.*

Take your fabric with the herbs and crystal and sit in a peaceful and sunlit spot, preferably outside in the garden or somewhere in nature and on the ground. With the red thread and needle, sew the top square to the bottom to seal the sachet. Use whatever stitch you please but make sure that you are focused on healing and bringing the body, mind and spirit together again with each stitch.

Place the sachet under your pillow.

Alternate Herbs

There are no alternatives for this spell.

Herb Robert is named after the 11th-century French Saint Robert Abbot of Molerne (*1028-1111*). He was known as a very saintly man during his lifetime and one who possessed great medical skills.

Adding Ginseng to chicken soup makes a very tasty and health-giving meal, which is popular throughout Asia.

Rosemary and Jojoba Hair-Growth Spell

This is my personal, secret hair blend and spell which I use with great success to ensure thick, long and healthy hair. If you begin using it the morning after a New Moon and then stop once the Moon is Full, each month, you will encourage your hair to grow long and healthy.

Rosemary is a well-known stimulant for hair growth, as is Cedar. Clary Sage helps balance natural scale oils and is a calmative, which is good if you feel your hair issues are stress–related.

Timings: New Moon, Friday, Midday

Find and Gather

- 4 tablespoons of jojoba oil
- a long, fresh Rosemary sprig in flower, if possible (*Rosmarinus officinalis*)
- 20 drops of rosemary essential oil
- 10 drops of clary sage essential oil
- 5 drops of cedar essential oil
- 4 tablespoons of coconut oil
- a sterilised glass bottle

The Spell

Wash the Rosemary sprig and hang to dry completely. Once ready, place in the glass storage bottle and fill the bottle with all the other ingredients. Shake well and say:

Plants of the Earth,
Help my hair grow.
Healthy and long,
With sparkle and glow.

Each night warm about a teaspoon of the mixture in your hands and then massage into your scalp. You will need to sleep with a protective pillowcase or towel dedicated to prevent staining of good bed linen.

Alternate Herbs

There are no alternatives for this spell.

Rosemary has been used since ancient times as a memory booster. Scholars in Greece would wear circlets to help them focus on their study.

Jojoba is native to North America. Native Americans crushed the seeds to produce oils and salves for skin conditions and to soften animal hides. Eating the seeds was also believed to make childbirth easier.

Saffron Happy Healing Spell

Saffron is included in this spell because of its healing abilities and its ability to instil mirth to any atmosphere. This spell would be very good to use when administering care to children or to those who respond well to a lighter attitude. In any case, this handwash will increase the healing powers of spell or magickal work and boost the impact of any type of care given to another.

Timings: Waning Moon, Saturday, Midnight

Find and Gather

- 1 cup of pure water
- 1 tablespoon of liquid Soapwort (*Saponaria officinalis*)
- 3 threads of dried Saffron (*Crocus salvia*)
- a small frying pan
- a glass bowl
- a spoon
- an empty handwash dispenser, preferably glass or ceramic

The Spell

Panfry the Saffron for a few minutes over a medium heat, then remove and allow to cool completely.

Pour the water into the bowl and add the Soapwort. Mix by stirring in a clockwise direction and say:

> *Healing hands,*
> *Cleansed in flowers.*
> *Happiness return*
> *with health in showers.*

Stir three times in an anti-clockwise direction and say:

> *Out you go, unhealthy foes.*
> *Take all that is wrong as you go.*

Drop the Saffron threads into the mix, one by one, and say with each:

> *One for healing,*

One for mirth,
and one for strength upon this Earth.

Bottle the mix in the handwash dispenser and then use to wash your hands before performing any magickal spells or work involving healing. The handwash can also be used when caring for those who are sick.

Alternate Herbs

There are no alternatives for this spell.

To stop lizards venturing into your home, folklore suggests that you keep fresh Saffron around the house.

Dried Saffron, as we use it, is created from the stigmas of the flowers of the plant. To produce 100 g/3.5 oz of dried Saffron it requires 60,000 flowers.

Dill and St John's Wort Joyful-Day Spell

Dill will fill you with enthusiasm for the day ahead when used in this magickal salt scrub. It has the added benefit of making you irresistible to others – another way to have a joyful day!

St John's Wort provides a great cure for melancholy. It also dissipates negative thoughts and moods, so will work beautifully with Dill to help you start your day with a positive vibe.

Timings: Full Moon, Friday, Morning

Find and Gather

- 2 tablespoons of fresh or dried Dill (*Anethum graveolens*)
- 2 tablespoons of fresh or dried St John's Wort (*Hypericum perforatum*)
- 5 drops of orange essential oil
- 6 drops of lemon essential oil
- 1 cup of sea salt
- approximately ½ cup of coconut oil
- a glass/crystal bowl
- an airtight glass jar

Herb Spells ✦ 187

The Spell

Add the salt and dried herbs to the bowl and stir well in a clockwise direction.

Add the essential oils and then gradually add the coconut oil.

Stop when you are happy with the consistency. You may like a wetter or drier mix and so may use more or less of the oil.

Place in the storage jar and then turn three times in an anti-clockwise direction and say:

Out you go, gloom.

Out you go, darkness.

Out you go, negative thoughts.

Now turn three times in a clockwise direction and say:

In comes sunshine.

In comes happiness.

In comes positive days.

When required:

Stir your mix with a wood spoon before use so the consistency is even.

You can either add a handful to a warm bath and soak or use as a scrub in the shower.

Alternate Herbs

St John's Wort » Valerian (*Valeriana officinalis*)

Along with being a revered sacred herb by many cultures, St John's Wort has been scientifically proven to be effective in the treatment of depression.

Dill seeds were once known as 'Meeting House Seeds'. Early settlers would chew them during sermons.

Cacao Physical-Energy Spell

This knot spell helps you maintain your physical energy.

Keep your hemp-string vessel handy for days when you feel your energy slipping.

The Cacao will impart vigour on your spell and will ensure that your own vigour does not slip away. You will be filling your vessel with the Sun at the beginning of this spell and can refill it as needed.

Timings: Waxing Moon, Tuesday, Midday

Find and Gather

- 9 Cacao beans (*Theobroma cacao*)
- a ceramic/terracotta vessel with lid
- a length of hemp string 23 cm/9" long

The Spell

Take your ceramic vessel outside and leave in the sun for three hours. Be sure to move it, if necessary, so that the sun directly fills the inside of your vessel all of this time.

Add your Cacao to the vessel and then hold it above your head towards the Sun.

Turn around nine times, clockwise, and say at the end of turning:

Powered by Sun,
The spell has begun.
Vessel of energy,
Mine to take.

Add your Cacao beans and put your hemp string in.

When you wish to use your spell, take out the length of string and make nine knots in it. With each set of three knots say:

Knot one, energy sealed.
Knot two, refilled with sun.
Knot three, energy keep.

Carry the string in your pocket to hold your energy fast. To dispose of used knots, burn and say:

Return to fire for another day.
I'll use again in another way.

Alternate Herbs

You can substitute the nine Cacao beans for nine pinches of dried Cacao.

It is from Cacao that chocolate is created and it is perhaps no surprise that its botanical name translates to 'food of the gods'.

The Aztecs used Cacao extensively in foods and drinks, and the beans were also used as a form of currency.

Angelica Return-What-Is-Lost Spell

This spell can be used to return anything at all – from lost keys to a lost lover or lost pet. If you do not have a tree on your property then find a tree nearby that you feel evokes strength and wisdom. Although this spell works by sending out energies for lost things to be returned to you, it may sometimes provide you with a vision of where your lost thing may be. Angelica is named after the Archangel Michael and while this will boost the spell's powers, especially for those who work with the Angelic Realm, the true power of this plant is its thick and twisting root system. This will pull in and hold the energy of return for you and ground it.

Timings: New Moon, Monday, Midnight

Find and Gather

- Angelica Root (*Angelica archangelica*)
- red thread
- a tiny piece of paper
- a pen/pencil
- gifts for tree:
    - a gold coin
    - a tiny piece of cake
    - a cup of spring water

The Spell

Draw the thing that you have lost on the paper and then wrap it around the piece of Angelica Root.

Tie the red thread around this bundle, leaving a long thread loose.

Take your spell out to a tree, tie it to a branch and say:

Oh great tree, look far and wide.

Find my treasure and return to my side.

Look inside my petition to you,

And grant my request, oh please do!

Feed the tree with your gifts of a gold coin, a piece of cake and a glass of spring water. Be sure to repeat this gift-giving when your thing is returned.

Alternate Herbs

There are no alternatives for this spell.

Angelica is native to Syria. Its leaves have a high sugar content and so it is popular in fruit recipes as a processed sugar substitute.

Angelica tea helps heal many conditions, including digestive ailments, and is thought to be a good general-health tonic that supports healthy circulation as well as providing mental harmony.

Chamomile and Vetiver Fear-Banishing Spell

Creating a selection of candle-anointing oils to keep in your personal apothecary, ahead of time, is good magickal practice.

Chamomile is added to this spell for its calming and soothing properties, which will help those who bask under the light of this candle to hold on until the fears dissipate.

Vetiver is a calming addition and helps ground and unify energies, allowing you to think clearly, from a balanced perspective, about your fears.

Timings: Waning Moon, Saturday, Midnight

Find and Gather

✦ 1 tablespoon of fresh or dried Chamomile (*Chamaemelum nobile*)
✦ 7 drops of vetiver essential oil
✦ 4 tablespoons of almond oil
✦ a strainer
✦ a glass/crystal bowl
✦ a glass bottle for storage

Herb Spells ✦ 191

- a white candle
- a candleholder

The Spell

Place the almond oil into the glass/crystal bowl. Mix in the Chamomile and say:

Fears will come and fears will grow,
Flower of calm will face them with grace.

Drop in the vetiver essential oil, mixing together, and say:

Together we shall stand,
and fear shall fall.

Light the white candle and set it safely in the holder next to the mixture.

Leave to steep for a few hours in a sunlit position.

Strain the mixture into a glass storage bottle and store in a cool, dry place.

Bury the Chamomile plant matter and the candle remains in a sunny spot in the earth.

To use, place a drop of the oil in the centre of a candle and gently massage in. You can use any colour candle, but white is the best because it wards off doubts and fears while also offering protection.

Alternate Herbs

Chamomile can be substituted with Lavender (*Lavandula*).

Chamomile is known as a 'Plant Doctor' because planting it beside another plant that is not doing well will improve the failing plant's health and vigour.

Vetiver is a type of grass prized for its roots, which have a beautiful sandalwood-type scent that is incredibly long-lasting. In many Asian countries Vetiver is woven into window screens to deter insects. The screens are sprayed with water each day to release the fragrance.

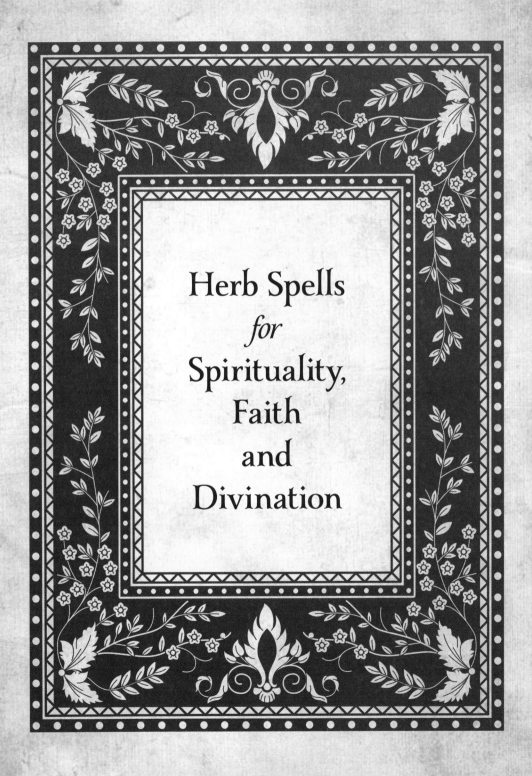

Herb Spells *for* Spirituality, Faith and Divination

Frankincense and Bilberry Mediumship-Improvement Spell

If you are working on your mediumship skills, you will find this incense very helpful. It will enable you to focus your energies more sharply. Included is Frankincense, which works to lift energy, to open up your vision and to offer protection. Most importantly, Frankincense supports spiritual growth. Bilberry ensures clarity, which is valuable when working in this field because it keeps unwanted visitors and entities from visiting you.

This incense should never be used to call on those in the spirit world unless you have extensive experience and training in this field.

Timings: New Moon, Monday, Late Night

Find and Gather

- 3 dried Bilberry leaves (*Vaccinium myrtillus*)
- 1 tablespoon of Frankincense resin (*Boswellia*)
- ½ cup of White Rose petals (*Rosa*)
- 2 Gardenia petals (*Gardenia jasminoides*)
- a mortar and pestle
- baking/non-stick paper and tray
- a glass jar

The Spell

Crush the Frankincense resin using the mortar and pestle.

Add the rest of the ingredients one at a time and macerate each as you combine.

When complete, turn the bowl three times clockwise and say:

The veil will open and I shall see.

Keep me safe and this side be.

Roll the resin into pea-sized balls and lay on the baking paper on the tray in the sun to dry. Once dry, store in the glass jar and keep in a cool, dry place.

To use, burn as you would any incense, especially during mediumship sessions, to offer protection, clear vision and focus.

Alternate Herbs

The Rose can be substituted for another colour Rose or for more Gardenias.

Bilberry is an important part of the Celtic harvest festival Lammas, or Lughnasadh. At these festivals, the berries are eaten for luck and the branches are used for decoration and protection.

The Ancient Egyptians burned Frankincense at sunrise in honour of their Sun god Ra.

Evening Primrose Psychic Energy-Replenishment Spell

If you are a divination reader or have had an energetically draining experience, you may like to try this bath spell. Evening Primrose speeds recovery of all types and will also bring you back to your usual state if you have been feeling under the weather. If you are lucky enough to have found, or grown, Evening Primrose flowers, add them to your bath for additional magick infusion. The inclusion of Evening Primrose will also allow your inner beauty to shine.

Sea salt will assist in grounding you while supporting your emotions, and the amethyst crystal helps to focus and replenish your psychic gifts.

Timings: New Moon, Monday, Late Night

Find and Gather

- 4 tablespoons of evening primrose oil
- an amethyst crystal
- 2 tablespoons of sea salt
- 2 white candles

The Spell

Set the candles safely on, or very close to, your bath.
Light them and say:

White light of protection,
Surround me in your grace.

Run your bath, add the evening primrose oil and say:

Heal and glow.

Then add the sea salt and say:

Ground and balance.

Once the bath is filled to your liking, take your amethyst crystal with you and immerse yourself in the healing and replenishing waters for as long as you like.

Alternate Herbs

None are completely suitable for this spell, although lavender essential oil (*only use 10–20 drops*) could make a similar bath.

Evening Primrose is native to North America, where Native Americans have used it as a sedative, a painkiller, to heal wounds, for muscle spasms and as a cough remedy.

Magickal uses for Evening Primrose include its use in spells connected with success and in increasing your desirability to lovers.

Brahmi and Rose Nerve-Calming Spell

This is a beautiful massage and skin oil, which you can use on yourself and on others. Brahmi assists us to remember happy memories and our true inner self while supporting our nervous system and bringing balance. Rose will share love and peace with you.

Use this tonic when you are feeling stressed, nervous or apprehensive.

Timings: Waning Moon, Monday, Midnight

Find and Gather

- 1 cup of fresh Brahmi (*Bacopa monnieri*)
- 11 drops of rose essential oil
- 1 cup of sweet almond oil or your preferred massage carrier oil
- a clear glass/crystal bowl

- ✦ a rose quartz crystal
- ✦ a pink scarf or tablecloth
- ✦ a large sterilised glass jar
- ✦ a beautiful sterilised bottle

The Spell

Wash and completely dry the Brahmi. This could take a day.

In a quiet place, lay out your pink cloth and place your clear glass/crystal bowl upon it. Place the rose quartz crystal inside the bowl and then gently pour your sweet almond oil and rose oil into the bowl while breathing softly and deeply over the bowl to bring calming energy into the space.

Drop the Brahmi into the bowl, stir in an anti-clockwise direction and say:

Release, release, release.

Take three deep breaths and then stir clockwise and say:

Relax, relax, relax.

Pour the oil mixture (without the rose quartz crystal) into the jar and store in a cool dry place for 14 days. After this time, take out and strain into the beautiful bottle.

Bury the herb matter in your garden.

Alternate Herbs

Rosemary (*Rosmarinus officinalis*) may be substituted for Brahmi. Brahmi oil can be substituted for the fresh plant. Use 2 tablespoons.

Brahmi has been used in India since ancient times as a multi-faceted healing herb. It works well to help with depression, stress, insomnia and fatigue, both physical and mental, while improving memory and concentration.

Roses have a long history dating back over 35 million years, making them one of our oldest flowering plants. The first cultivators of the Rose were probably the Persians.

Herb Spells ✦ 197

Dandelion Divine-Guidance Spell

This is a rather fun spell to create, and it provides a very good way to work out a direction in a matter or to find the answer to a question. Try to keep all your questions and workings with this spell focused on one issue or area. You will need to do this spell inside, or your Dandelion seeds will blow completely away. Dandelions not only grant wishes, they assist us to see clearly and offer the gift of second sight.

Timings: New Moon, Wednesday, Sunrise

Find and Gather

- 3 Dandelion seed heads (*Taraxacum officinale*)
- a very large sheet of paper or cardboard (*at least A3*)
- pens and pencils
- a glass/crystal bowl

The Spell

Lay out your large sheet of paper and, using your pens/pencils, divide the paper into three sections reflecting the directions/paths you seek. In each section draw something that relates to these directions, even if you don't know outcomes. For example, perhaps you are wondering if you should leave your job and either study or find something else. One section could have a drawing of the study institution, another a picture of you dressed in your current work uniform and the third could be a question mark.

Pick all the seeds carefully from the Dandelion and place them into the bowl.

Standing over your paper, close your eyes and start sprinkling the seeds and say:

Fall where you like, fall where you may.
But show me sweet seeds, my brand new way.

Open your eyes and study the results.

You will be able to find guidance from the seeds via their patterns and the places where they have fallen. Are they all in one section? Are more in one than another? What do the patterns remind you of? See if you can recognise any symbols or shapes in the way the seeds have fallen. If you are unsure of what they may mean, consult a tea-leaf-reading book or online resource for additional insight.

Take photos so you can refer to your patterns later. Take the paper outside, blow the seeds to the wind and say:

Fall where you like, fall where you may.
Thank you, sweet seeds, for your divine insight.

Alternate Herbs

None are suitable for this spell but you can collect and dry Dandelion seed heads for later use. Store in clean dry jars in a cool, dry place.

The common name 'Dandelion' is from the French 'dent de lion' or 'lion's tooth', which refers to the jagged leaves of the plant.

The 'Dandelion Clock' is a popular folklore tradition and childhood game: blow the seed head and the number of breaths it takes you will tell you what time of day it is.

Lemon Balm 'Yes, No, Maybe' Spell

Lemon Balm helps us to reflect deeper on issues we are trying to make decisions about. In this spell you will be creating a type of divination vessel from a bowl of water. This method is usually known as scrying.

Timings: New Moon, Monday, Late Night

Find and Gather

- a handful of Lemon Balm leaves (*Melissa officinalis*)
- a large bowl
- pure water
- a clear quartz crystal
- a black tourmaline crystal
- a smoky quartz crystal
- a beautiful purple cloth
- a green candle
- a blue candle
- a red candle
- a yellow candle

Herb Spells ✦ 199

The Spell

Place your purple cloth on a flat surface. This cloth represents 'spirit'.

Rest your bowl on your cloth and half-fill with water.

Place each of your candles around the bowl, to suit your hemisphere/spiritual practice. The usual placement is: Earth – North (green), Fire – South (red), Air – East (yellow), Water – West (blue). You may like to reverse this format to suit the Southern Hemisphere or your geographic location to correspond with the geography of the land. Light your candles. Place your crystals into the centre of the bowl and say:

Above and below, from the East and the West,
Herb of vision, now come to rest.
Herbs divine, from below to above,
Help me to see, with truth and with love.

Toss the Lemon Balm leaves into the water and swirl around with your fingers three times in a clockwise direction. Ask your question out loud. Once the water settles, take note of where the majority of the leaves have settled. The crystal they are closest to will be your answer.

Clear Quartz = Yes, Black Tourmaline = No and Smoky Quartz = Maybe.

Alternate Herbs

None are suitable for this spell but you could try Lemon Blossom flowers (*Citrus × limon*).

Lemon Balm is also widely known as Bee Balm because of the love bees have for the flowers of this special plant.

In 1696, the London Dispensary told its readers that a wine created from Lemon Balm would 'renew youth, strengthen the brain, relieve a languishing nature and prevent baldness'.

Bay Laurel Oracle-Boosting Spell

This bath is very good for those who work with, or who are learning, oracle modalities. It is best used when the moon is Full. Bay Laurel is a plant with powerful oracle energies and protective qualities. Rose water will increase psychic abilities and help facilitate any changes you are seeking.

Timings: Full Moon, Wednesday, Late Night

Find and Gather

- 9 fresh or dried Bay leaves (*Laurus nobilis*)
- ½ cup of rose water
- 2 cups of sea salt
- ½ cup of baking powder (*baking soda*)
- 2 white candles

The Spell

Carve a Full Moon on each candle to help increase your powers.
    Set candles safely on or near the bath. Light the candles and say:
        Precious light of the Moon,
        Shine the way.
    Mix together the sea salt and baking powder and add to the running bath water.
    Stir in the rose water.
    Float the Bay leaves upon the bath water once it is fully drawn.
    Lie in your bath and completely relax.
    When you have finished your bath, drain the water and collect all the remains of the spell, including the candle ends, and bury in a dark place on your property.

Alternate Herbs

None are suitable for this spell, although you can substitute the rose water with rose essential oil (*10–20 drops*) or a good handful of organic Rose petals.

Bay Laurel was used to create the wreaths that adorned the champions' heads at the very first Olympic Games in 776 BC.

The Ancient Romans loved Bay Laurel and would seal letters containing good news with a Bay leaf. They believed that the apparent abundance of the trees was due to them being able to magickally avoid being struck by lightning.

Star Anise and Cinnamon Intuition Spell

This brew will make two mugs of delicious intuition-boosting magick. If you are partaking alone, you can either halve the quantities to make one mug and keep the extra in the fridge for the next day, or perhaps come back for seconds!
   Star Anise will increase intuition and psychic awareness.

Timings: New Moon, Wednesday, Morning

Find and Gather

- 1 Star Anise (*Illicium verum*)
- 2 Cinnamon sticks (*Cinnamomum verum*)
- a fresh pear
- 2 teaspoons of sugar
- 2 cups of pure water
- 2 beautiful mugs
- additional Star Anise and two Cinnamon sticks

The Spell

Chop up the pear and place it in a saucepan with some water and the Star Anise and Cinnamon. Bring to the boil and then lower the heat. Cover and simmer for another 10 minutes. Take off the heat and leave to cool for about 15 minutes.

Warm the mugs and then strain the mixture into the mugs and add a teaspoon of sugar to each. Place a Cinnamon stick in each and an extra Star Anise.

Stir the brew with the Cinnamon sticks in a clockwise direction and say:

   Open to knowing
   Clear I shall see.

Warmed by the herbs,
So let it be.

Any remains from creating this spell and brew should be buried in your garden or a place close by in nature.

Alternate Herbs

There are no alternatives for this spell.

Star Anise is a herb strongly connected with the New Moon and can be carried with you to bring luck or it can be placed under your pillow to help you dream of another who is far away from you.

Cinnamon raises the vibrations of other herbs it is mixed with. It will also raise psychic powers and open spiritual elements. Cinnamon was a vital essential oil in the Ancient Egyptian embalming process.

Coriander and Wormwood Purpose-and-Path Spell

When working out your purpose, this mist will assist you at every stage. If you ever get lost on the way, just use it again to set yourself back on your path.

Coriander will help you to find your hidden talents and skills and will uncover your true purpose. It will calm passionate ideas that may be hindering your true path.

Wormwood will support you by showing you deeper possibilities and strengthening your intuition. When the mist runs out, cast the spell again.

Timings: Full Moon, Wednesday, Midday

Find and Gather

✦ 1 sprig of fresh Coriander (*Coriandrum sativum*)
✦ 1 sprig of fresh Wormwood (*Artemisia absinthium*)
✦ a glass/crystal bowl
✦ 4 cups of pure water
✦ a clear quartz crystal ball

- ✦ glycerin
- ✦ a large glass bottle
- ✦ a small glass misting bottle
- ✦ a purple cloth

The Spell

Find a place, preferably outside, where you can leave your essence for an hour in the sunlight. Place your clear quartz crystal ball into the bowl. Neatly lay out your purple cloth and place your clear glass/crystal bowl upon it.

Slowly pour your pure water into the bowl and say:

In bright of sun and water pure,
My purpose I seek.
So that in life I am sure.

Put your herbs into the water, one by one. As you place each into the water say (each time):

I welcome sunshine, I welcome happiness, I embrace my purpose.

Leave your essence water and herbs in the sunlight for an hour and then strain into your large bottle. Fill to 4/5 with the water and then top up with the glycerin. Decant what you need into the smaller misting bottle.

Spray into the air in your space (home/work) each morning and repeat the above chant each time. The herbs remaining should be buried in a spot that is always sunlit.

Alternate Herbs

None are suitable for this spell, but if you cannot obtain the preferred fresh herbs then a teaspoon of each, dried, will do. Try to create the master stock when you do have fresh plants, for later use in spells like this one.

Coriander is a favourite in love spells because of its warming qualities. If added to warm wine it will supposedly promote lust in the drinker.

Wormwood is a main ingredient in the drink absinthe. The herb can be toxic, so care must be taken in all use with it. Hanging it from the rear-view mirror in your car will prevent accidents.

Sage and Nutmeg Faith-Keeping Spell

You will need to find a locket or create one to contain this spell. The locket will remind you of your faith, whether this is simply your personal way of living or a tradition you may follow. Wearing the locket every day will assist you in keeping true to what you believe in.

Sage imparts wisdom, spirituality and faith in this spell, and will help you find your way back to your faith when you feel challenged. Nutmeg, although traditionally thought of as a good-luck charm, warms the soul. It also brings elements and people closer together.

Timings: Full Moon, Sunday, Late Night

Find and Gather

- 1 teaspoon of dried White Sage (*Salvia apiana*)
- 1 teaspoon of dried Nutmeg (*Myristica*)
- ½ cup of sweet almond oil
- a glass jar
- very small squares of white flannel 2 x 2 cm/0.5 x 0.5"
- a beautiful locket
- a mortar and pestle

The Spell

Mix together the White Sage and Nutmeg in the mortar and pestle and then pulverise it.

Drizzle in the sweet almond oil and work together in a clockwise direction.

Once these ingredients are well mixed, turn the mortar three times clockwise and say:

The faith I shall keep
No matter the day,
No matter the weather.

Pour into the glass jar and fill with small white flannel squares.

Leave to soak for seven nights.

To use, take out a square, squeeze well and trim to fit your locket.

Use a new square each seven days.

Bury the squares in a sunlit place.

Alternate Herbs

The White Sage can be substituted with any Sage.

A Creole spell includes sprinkling Nutmeg in a woman's left shoe every night at midnight so you can make her crazy with love for you.

The botanical name for White Sage, 'Salvia', comes to us from the Latin 'salvere', which means to heal, preserve or redeem. An Italian proverb relates to us: 'Why should a man die when he has Sage in his garden?'

Sage Blessing Spell

This water can be used any time you would like to bless an object, place or a person. You will be creating it under a Full Moon (the timing is non-negotiable on this one!). Once made, you can use this blessing water at any time and share it with others, so make a nice quantity. If it is raining, collect the water for an added magickal boost.

Timings: Full Moon, Sunday, Late Night

Find and Gather

- Sage (*Salvia officinalis*)
- a mirror
- a cup of rose water
- pure water
- a small handful of salt
- a beautiful white cloth
- a large, beautiful bowl
- a special bottle

Earth Magick

The Spell

Find a place outside where you can see the Full Moon.

Lay your white cloth out on the ground and say:

Gently touched with cloth of white,

Ground in Earth for magick tonight.

Set your bowl upon the cloth and add the sage.

Pour the pure water in and say:

Water of heart, of love and of care,

Support and bring comfort to all that is there.

Pour in the rose water and say:

Empowered with flowers,

Their love and light.

Sprinkle in the salt and say:

Strengthen and ground,

With all of your powers.

Taking the mirror, angle it so you catch the reflection of the Moon and bounce it into the bowl of water and say:

Light of the Moon,

Add your blessings tonight.

Leave the bowl out for the night. The next morning, bottle the water. This will be best kept refrigerated but you can add a little glycerin to preserve if you wish.

Alternate Herbs

You may include your favourite herbs in this spell.

Rose water is created by steaming Rose petals. which was a common practice in Ancient Persia.

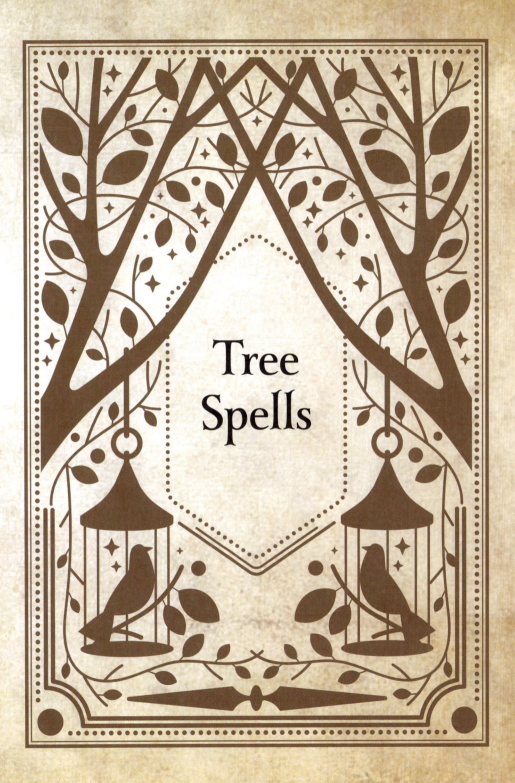

Introduction

Spellwork is energy work, and listening to and understanding the language of plants helps you raise and impart the energy of trees into your spells. If you can sit by a majestic Oak tree, using its fallen leaves to weave your magick, then that would be divine, but if not? I'll show you how to still bring the magick, the love and the power of an Oak tree – of any tree – into your spellcrafting and casting.

To immerse yourself in the world of Tree Magick make sure you are spending mindful time with trees – any tree. Although you may not be able to share time with particular members of each botanical family, all are connected by the universal threads of Nature, so being immersed in their spaces, listening to their language and slowing to the time and pace of trees will ensure you open the door to all.

In this section, I've included instructions on how to create your own spells with trees you already know, those you feel drawn to and those you may need to bring into your life. I've also shared 60 tree spells that I've crafted just for you. Wishing you a wondrous time exploring the trees and may you find the forest and the trees full of the magick you seek.

Working Magickally with Trees

+ Step one: plant a tree.
+ Step two: look after it.

I believe that you can't truly know something unless you do it yourself. And you can't just do it once then forget about it or hire someone to do it for you. In magick this is even more relevant.

There is real magick in doing and in following up and caring for plants. I know, as I've seen it for myself and others have written about it for centuries, and I'm sure you have your own experiences as well.

If you do not have a garden, plant the tree somewhere else! Simple. There are no excuses: even in our largest cities there are community gardens, tree-planting days and nature regeneration programs. Go on: off you go and do it now! When you come back I promise you will have the magick right there in your hands.

It's living in the dirt under your nails, it lingers in the scent of leaves in your hair and it lives in the energy you exchanged when you held that plant and put it in the earth. It will grow stronger with each day you check on your tree friend, when you quench its thirst, feed its roots and protect it from harm. When you sit with it and chat, but especially when you are quiet and just listen.

Go and spend time with the family and friends of this tree. Walk through forests; lie under the branches of that tree in the park; stop by the street tree and say hello. You are now working magickally with trees.

Create a Magick Proxy Tree

If a spell calls for you to work with a living, growing tree and you do not have access to one, then you may like to create a magick proxy tree instead. All trees, plants and their flowers are connected energetically, and you can call this energy to you. To make it, use a fallen branch of any tree stuck into the earth, with the image of the tree you wish to work with before it, together with any botanicals derived from it (*such as oils, essences, leaves and bark*) that you have been able to locate. Size will not matter. Once you've created it, say:

> *Brother, sister, old tree I have faith,*
> *Find the energy of Bodhi,*
> *And bring here to this place.*

How to Create Your Own Tree Spells

To use a tree in a spell you should understand its energy, and to do this you need to know its meaning and attributes. You can find these by exploring the properties it has or look to resources such as aromatherapy, herbal medicine guides and botanical history resources that discuss the properties of plants.

Tree Spells ✦ 211

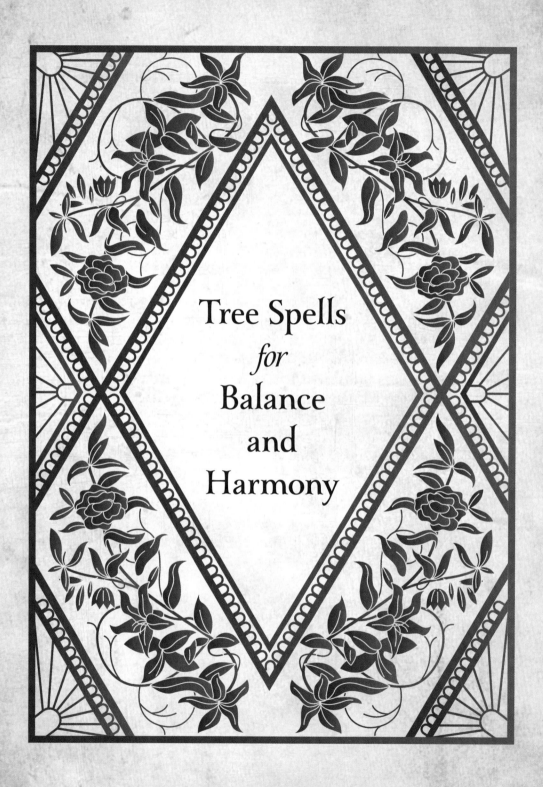

Tree Spells
for
Balance
and
Harmony

Maple Tree Positive Energy Spell

Maples are generally found in temperate northern regions and occasionally subtropical areas of Asia. Mostly deciduous, there are more than 100 species of Maple as well as numerous cultivars.

As well as being a very effective positive energy encourager, Maple leaves can be used in love spells and spells that are crafted to attract abundance and success. The name of this genus, Acer, *means 'sharp' and refers to the use of the wood to make spears. It may also refer to the shape of the leaves. This spell will create a handy happiness booster essence that will last for about a week on the shelf or a month in the refrigerator.*

Timings: Full Moon, Sunday, Midday

Find and Gather

- a yellow cloth
- a clear glass or crystal bowl - it is preferable to obtain a bowl that you will only use for the making of essences
- 1 cup of rainwater/water
- 4 Maple leaves (*Acer* spp.)
- a glass misting bottle

The Spell

Find a place, ideally outside, where you can leave your essence for a good hour in full sunlight. Lay out your yellow cloth and then place the bowl on it. Slowly pour the water into the bowl and say:

> *Sparkle water,*
> *Dance in the sun.*
> *Take in the joy,*
> *A new day begun.*

Put the Maple leaves into the water one by one, each time saying:

> *With Maple,*
> *Positive energy be,*
> *With this leaf,*
> *Positive energy free.*

Place the essence and leaves in the sunlight for an hour and then strain into the misting bottle. Use each morning in the air of your space (home/work) and repeat the second chant each time. The leaves should be buried in a spot that always has sunshine upon it during the day.

Passing a baby or young child through the branches of a Maple tree will ensure they have a long, happy and healthy life.

Will it rain? If you are lucky enough to be in the vicinity of Maple trees, look at their leaves. If they have turned so that their underside is seen, then a downpour is imminent.

Cedar Tree Gain Control Spell

Although there are many trees bearing the common name 'Cedar', there are only four true Cedars in the world and these are of the Cedrus *genus. Perhaps the best known is the Cedar of Lebanon (*Cedrus libani*), a majestic tree that has been revered since ancient times and is today widely grown as an ornamental tree in parks and gardens.*

The use of cedar in this spell will assist in not only regaining control of situations and yourself by imparting calming energies, clearing and offering protection, but also by providing the strength and wisdom of this large and ancient tree.

Spell boxes can be created for any purpose and are good for issues you feel may be recurring. If you find that at times you lose yourself, emotions or power over situations, then this spell could provide you with a valuable tool.

Timings: Waxing Moon, Tuesday, Midday

Find and Gather

+ a black Orchid (*Trichoglottis brachiata*) or any species of Orchid that has a dark colour
+ cedar essential oil
+ a small, plain, wooden box with a lid - if you can find a Cedarwood box that would be perfect!
+ a white fabric bag or cloth to place the box in

The Spell

First, let your Orchid dry out completely. This will take about a week.

Place the dried Orchid and the essential oil into your box and say:

In you go, one and then one,
Together combined, for the work to be done.

Close the lid and say:

Magickal box,
Hold and calm,
Bring steady control,
With a thrice times roll.

Rub three drops of the cedar oil on each side of the box and the lid.

Close and roll it over three times in your hands. Put the box in the white fabric bag/cloth then find a dark, quiet place to keep it. When you would like to experience the magick of your spell to assist in gaining control of a new (or even an old) situation, take the box out and repeat the chant, then roll the box three times.

Used by the Ancient Egyptians for embalming, Cedar oil and wood was prized throughout the ancient world as being incorruptible and therefore sacred. The wood has often been used in the making of boxes for the safekeeping of sacred or valuable texts as well as in the building of religious temples.

The essential oil gained from Cedar is believed to be the very first oil that humans distilled. It is used for its calming, soothing and rejuvenating properties as well as being a very good antiseptic.

Lemon Tree Inspire Joy Spell

Citrus trees originated in south-east Asia from just three types: the mandarin, the pomelo and the citron, so what you find in the citrus world today is the result of years of cultivation and hybridisation. This is thanks to the rare ability citrus trees have to mutate easily as well as the sexual compatibility between the species.

Lemon trees are naturally uplifting and provide a measure of protection as well. This uplifting spell creates a beautiful candle that you could add a gorgeous golden ribbon to and gift to someone needing more joy in their life. Lemon is well known for its cleansing properties so its use will not only impart sparkling joy but clear away dank and dark energies as well.

Timings: Waxing Moon, Friday, Evening

Find and Gather

- a Lemon (*Citrus × limon*)
- a small Lemon tree leaf
- wax/baking paper
- a large yellow or other light-coloured pillar candle
- a white taper candle
- a metal spoon

The Spell

Finely grate the zest of the Lemon (*just the yellow outer skin*) and then air-dry on a plate for a few days before using. Dry the leaf in the same way for a few weeks or by using a flower press. Lay out the wax/baking paper on a heat-proof surface to protect your work area and your candle. Set the pillar candle on the paper. Light the taper candle and drip wax onto the pillar candle. You will need to spread the wax very quickly with the back of the metal spoon. Press the Lemon leaf into the wet wax and onto the pillar candle and then melt a little more wax over the top of the leaf and spread with the spoon.

When you have finished say:

Lemon tree bright,
Clear and make right,
Joy each time,
Your wick is alight.

Once you are happy with the result, melt more taper wax and cover the pillar candle with the dried Lemon zest, finishing with a layer of wax to seal and using the metal spoon to gently spread and push down the pieces into the wax.

To bring joy into an area, to an occasion or a situation, simply light your candle.

While you are drying Lemon zest, you might want to make extra as it is a powerful love charm spell ingredient to help win the affection of the one you desire. The leaves are said to inspire lust when added to teas.

To honour the love of your life and to ensure the longevity of your relationship, grow a Lemon tree from a pip and give it to them.

Bodhi Tree Healing Spell

The Bodhi tree can live up to 2,000 years and this attribute may have created its status as a sacred and holy tree in many religions in its native homelands of south-east Asia and India. This is the tree that the Buddha sat beneath when reaching enlightenment.

Bodhi will help you find personal healing. This spell is a walking spell, a way to raise energy to facilitate change. Doing this, as well as focusing energy with a simple meditation on your outcome, will help create a very good all-round healing spell. This could be used to heal rifts in relationships as well as offer support for physical, emotional and mental healing.

Timings: Full Moon, Thursday, Any Time

Find and Gather

- Bodhi tree (*Ficus religiosa*)
- a pink Rose (*Rosa* spp.)
- a spoonful of honey in a beautiful glass

The Spell

Stand in front of the Bodhi tree and say:
> *Brother, sister, old tree, I have faith,*
> *Find the energy of Bodhi,*
> *And bring here to this place.*

Holding the rose, walk around the tree slowly in a clockwise direction. As you walk, gently loosen the petals and let them drift to the earth. As each petal falls to the ground say:

The circle of healing grows in the dirt,
Healing will come from deep in the earth.

Repeat until all petals have been released and your circle is formed, then take the honey and pour it onto the bark of the tree and say:

A gift of thanks, for work to be done.

Sit down, close your eyes and focus on the way you would like to see the situation, person, animal or thing healed. Stay as long as you feel you need to. Leave the petals to do as nature pleases with them.

Walking around a Bodhi tree can also rid you of evil influences. You will need to do this at least three times but it should drive away any negative entities that are attracted to you.

A folklore cure for female infertility in many Asian countries involves walking naked around a Bodhi tree.

Blackthorn Tree Remove Negativity Spell

A very common wild shrub throughout Europe, the Blackthorn produces fruit that are used to make jams, syrups and wines. Another name for both the tree and its fruit is 'Sloe'. The fruit is also traditionally used to produce the drink sloe gin.

Not only will Blackthorn help remove negative energies, it will also stabilise emotions and reveal hope for you going forward. This spell creates a somewhat bitter though refreshing drink to clear away negative energies. When you drink your magickal sparkling brew make sure that you visualise the negativity you are trying to get rid of leaving.

Timings: Waning Moon, Saturday, Midnight/Dusk

Find and Gather

- 3 Blackthorn sloes (*Prunus spinose*) - if unobtainable replace with any dark edible fruit but also use an image of Blackthorn
- 2 tablespoons of lemon juice
- a wooden spoon
- a beautiful clear glass

Earth Magick

- 1 teaspoon of honey
- champagne or sparkling wine or water

The Spell

Prick the sloes and soak them in the lemon juice overnight. The next day, squash the sloes into the juice with the spoon and then strain, retaining the juice. Say:

Juice of Blackthorn,
Bitter and sour,
The things that have darkened me,
Will go with this hour.

Bury the fruit in a dark place in the garden.

Pour the juice into the glass and say:

Magickal juice,
With each sip this will end.
Negative leaves,
While positive mends.

Add the honey and while stirring say:

Sweet mender and healer mix well.

Top with the champagne or sparkling or wine or water and say:

Bubble and fizz,
Alive is the brew.
The dark disappear,
The light is anew!

Drink all but a mouthful and throw this out the front door, saying:

And now be forever gone!

The wood of the Blackthorn is traditionally used in Ireland in the making of shillelaghs. These sticks are used as both walking sticks and magickal wands.

Thorn trees have strong links with faeries and Blackthorn have their own guardians, the Luantishees. These faeries have their own special day, 11 November, and on this day black ribbons tied around the trunks of Blackthorns and blessings of gratitude for their work are greatly appreciated. However, you must never harvest anything from a Blackthorn tree on this day, as to do so will cause great harm to come to you.

Tree Spells ✦ 219

Holly Tree Find Balance Spell

The evergreen Holly is native to Europe as well as western Asia. It is a smaller understory tree that thrives in shaded woodland. Synonymous with Christmas, it also was – and still is – an important pagan tree that is a symbol of life and renewal as part of midwinter observances. Holly shares the energies of peace, protection and cheerfulness and can help with finding balance.

Witch bottles, also known as spell bottles, have been in use since at least the early 17th century in the UK and USA. They can be created for any purpose, but I particularly like making witch bottles that symbolise your challenges and provide a focus point for you to watch. Whatever you place inside, how it reacts when shaken will be like all the pieces mixing up and then settling in your own personal puzzle.

Timings: Full Moon, Wednesday, Twilight

Find and Gather

- 12 Holly leaves (*Ilex aquifolium*)
- a beautiful clear bottle and cap
- 6 red beads
- 2 tablespoons of rose water
- a stone from the garden
- water

The Spell

Divide the Holly leaves into two piles of six leaves each before you and say:

> *Balanced before me and balanced shall be.*

Add them to the bottle and say:

> *Twelve leaves of the Holly,*
> *Dance, play and just be,*
> *But always dear Holly,*
> *Find balance for me.*

Add the red beads, the rose water and water to fill and say:

Guiding love and true heart.

Add the stone and say:

Grounded balance will start.

Seal the bottle. Whenever you are seeking balance, simply shake the bottle then sit quietly and watch the contents completely settle. You should receive thoughts that will help you ground and be more balanced. This bottle will last about a month before the contents degrade. Empty and clean well then create a new witch bottle.

The origin of the festive wreath on the front door at Christmas time is in the practice of hanging Holly wreaths on doors to provide a place for faeries and wood spirits in midwinter. This would also ensure good luck for the coming year.

To bless your garden, try holding nine holly berries out under the light of a Full Moon for an hour. Pop them into a glass of beer (*DO NOT DRINK: Holly berries are poisonous!*) and then pour it over your garden. This potion is said to improve the qualities of the blossoms of any plant but particularly those of Foxgloves and Hollyhocks.

Linden Tree Remove Stress Spell

The most outstanding feature of this widespread Northern Hemisphere native is its huge heart-shaped leaves. These, combined with its gorgeous, highly perfumed flowers, make Linden a popular street and parkland tree in that part of the world. The inner bark (liber) was once used as a form of paper and is where the word 'library' comes from.

Linden provides soothing energies for this spell. The creation of your own teas is something magickal all by itself. Finding botanicals that you are drawn to and mixing them together to make warming drinks to delight, calm and please you is real kitchen magick. Here you will be adding a few chants to empower a selection of botanicals that I have found personally beneficial for stress removal. If you cannot find Linden flowers, you may like to try Chamomile.

Timings: Waning Moon, Saturday, Midnight/Dusk

Tree Spells ✦ 221

Find and Gather

- 1 cup dried Linden flowers (*Tilia* spp.)
- ½ cup Lemon Balm leaves (*Melissa officinalis*)
- 2 dried heads of Lavender flowers (*Lavandula* spp.)
- an airtight container
- boiling water
- a beautiful teapot and cups
- honey
- a few Linden tree twigs (*if possible*)

The Spell

Place the Linden flowers, Lemon Balm leaves and Lavender flower heads (*intact*) in the airtight container and leave for about a week so that the fragrances and tastes can combine.

As you pop them in say:

Linden and Lavender
So healing and calming,
Together with Balm,
So lovely and soothing.

When you wish to use, add 2 tablespoons of the mixed Linden flowers and Lemon Balm leaves for each cup to your teapot. (Leave the Lavender in the container as an aromatic flavouring for your tea.) Add enough boiling water for each cup. Leave to stand for a few minutes. Turn the pot clockwise three times and say:

Calm come in,
Stress go out.

Pour, sweeten with honey if desired, stir with a Linden twig, then sip slowly.

Planting a Linden tree in your home's garden will offer protection for everyone within. The branches can be cut (*or fallen ones used*) and placed over the front and back doors to prevent evil and misfortune entering.

The bark and branches of Linden trees are considered very lucky and Linden leaves, also edible, are used in spells for immortality. You might like to add a leaf or two to your tea mixture.

Rowan Tree Energy Protection Spell

The Rowan tree is a native of Europe and Asia and is often found near sacred sites, especially stone circles throughout the UK and Ireland. Legend tells us that it grows 'thrice as well' in these places. Common names for this tree include Witch Tree, Wicken and Witchbeam, all indications of its long history as an important tree of magick. Rowan is regarded as an all-round protection tree.

An amulet is a magickal object that contains energies, usually to protect the holder, so they should be carried. This spell requires you to create such an amulet from items that will offer energy protection. I find this very helpful if I am going to places where I am sharing what I do, or going to places that are very busy or contain too much negative or drawing energy.

Timings: Full Moon, Saturday, Late Night

Find and Gather

- a Rowan tree or the photo of a Rowan tree (*Sorbus aucuparia*)
- pencil and paper
- a small gold bag
- 3 Rowan leaves
- 3 White Sage leaves (*Salvia apiana*)
- 3 Basil leaves (*Ocimum basilicum*)

The Spell

Traditionally this type of amulet would have contained three Rue leaves (*Ruta graveolens*). As Rue can cause severe dermatitis on contact with skin and the charm bag will be worn or carried, I replace Rue with White Sage.

If you have access to a Rowan tree, sit before it and draw it using the pencil and paper. If not, find a suitable photo of a Rowan tree to draw and say:

Alive on the paper,
Witch tree you will be,
Protect my energy,
For all and for me.

Tree Spells ✦ 223

Fold the artwork three times and place in the gold bag. Add the leaves. Carry it with you to provide protection of your energy in times of need. To use, close your eyes and touch the amulet bag. Visualise your energy as a huge bubble around you, transparent but strong and unbroken – any corruption or hole you have felt in it repaired. Place the bag next to your ear for a few moments. If you ever feel you need to replace this amulet for any reason, bury it in a cool dark place away from your home or workplace.

If you would like to ensure a successful flower garden, collect Rowan berries on Rowan Tree Day (*1 May*) and fill an old leather boot or shoe with them. Bury in your flower bed on a Wednesday or Friday.

Carrying the berries or the wood of Rowan is said to heighten psychic abilities and intuition, while a staff or walking stick of Rowan will not only offer protection but ensure you do not become lost.

English Oak Tree Inner Strength Spell

Living for hundreds of years, the mighty English, or European, Oak tree is a haven for many woodland birds and animals. All Oak tree species have been celebrated as symbols of grounding, longevity and strength throughout time by many faiths.

In this spell you will be tapping into the strength of the Oak tree. Using a candle of a colour that corresponds with strength will further empower your spell. This spell could easily be cast using items from any large, powerful tree in your area, but check the meanings and attributes of the tree first.

Timings: Full Moon, Sunday, Midday

Find and Gather

- a large flat tray
- a cup of sand (*Note:* if it's illegal to take sand from the beach in your area, sand can be purchased from home-improvement and art and craft stores)

- ✦ an Oak twig (*Quercus robur*)
- ✦ a red candle
- ✦ a candle holder
- ✦ matches
- ✦ an acorn

The Spell

Set your tray before you, pour the sand onto it and say:

> *Sand from the earth,*
> *Sand from the sea,*
> *Ground and protect,*
> *What is within me.*

With the Oak twig, draw the outline of an Oak leaf and say:

> *Strong and steadfast,*
> *Leaf of the tree,*
> *Within you lives a strength,*
> *That will grow within me.*

Place the red candle in its holder in the centre of the Oak leaf outline and light. Hold the acorn in front of the flame and say three times:

> *Light from the Oak,*
> *Light from the flame.*

Let the candle burn completely out. Carry the acorn with you when you need a boost in inner strength. All ingredients used in this spell (except for the tray and candle holder) should be buried under a large tree when complete.

The shape of modern blind-pulls is not accidental. It is believed Oak trees protect against lightning strikes. Blind-pulls may be shaped like acorns and other decorative window elements were often made of Oak or embellished with Oak motifs for this reason.

Hollow Oak trees are thought to be the home of faeries, elves and woodland spirits. In Ireland and Scotland these trees are known as 'Bell Oaks' and in England as 'Bull Oaks'.

Tree Spells ✦ 225

Elm Tree Psychic Attack Shield Protection

Elm, being one of the few woods that do not rot in water, has been used to make ships, bearing posts in buildings and pipes. This tree dominated the European landscape until the Dutch Elm disease (first recorded in 1910) severely reduced the population of most species over time.

Elm has very strong grounding energies and also offers stability. The use of loud noises in spells will often indicate the beginning or end of the spell; however, in this spell sound is used as a correspondence. Imitating thunder, the sound of lightning, is meant to frighten off the negative energy you may have experienced or are trying to avoid. It is believed in many folklores that Elm trees are never struck by lightning as they have command and power over it.

Timings: New Moon, Sunday, Midnight

Find and Gather

- a large shallow bowl
- rainwater
- a pen and paper
- a large metal saucepan
- a large metal spoon
- a good handful of Elm leaves (*Ulmus* spp.)

The Spell

Fill the bowl with water and say:

> *Water of storms,*
> *Of sky and clouds.*

Swirl the water around briskly.

Use the pen and paper to write down your psychic attack experience or simply write that you wish to be protected from a psychic attack. This spell will last a month.

Rip up the paper and drop it into the water while swirling it briskly again and say:

> *Take this attack,*
> *Reversed it shall be.*

Bang the saucepan with the spoon three times. This represents the sound of thunder. Throw the Elm leaves into the air so they fall around you and say:

Surround me with protection,
Create your great shield.
Elm tree I ask you,
To look after me.

Pour the water onto the ground and dig the paper into the earth. Bang the saucepan with the spoon three more times.

Elves are said to be fond of the Elm tree and this has led to the common name of Elven for Elms in some areas. The reputation of the tree and its wood for never being struck by lightning is perhaps because elves offer this protection.

References to Elm can be found in the stories of the Roman god of wine, Bacchus. The planting and pollarding of this tree in vineyards throughout time in many areas is due to the belief that these are the best trees to offer shade, support and protection to the growing vines.

Tree Spells
for
Modern Problems

Larch Tree Social Media Protection Spell

The European Larch tree is a long-lived conifer that thrives at high altitudes. A native of Europe, it is found from the Southern Alps through to the Carpathian Mountains. It is also a popular forestry tree throughout North America and Europe.

Larch is a brilliant self-confidence booster and helps dissolve negativity. Creating the symbol of a cross in spells can mean that you are crossing the path or blocking the way of something. In this spell you make this symbol to stop or slow the effects of negative social media activity. Another wood can be substituted but you must use Larch or at least Pine (Pinus spp.) needles for this spell to work.

Timings: Waning Moon, Saturday, Midnight/Dusk

Find and Gather

- Larch wood (*Larix decidua*) - 2 small twigs or pieces of wood, any size you desire
- black string - length to suit
- 3 Larch needles (*leaves*)

The Spell

Take the two pieces of Larch wood and hold them in front of your computer screen in the form of a cross. Bind in the middle with the black string and say:

> *Social media,*
> *Stay good and stay true,*
> *This cross to stop,*
> *Harm and undue influence.*

Place the three Larch needles in the centre of your cross, bind them with the black string and say:

> *Leaves that are sharp,*
> *Leaves that are three,*
> *Together watch over,*
> *And repel negativity.*

Tree Spells ✦ 229

Place in front of your computer screen and leave. If you think it needs a boost at any time, burn dried Larch and pass through the smoke. Use this on phones and tablets by tapping the screen with the cross three times each morning.

Due to the belief that Larch wood was impervious to fire, it was and still is used to create amulets and talismans that offer protection from fire and enchantment, and to ward off the evil eye.

In Siberian mythology, the first man is said to have been created from a Larch tree. To the Lapp and Siberian people, Larch is considered to be the 'World-tree'. This is a tree in many religions and beliefs that is thought to hold up and support the heavens and be a connection of sorts between heaven and earth – and sometimes the otherworld below.

Alder Tree Dispute Shield Spell

The Alder tree grows best close to waterways throughout Europe, where it enjoys damp, even waterlogged, marshy grounds. The timber produced from Common Alder (Black Alder) is water-resistant and was used for the foundations of many buildings in the water-filled city of Venice in Italy. Other uses included boat-building and bridge piles.

Alder provides shielding and helps release negative and destructive energies. This spell creates a water mist to be sprayed around you to provide shielding from disagreements. It would be very beneficial in the workplace or in social circles when you do not wish to become involved with the disputes of others.

Timings: Waning Moon, Tuesday, Midday

Find and Gather

- 1 cup of pure water
- a large crystal/glass bowl
- Alder (*Alnus glutinosa*) - a twig, leaf, seed or other Alder-based botanical
- a glass misting bottle

230 ✦ Earth Magick

The Spell

Find a place, preferably outside, where you can leave your essence for an hour in the sunlight.

Pour the pure water into the bowl and say:

Water of emotion,
You will hold and shield.

Place your Alder wood or other Alder items in the water and say:

As Alder resists,
So might I.
Troubles meant for others,
Will not find me.

Leave in the sunlight for an hour, then strain the essence water into your misting bottle. Use each morning in the air of your space (home/work) when you know disputes are imminent or when they occur. Repeat the last four lines of the chant each time.

If you wish to use the Alder pieces for another purpose, first dry them in the sunlight and smudge them to cleanse.

The term 'Alderman' comes to us from the common name of this tree. It is derived from 'ealdor', the old English word for 'chief'. The red dye obtained from the tree was also used as a ritual face paint for sacred kings in ancient times.

Three different dyes are obtained from the Common Alder tree: red from the bark, brown from the twigs and green from the leaves and flowers.

Hazel Tree Study Spell

Hazel can be classified as either a tree or a shrub, but most experts agree that it is a tree as it can reach the 6 m/20' height requirement. However, it has low branches like a shrub. Found growing naturally across Europe, western Asia and North Africa, this is the tree that produces the widely consumed Hazelnut.

Tree Spells ✦ 231

Hazel is a tree of knowledge and skill with words. In this spell you will be combining the learning- and focus-enhancing qualities of the crystal green fluorite with the energies of the Hazel tree – leaving you with a little study snack as well!

Timings: Waxing Moon, Wednesday, Daytime

Find and Gather

- a baking tray
- baking paper
- 1 cup of raw hulled Hazelnuts (*Corylus avellana*)
- a clean tea towel
- a violet candle
- a candle holder
- matches
- a green fluorite crystal bracelet

The Spell

First you will need to roast the Hazelnuts.

Preheat the oven to 180°C/385°F. Line the baking tray with baking paper and spread out the whole Hazelnuts in a single layer. Roast for 10 minutes or until lightly toasted and the skins have started to crack.

Remove the skins. To do this, place the Hazelnuts in the tea towel and gently rub together until the skins come away. As you rub say:

Wisdom and knowledge,
Warm within me.

Set up your study area by lighting the violet candle in its holder and placing the green fluorite crystal bracelet in front of it. Take one Hazelnut and crush it.

Sprinkle a tiny bit carefully into the flame and say:

Alive the words, ideas and concepts,
I promise to do my very best.

Put the bracelet on and commence your study. Let the candle burn down. You can nibble the rest of the Hazelnuts for a study mind-power boost as you work. Wear the bracelet at any other time to ensure good study sessions, and in exams and during assessments so that the knowledge you gained while studying is in focus again.

Hazel trees are said to be portals and doorways into the faerie world. It is said that Wild Thyme, olive oil, rose and marigold water mixed with the buds of young Hazel can be used to open the way.

May Day is the traditional day to gather Hazel wood that can be used to create protective talismans. The use of Hazel wood to create hurdles around farms in many parts of the world probably stems from this belief as well.

Baobab Tree Traveller Spell

An African native tree, the Baobab is one of the widest trees in the world. The hollow trunk becomes swollen with water, attaining a circumference of up to 30 m/100' while holding up to 1,200 litres/2,540 pints of water.

You will be crafting a tiny Baobab tree trunk using a Walnut shell as a base. This talisman can be easily slipped into a cotton crotchet crystal holder. You can also place the talisman in your bag or suitcase. Walnut shells make excellent natural lockets as they are guardians of magick. The crystal malachite is used in this spell for its ability to offer protection to travellers, ward off the evil eye and for the additional gift of helping those who fear flying.

Timings: Full Moon, Thursday, Midday

Find and Gather

- a Baobab tree (*Adansonia digitata*) - or an image and (*if possible*) any part from a Baobab tree (*essence, leaves, bark, twigs*)
- water
- two clean dry Walnut shell halves (*Juglans regia*)
- a very small malachite crystal
- strong glue
- crotchet crystal holder or tiny mojo bag (*optional*)

The Spell

Either sit beneath a Baobab tree or create a little shrine to the tree with an image and the Baobab tree parts.

Pour the water into one Walnut shell half and say:

Travel well within this shell.

Where we go, travel well.

Pour this water into the other Walnut shell half and say:

To return safe, so it will be.

Pour the water on the ground and say:

Come back to here, safe.

Place the Walnut shells somewhere they can air-dry for a day and place the malachite crystal in one half. When completely dry, glue the two shells together, retaining the crystal inside, and leave to dry as per the glue instructions. You may like to decorate or paint the closed shells or cover them in air-dry clay. Wear when travelling or place it in your luggage.

The kings and elders of Africa would hold their meetings under Baobab trees as they felt that the tree's spirit would guide them in their work and decisions. To this day, this tree is used as a community meeting place in many regions.

Known also as 'upside-down' trees due to their appearance, Baobabs are in fact the largest succulent plant in the world. Because they hollow out to store water, their trunks have been used as shelter and some have been used as shops or bars.

Coconut Palm Tree Relaxation Spell

Extensively naturalised in warmer climes throughout the world, the Coconut Palm was originally native to the Eastern Tropics. They can grow to 18 m/16' and are planted not only for their beautiful appearance but for their usefulness, as every part of this remarkable tree can be utilised: the fruit as a food, drink and an oil of many uses; the leaves and trunk for construction; the flower as a base for a type of wine called 'toddy'; and the Coconut fruit husks as a fuel and textile matting.

This spell creates a gorgeous oil that can be used directly on the skin or added to a bath.

Use this oil when you are feeling stressed, nervous or apprehensive. The addition of Rose will give you some additional love and peace.

Timings: Waning Moon, Monday, Midnight

Find and Gather

- a Palm leaf (*any type*) - if you cannot obtain one, be crafty: for example, create one from paper
- a clear glass/crystal bowl
- a rose quartz crystal
- 1 cup Coconut oil - carefully melted in a double boiler
- 11 drops of rose essential oil
- a beautiful bottle, sterilised

The Spell

In a quiet place, put your Palm leaf on the ground and the bowl upon it. Place the rose quartz crystal in the bowl and then gently pour the Coconut oil into the bowl while breathing softly and deeply over the bowl to bring calming energy into the space.

Drop the rose oil into the bowl, stir in an anti-clockwise direction and say:

Relax, relax, relax.

Take three deep breaths and then stir clockwise and say:

Relax, relax, relax.

Take out the crystal then pour the oil mixture into the bottle and store in a cool, dry place out of direct sunlight.

The people of Samoa share the myth that the Coconut Palm originally grew at the entrance to the spirit world and was known as 'Leosia', 'the spirit watcher'. If a spirit struck the tree, they would return to the mortal world.

You can provide protection to your home or any building by hanging a fresh coconut in a high place within. Another method is to drain the coconut of its milk and then fill with herbs that provide protective qualities. Seal and bury next to the place where you require protective energies.

Jacaranda Tree Lucky Money Spell

This fast-growing tree is a favourite street tree in suitable climates. Jacaranda is native to Paraguay, southern Brazil and northern Argentina. The mauve-blue flowers completely cover the tree before falling to create a colourful carpet below.

Jacaranda brings with it the meanings and energies of wisdom, luck and also a bit of love! In this spell, you will also be using Basil as it is a naturally lucky herb and also a good friend of money. The use of a citrine crystal will help with prosperity.

Timings: Full Moon, Thursday, Morning

Find and Gather

+ a green candle
+ a candle holder
+ 3 gold coins
+ 3 citrine crystals
+ a beautiful box with a lid
+ a handful of dried Basil (*Ocimum basilicum*)
+ Jacaranda flowers (*Jacaranda mimosifolia*)

The Spell

Place the green candle in the holder in front of the box and light. Pop the coins into the box, add the citrine crystals and say:

> *Golden coins and crystals gold,*
> *Glow with growth within.*

Sprinkle in the Basil and say:

> *Abundance and success,*
> *Grow for me and do your best.*

Sprinkle in the Jacaranda flowers and say:

> *Wisdom and luck,*
> *So it will be.*

When you wish to boost your luck with money, open the box and ask for it. Keep your box in a private, quiet and dark place to protect the energies.

236 ✦ Earth Magick

The Amazonia Moon goddess visited earth as a beautiful bird named Mitu, who landed upon a Jacaranda tree. She spent her time living with the people and sharing wisdom and knowledge with them. When her time was over, she ascended through the Jacaranda, covered in flowers.

In many parts of the world, if a Jacaranda bloom falls on your head it is considered to be good luck. A modern Australian superstition suggests that if you have not begun your study for final exams by the time the Jacarandas bloom, it is too late.

White Mulberry Tree Wholeness Spell

Native to northern China, this tree is the food source of silkworms. While the fruit of the White Mulberry is edible, it is the Black Mulberry that produces the berries most people are familiar with.

This is a spell for those who feel they might not be as healthy as they would like to be. White Mulberry will provide harmony and help with connecting with what it is you may need for yourself to achieve wholeness. The colour turquoise is used in this spell as it is associated with wholeness, emotional balance, spiritual grounding and patience.

Timings: Full Moon, Monday, Morning

Find and Gather

- A few White Mulberry leaves (*Morus alba*)
- a tree
- a real silk scarf, hanky, tie or ribbon – preferably turquoise or white
- a ball of white string
- a pair of scissors
- a fire

The Spell

If you do not have the leaves, create some from paper and have an image of the White Mulberry tree nearby. Go to your tree and tie your silk item to it. Tie one end of your ball of string to the tree also. Walk away from the tree while unwinding the ball of string, saying:

Away I go and all I will see,
From small to larger,
What I need released to be me.

Walk as far as you can without losing sight of the tree, taking the leaves with you.

When you are happy, drop the leaves on the ground and then walk back and wind the string that has been released from the ball back into your hand, making a new ball. Cut the string so you have two string balls.

Create your fire, making sure it is safe (perhaps) in a cauldron or a fire-proof bowl).

Throw the new ball of string on the fire and say out loud all the things you want to release so you can be whole. Take the rest of the string and wind it around the tree three times. Cut the end. Place this string under your pillow with your silk item. You should dream of ways to healthy wholeness.

Wear your silk item when you are seeking healthy outcomes, paths and answers.

In 1608, King James I of England was keen to establish a silk industry so encouraged the planting of Mulberry trees throughout England. The story goes that people did just that but, unfortunately for the industry, planted Black Mulberry, which produces the more delicious fruit but is not the tree that supports silkworms.

Mulberry is a very good protector against evil in any form and also makes a powerful wand that can be used in general spellcasting as well as protection, exorcism and magickal cleansing work.

Eucalyptus Tree Stop Me Texting Spell

All native to the Southern Hemisphere, with most being also evergreen, there are over 800 species of Eucalyptus. The timber is widely used and the tree grown also for its beauty and fast-growing habit in temperate locations throughout the world.

A modern dilemma is how to stop yourself texting, messaging or posting updates on social media at times when you probably shouldn't. In this spell, the use of Eucalyptus helps to bring in the energies of division between worlds, ideas and places and is a purifier. You are also smudging by using the smoke of the Eucalyptus and protecting with the energies of this tree through its image.

Timings: Waning Moon, Wednesday, Midnight

Find and Gather

- a heat-proof dish
- a pen and paper
- matches
- dried Eucalyptus leaves (*Eucalyptus* spp.)
- a digital image of a Eucalyptus tree
- your phone

The Spell

Set up your heat-proof dish outside.

On the piece of paper, write down the last few texts, messages or social media posts that you sent but wish you hadn't. Drop into the dish, set them carefully alight and say:

The last of my words,
I cannot undo,
This day forward,
I wish to be true.

Empty the ashes out onto the ground and stamp them in with your feet.

Place the Eucalyptus leaves in the dish and set them alight.

Pass your phone very carefully through the smoke and say:

Cleanse out the things,
I've done before.
Stop me from doing this any more.

Keep the image of the Eucalyptus tree on your phone, and in times of need set it as your screensaver. It will help stop you from texting, messaging and posting when you probably shouldn't.

Eucalyptus trees are natural purifiers and will assist with rejuvenation, healing, gaining clarity and mental focus. They can also help to boost your immune and energy systems. Perhaps one of the easiest ways is via eucalyptus oil, which can be used in aromatherapy preparations and in various direct applications.

The leaves of Eucalyptus change shape over the tree's lifetime. While young, the leaves stand out horizontality to collect maximum light. As the tree ages, the leaves twist so that they present vertical to the tree, protecting it from too much heat radiation and light.

Coral Tree Job Hunting Spell

An incredibly fast-growing tree that is native to Brazil, most of the Coral Tree is covered in thick thorns. It produces beautiful downward-hanging flower panicles. Each of these appear in six-week cycles and can contain up to 100 flowers.

The use of Coral Tree in a job hunting spell is due to the energies of positivity and confidence and its ability to help you to stay focused on what it is you are trying to achieve. If you cannot find Coral Tree flowers, substitute Coral Tree essence sprinkled over red Rose petals. I have given timings which will provide you with a really important booster but you can and should do this spell on the first day of each week while you are job hunting. The especially keen may like to do it every job hunting day.

Timings: New Moon, Wednesday, Sunrise

Find and Gather

- a handful of Coral Tree flowers (*Erythrina* spp.), fresh or dried
- a big handful of multi-coloured flower petals and leaves, fresh or dried
- a beautiful bowl
- a compass

The Spell

The night before the spell, place the Coral Tree flowers and the multi-coloured flower petals and leaves in the bowl and say:

> *A celebration awaits,*
> *When I return to my gates.*

Place the compass on top of the botanicals and say:

> *Take me to where my new job awaits.*

240 ✦ Earth Magick

In the morning, before you leave for the day, walk out your front door with the bowl for a few paces, turn around and start to walk back while throwing the botanicals into the air and saying three times:

The next time I return,
A job I will have earned.

Take one Coral Tree petal and place it in your pocket or bag to take with you for additional luck.

Thought to be *E. variegate*, a Coral Tree is found in Tibetan Buddhism as the tree referred to as 'man da ra ba' in Sukhavati. In the Hindu faith, it is believed that the Mandarah tree in Indra's garden in Svarga is a Coral Tree (*E. stricta*).

Many Coral Trees are used as supporting plants for crops. Some are used to provide shade for Coffee and Cocoa plantations while others provide support for climbing vines such as the Vanilla Orchid.

Walnut Entrepreneur Spell

The Walnut tree has been widely cultivated for both its beautiful timber and delicious nuts. The Romans introduced the Walnut to Britain and from there it was taken to the USA and beyond. Its natural distribution spreads from Greece through to central China and Japan.

This spell will create a type of Florida Water with the added energy of Walnut. This tree will help support you as you head for change or forge new relationships. It will give you inner strength and provide fertile ground and longevity. In many communities, especially those connected with the practice of Vodoun, Florida Water is a powerful spiritual protector and cleanser. Not for consumption, it can be used lightly as a personal fragrance, added to a bath or sprinkled around your place of business or work.

Timings: Waxing Moon, Thursday, Daytime

Find and Gather

+ 1 Walnut (*Juglans regia*), crushed - or about 1 teaspoon
+ 2 cups of vodka

Tree Spells ✦ 241

- 2 tablespoons of orange flower water
- 2 drops of jasmine essential oil
- 16 drops of bergamot essential oil
- 12 drops of lavender essential oil
- 3 drops of lemon essential oil
- 2 drops of rose attar essential oil
- a gorgeous bottle, sterilised

The Spell

Mix all the ingredients together and place in the bottle while saying:

Ventures I'm taking,
Plans I will make,
Success will come to me,
Each day as I wake.

Use as needed to provide protection and to ensure success to your business endeavours.

You may find it useful to use at the beginning of your working week and again at times when you are attending important meetings, making decisions or working on anything especially challenging.

If you wish to use on your skin as a fragrance, do a small patch test on your inner arm first and monitor for 24 hours. Adding to a sterilised spray bottle can also make it easier to use.

Traditionally, ink has been made from Walnuts and it makes a very magickal way to write your own spells or keep your journal or Book of Shadows. You can also use it to stain wood.

The Walnut is often referred to as the 'Tree of Prophecy' or 'The Royal Tree', as the health of the tree would foretell the fortune of those residing nearby. For example, if the tree fell it was a very bad sign.

Tree Spells *for* Relationships and Love

Myrrh Tree Divorce Ritual

From eastern and north-eastern tropical Africa, the bark of the Myrrh tree produces a resin prized as an incense, in perfumes, as a flavouring in food and as a complementary healing ingredient. More of a shrub than a tree, it is covered in thorns and will only grow in full sun.

Myrrh will bring the energies of emotional balance, healing and wisdom so will help with any stage of a divorce in which you need support. Cyclamen flowers assist us to say goodbye and to leave a situation cleanly. Cyclamen plants are poisonous so please take care when using in this spell. Beware of the place you are planting the cyclamen and keep out of the reach of young children and pets.

Timings: Waning Moon, Saturday, Midnight

Find and Gather

- a Cyclamen plant (*Cyclamen* spp.)
- a plant pot and potting mix
- a heat-proof dish
- matches
- a charcoal disc or block
- Myrrh resin (*Commiphora myrrha*) - a few small pieces

The Spell

This spell needs to be done in a place where you and the person you wish to separate peacefully from have both been together. Carefully replant the Cyclamen in the new pot and say:

It is time for goodbye,
I wish us to part,
But peacefully go,
And make a new start.

Place the charcoal disc on the heat-proof dish and light it. Place the Myrrh on the glowing charcoal. Pass the dish over and around the Cyclamen plant and say:

Separate calm,
Peaceful we go.

244 ✦ Earth Magick

Leave the Cyclamen in the place you planted it for seven nights and then gift it to the person you are parting with. If you cannot do that, place it at the back door, in the rear yard or towards the back of your home.

The ancient Egyptian ruler Queen Hatshepsut was one of the first plant hunters and sent out expeditions to Somalia to collect the resin of the Myrrh tree to be burned in the temples.

Myrrh used as an incense provides a very conducive atmosphere for deeper meditations. It can also be used to help heal grief and sorrow and to connect with the dead.

Flowering Dogwood Tree Boundary Spell

Common in its native North America and Europe, the Flowering Dogwood is noted for its bark. The trunk will fissure as the tree grows, splitting into small, square blocks. What appear to be white flowers are actually large, long bracts surrounding much smaller clusters of green flowers.

Dogwood provides purity and helps set boundaries. Mirrors are a good means of creating a boundary of protection by bouncing back and deflecting any negative energies. Used together, you can cast a spell to quickly disperse unwanted intrusions into your world.

Timings: Waning Moon, Saturday, Midday

Find and Gather

- a black cloth
- a mirror
- 4 black candles
- candle holders - if required
- matches
- a pencil and paper
- 4 flowers or leaves of the Flowering Dogwood (*Cornus florida*)

Tree Spells ✦ 245

The Spell

Lay out the black cloth and place the mirror in the centre.

Place the candles around the mirror, forming a square, and say:

All that falls on the silver light,

Protected within the boundary right.

On the paper, write down what it is that you are seeking boundary protection for. Fold the paper and place it in the centre of the mirror.

Place the Dogwood flowers or leaves next to each candle and say:

Tree of Dogwood,

Pure and bright,

Hold what is within,

All safe and tight.

Dry out the flowers or leaves and bury near the entrance to your property.

The boundaries of Rome were created by Romulus using his javelin, which he then threw at Palatine Hill. It landed and took root, becoming a Dogwood tree. It was also a popular timber for the creation of weapons such as spears during Ancient Roman times.

Collecting a little sap from a Dogwood tree during midsummer in a handkerchief creates a talisman that will help your wishes come true. Carry it with you always to ensure this.

Italian Cypress Tree Peaceful Separation Spell

The Italian Cypress has a distinctive tall, column-like appearance. These are the trees that are synonymous with Tuscany as they grace the rolling hills of this Italian landscape. Unlike other Cedars, the leaves of the Italian Cypress have no scent.

The Cypress tree helps us find our personal path and can help lead us out of difficult or unwanted situations. It can also help support you through the mourning of loss and departure. This spell creates a relaxing bath salt blend that can help release and soften negative feelings surrounding a separation. The addition of Rose petals will further support you with courage and love. This spell makes about just over a cup of magickal bath salts.

246 ✦ Earth Magick

Timings: Full Moon, Monday, Evening

Find and Gather

- 1 cup of Himalayan salt
- ¼ cup of bicarbonate of soda
- a glass mixing bowl
- 1 teaspoon of dried Rose petals (*Rosa* spp.)
- 5 drops of lavender essential oil
- 11 drops of cypress essential oil
- a wooden spoon
- a gorgeous jar
- an image of the Tuscan landscape featuring Italian Cypress trees (*Cupressus sempervirens*)

The Spell

Mix together the Himalayan salt and the bicarbonate of soda in the glass bowl. While stirring say:

Ground and release, earth and peace.

Then add the Rose petals and say:

Love has come, now softly part.

Add the essential oils, mix well and say:

Find me a path of peace and of love,

Take me from here to something better thereof.

Decant into the jar and store in a cool, dry place for about a month.

To use, simply tip the entire contents into a running bath, set up your image of the Tuscan landscape in front of you and enjoy a relaxing bath.

The Ancient Greeks and Romans called the Cypress the 'mourning tree' and planted it in graveyards and in front of homes when someone within had died, as they considered the tree sacred to the gods of the underworld.

The Cypress is also considered a symbol of resurrection and healing and so is perfect for magick and spells that require these energies. Traditionally a branch is cut from a Cypress tree very slowly, taking three months, and then this can create a healing wand. Pass over afflicted areas and cleanse by dipping the end in a flame after each use.

Pear Tree Regain Harmony Spell

Originating as a hybrid in western Asia over 2,000 years ago, the Pear has been cultivated for hundreds of years, giving it a wide natural distribution throughout Europe. Such has been the popularity and extensive breeding of the Pear, it is impossible to discern what the Pear originally looked like.

Pears offer comfort, harmony, affection and balance and so are a lovely base for this peace-bringing drink. Share with those you may be experiencing some disquiet with to bring emotions and minds back into a more harmonious balance.

Timings: Waning Moon, Wednesday, Dusk

Find and Gather

- 1 cup of boiling water
- ¾ cup of castor (*superfine*) sugar
- 1 cup of fresh Lemon juice (*Citrus × limon*)
- 4 cups of cold sparkling water
- a large glass jug (*to store the lemonade in the fridge*)
- 3 ripe Pears (*Pyrus communis*)

The Spell

Mix together the boiling water and sugar and stir until dissolved.

Remove from heat and let cool completely. Pour into the jug. Add the Lemon juice and cold sparkling water to the sugar mix and say:

> *Sweet and sour,*
> *Mix and flow,*
> *Bring harmony now,*
> *With those that I know.*

Slice the Pears, add to the jug and say:

> *Pears, in you go,*
> *Balance and harmony be.*

Use immediately, serving in beautiful tumblers full of ice cubes. If you wish to keep longer, omit the sparkling water and store in the fridge for up to three days, adding sparkling water when serving or substitute still for sparkling water.

If you dream of Pears, it is a very good omen and means great riches are coming your way. Should you be single, it indicates you will marry above your current socio-economic situation and should the Pears be cooked, such as in a pie, business success is on its way to you.

In Switzerland a lovely tradition sees families planting an Apple tree to commemorate the birth of a boy and a Pear tree for a girl. The trees are well cared for as the health and wellbeing of the child is said to be linked to their tree.

White Willow Tree Healing Heartbreak Spell

Growing in water meadows and along waterways, the beautiful Willow has leaves that are covered with fine soft hairs. When the leaves are moved by the wind, the tree has a beautiful silvery appearance. White Willow is found throughout much of Europe and western Asia.

Willow helps comfort those who have lost love and gives hope for a healed heart tomorrow. Find a place outside that you find comforting to create this spell. You will need to find a few items that you love: for example, if you love gardening, perhaps you might add a gardening tool; if it is crystals, you could add your favourite ones; if it is art, perhaps a paintbrush.

Timings: Full Moon, Friday, Evening

Find and Gather

- a few items that you really love
- a white Rose (*Rosa* spp.)
- a tiny jar of honey
- a small glass of milk
- a lovely cupcake or biscuit
- a stick of White Willow (*Salix alba*) - any size

Tree Spells ✦ 249

The Spell

Place your loved treasures upon the ground. Holding your white Rose, slowly walk around your treasures in a circle, in an anti-clockwise direction, while gently loosening the petals and letting them drift to the earth. Repeat until all the petals have released and your circle is formed and say:

Let heartbreak leave,
The tears of mine cease,
With each petal released.

Tip a tiny dash of honey into the milk. Sit and enjoy your milk and sweet treat while imagining your heart healing. You should also be open to messages and ideas that should come to help find avenues to heal. Then pick up your Willow stick, draw a big heart on the ground around your treasures and say:

Within my heart love,
The things that glow.
Within my heart,
The healing grows.

Let the petals and heart blow away on their own.

It is believed that simply sitting beneath a Willow tree will give rise to great inspiration and confer eloquence upon artists, writers, speakers, poets, actors, priests and musicians.

In China the Willow is considered a symbol of immortality because it can grow from the smallest cutting. It is also thought to be a very lucky plant and able to protect against harm, evil and illness.

Cherry Tree Love Reality Check Spell

Wild Cherry is the parent tree of most of the Cherries we enjoy today and is also used as the rootstock onto which many other of the Rosaceae family are grafted. It is the largest of Europe's native Cherry trees and has a natural distribution across the continent.

This spell will help you sort out your feelings for another. Is it lust? Love? Or something else? Cherries have been used for centuries in love spells to attempt to gain the affections of the one desired. In this spell we are harnessing the lusty powers of Cherries with their ability to weed out insincerity while learning/remembering life lessons.

250 ✦ Earth Magick

Timings: Full Moon, Friday, Late Night

Find and Gather

- a Cherry (*Prunus avium*) with the stalk still attached - it is preferable to pluck the Cherry from the tree yourself if possible
- a beautiful plate
- a hair from your head
- a hair from your love interest
- a camera, pen and paper or your phone

The Spell

Stand before the fruit-laden Cherry tree or before a tree proxy (*see page 211*) or an image of the tree and say:

> *Is it love or is it lust?*
> *Is it real or is it dust?*
> *Cherry tree ripe and filled with fruit,*
> *Please tell me tonight and don't be too cute!*

Pluck a Cherry, being careful to leave the stalk on.

Place the Cherry on the plate and squish it down with your finger until the skin splits to reveal the flesh. Lay each of your collected hairs across the Cherry and say:

> *Here we are,*
> *Them and me,*
> *So what is it, Cherry?*
> *What do you think it will be?*

Take a photo (or make a sketch) of your arrangement, noting which hair belongs to whom. Leave overnight.

In the morning if both hairs remain it's love. If both are gone then it's lust, and if only one remains? Well, then, the one that remains is more invested in the relationship than the other. Not all is lost but you might want to rethink things.

In the botanical name for Cherry, '*avium*' means 'of the birds' and is named for the birds that love this fruit. Some of its common names hint at this, such as Bird Cherry and Hawk Berry.

Linden Tree Forgiveness Spell

Found naturally from Portugal to the Caucasus, this very long-lived tree (some have been found to be up to 2,000 years old) is an indicator of ancient woodland. Sweetly perfumed yellow flowers and heart-shaped leaves make this a very attractive tree.

Linden trees work very closely with energies surrounding friendships, peace, justice and love and in this spell you will be harnessing these energies to assist you in asking for forgiveness and to convey that you are truly sorry.

Timings: Full Moon, Sunday, Evening or Morning

Find and Gather

- a tray
- a white cloth
- a white candle
- a candle holder
- boiling water
- a beautiful teapot
- dried Linden flowers (*Tilia cordata*) or Linden tea
- 2 white, or predominantly white, teacups
- a pot of organic honey
- spoons
- a white Rose (*Rosa* spp.) (optional) clear quartz crystal (optional)
- a Linden stick to stir your tea with

The Spell

Set the tray with the white cloth. Place the candle in its holder on the tray and light it.

Add the boiling water to the teapot then place it, the dried Linden flowers, the teacups, the pot of honey and the spoons on the tray and take to where you will be drinking the tea. You might like to add a white Rose (to indicate peace and purity of action) and perhaps a clear quartz crystal (to boost the power of your intentions) to the setting.

Earth Magick

Sit with the person you wish to ask forgiveness from and share a cup of tea. If this is not possible, set up tea for two and imagine them there with you then go through the spell as follows: Add 1 teaspoon of Linden flowers for each cup of water in the teapot. When you put the flowers into the teapot, make sure you say you are sorry to the other person in some way. Sweeten the tea with honey if required and stir with the Linden stick.

The Linden tree is usually considered to be female in many customs and traditions. In Lithuania, men make sacrifices to an Oak tree deity whereas women make sacrifices to that of the Linden tree.

The flowers of the Linden tree are useful as a support for the ailments associated with respiratory conditions including colds and flu. All parts of a Linden tree are edible - the leaves, bark, sap and the seeds along with the flowers.

Hawthorn Tree Strengthen Love Spell

Found in many parts of the world, these trees have proved to be extremely adaptable and tenacious. They cope with heavy pollution in cities, salt spray in rugged coastal areas and very low temperatures. Because of this, and their beautiful form, flowers and fruit (known as haws), they are popular garden and street trees.

This is a recipe to share and strengthen a couple's love for each other. It is a good spell to do when there have been challenging times in your relationship and you are in rebuilding mode. Hawthorn is included because it provides balance and purification. Hawthorn also protects hearts, offers hope and is symbolic of a sacred union. If you have no access to Hawthorn you could substitute any other edible red fruit, but bring Hawthorn into your magickal working through imagery.

Timings: Full Moon, Monday, Morning/Midday

Find and Gather

- ✦ 1 kg/2.2 lb ripe Hawthorn haws (*Crataegus monogyna*)
- ✦ a towel
- ✦ water (*as needed*)
- ✦ 2 saucepans (*1 large*)

Tree Spells ✦ 253

- a sieve
- a masher or spoon
- sugar (*as needed*)
- a sugar thermometer
- sterilised jars with lids

The Spell

Remove the stalks from the haws by rolling them in the towel and say:

Away with past and what has divided,
Strengthen our love with what is now decided.

Wash the haws very well, picking out any that are spoiled. Place in the large saucepan and add enough water to cover. Cook until they are very soft.

Strain through a sieve into a large bowl, pressing the haws with a masher or spoon to extract as much liquid as possible. Discard the haw pulp and seeds.

Pour the resulting liquid into the second saucepan and add 1 cup of sugar for each cup of liquid. Bring to the boil, stirring to dissolve the sugar. Continue to boil until the setting point is reached: 105°C/220°F.

Pour into warm sterilised jars and seal. Store in a cool, dry place for up to 12 months. Refrigerate once opened and use within two weeks.

When using, spread a little on a sweet biscuit or cake to share and say:

Strengthening hearts,
Together we fare.
Let the challenge scars heal now,
And our love be given new care.

Other types of Hawthorn are also edible and can be used in this jelly. Check local guides as to their availability. Note the seeds are not edible as they contain small amounts of cyanide, much like apple seeds, so always discard.

Traditionally, winter is considered over when the Hawthorn flowers. This is probably why dreaming of Hawthorn when single means a new lover is assured pretty much immediately!

Apple Tree Love Spell

The Apple we are all familiar with comes from a tree that was originally from Central Asia, where the wild trees are still found today. Humans have been planting Apple trees across the world for centuries. They have found their way from Asia through Europe and on to North America and beyond and have inspired myths and folklore.

This spell creates an old-fashioned Apple shampoo that will surround you with positive love energies to attract the right love for you. It will also help you see yourself in a positive light and love yourself more! Apple is used in this spell because it helps purify emotions, is an excellent self-care supporter and is symbolic of fertility, sensuality and love in general.

Timings: Full Moon, Friday, Morning

Find and Gather

- about 4-6 Apples (*Malus pumila*)
- a juicer
- a large glass or ceramic bowl
- 1 cup of distilled water
- ¼ cup liquid Castile soap
- 8 drops of rose essential oil
- a wooden spoon
- a fine strainer
- a beautiful glass bottle with lid
- a funnel (*optional*)

The Spell

Juice the Apples until you have 1 cup of juice. (*You can substitute purchased Apple juice but make sure it is fresh pressed/juiced with no additives.*) Pour into the bowl and then add the distilled water. Add the Castile soap and the essential oil, stir well and say:

> *Rose oil, Apple tree,*
> *Together for me,*
> *A love that is true,*
> *A love that is right,*
> *Breathe love through my hair,*
> *Bring love's heart delight.*

Tree Spells ✦ 255

Strain into the glass bottle, store out of direct sunlight and use within six weeks. To use: shake well and use as you would your regular shampoo.

If you would like to see a unicorn, it is said your best chance is to visit an orchard early on a misty spring morning, as they make their homes beneath Apple trees.

To find out if the one you desire loves you, throw an Apple pip (*seed*) onto a fire. You can say: 'If you love me pop and fly, if you do not lay and die.' If it pops, your love is returned, if it does not then they do not feel the same about you.

Sweet Orange Tree Friendship Spell

Found growing naturally in China and naturalised in many parts of the world, the sweet Orange is an important commercial crop. Sweet Orange is also grown by home gardeners as an ornamental tree as well as for its fruit.

This is a sparkling treat to share with friends to strengthen bonds, heal rifts and encourage warmth and clear communication. Orange is the base of the spell because it raises the energies of friendship, joy, enthusiasm and bonds. The sharing of food and drink is a bonding experience that humans have engaged in since time began so it makes the perfect format for any friendship spell.

Timings: Waxing Moon, Friday, Midday/Evening

Find and Gather

- 12 Oranges (*Citrus sinensis*)
- a juicer (*hand or electric*)
- a beautiful clear glass/crystal jug
- 1 bottle of champagne/sparkling wine or sparkling water
- 3 teaspoons of orange blossom water
- a wooden spoon
- gorgeous glasses for you and your friends

The Spell

Juice the Oranges, add to the jug and say:

Sweet Orange tree,
Your fruit before me,
Fallen from up high,
Bring the joy from the sky.

Pour in the champagne/sparkling wine or sparkling water and (using the version that suits) say:

Joyful wine (or water),
Sparkle and dance,
When friends gather round,
Our bonds to be grown.

Drop in the orange blossom water and stir with the wooden spoon while saying three times:

Flowers grow friendships.

Pour into the glasses and serve.

Wine features in many old spells that you may come across. Orange juice itself has always been considered a perfect substitute for any alcoholic beverage called for in spells and ritual work.

Don't throw away Orange peel. Added to a bath, it can make you more attractive to those you may have a romantic interest in. Carrying it in your wallet or purse with an Orange pip can help attract wealth.

Tree Spells *for* Change and Empowerment

Eastern Cottonwood Tree Communication Spell

The hybridisation of the Black Poplar (Populus nigra) *and this tree, the Eastern Cottonwood, has produced the extensively planted and well-known P. x canadensis. The Eastern Cottonwood is found naturally from the eastern Rocky Mountains from Quebec through to Texas.*

Eastern Cottonwood is suggested for this spell because it assists with the opening of communication channels. These types of spells are helpful in times when you feel you are not being clearly heard by another person or group, and while you cannot energetically change their opinion you can raise energy to ensure you are better understood.

Timings: Full Moon, Wednesday, Dusk

Find and Gather

- a blue tablecloth or scarf
- 4 leaves from an Eastern Cottonwood tree (*P. deltoides*)
- 2 bells
- a pen and paper
- a clear vase
- a small beautiful bottle with an airtight top
- water
- glycerin

The Spell

Lay the cloth out neatly and place the leaves in a line on the cloth. At either end of the line, place a bell. Take the pen and paper and write what it is that you need to be understood. Ring the first bell then say:

Hear these words,
And the things that I mean.

Then read what you have written.
Ring the second bell and say:

Make no mistake,
To take them to thee.

Fill your vase with the water and place the leaves in it. Place the vase on top of the paper you wrote on and put them outside in the sunlight for a day.

Add water from the vase to your bottle till three-quarters full then add one-quarter glycerin. Whenever you wish your message to be heard, ring a bell and shake your bottle.

The distinctively triangular leaves is why this tree bears the botanical name '*deltoides*', meaning 'triangular-shaped'.

Sacred to many Native American peoples, the Cottonwood is often thought of as a symbol of the sun and to some it symbolises the afterlife. The Hidatsa believe that by approaching with great respect and then standing in the shade of a Cottonwood you could have questions answered and be given insight and solutions to your problems.

Bay Laurel Tree Success Spell

Native to areas throughout the Mediterranean, the Bay Laurel was used by the Ancient Greeks to create wreaths to crown their sporting champions. The fragrant leaves are also used in cooking as an aromatic.

Bay leaves are used in this spell to raise the energy of victory and success that Bay Laurel shares. This tree symbolises immortality and provides protection from disease, misadventure and even witchcraft. In this spell you will be creating a headband decorated with Bay Laurel leaves. It is preferable that you carefully stitch them to the headband and focus on your success, but you can glue on the leaves using a cool-temperature glue gun.

Timings: Waxing Moon, Thursday, Daytime

Find and Gather

- fresh Bay Laurel leaves (*Laurus nobilis*) - at least 12
- a soft fabric headband
- a thick needle and thread
- a pen and paper

260 ✦ Earth Magick

The Spell

Sit in a sunny and bright spot and carefully sew your Bay Laurel leaves onto your headband in a straight line so that the leaves circle the band. Use two or three large straight stitches and overlap the next leaf slightly. After each leaf is secured say:

Leaf of the circle,
Take me on high with you too,
Together may victory,
Come swift and come true.

Once your wreath is complete, place it on your head, then take out the pen and paper and write down your success goals. Stand and read them out loud. Put the sheet of paper somewhere high in your home and place the Bay Laurel headband upon it.

The term 'poet laureate' comes to us from the Ancient Greek practice of also adorning acclaimed poets with fruiting branches of the Bay Laurel formed into wreaths.

If you feel you are going into a situation that may cause you to have bad luck or if you think you have bad luck at the moment, then try holding a Bay leaf under your tongue. Bay Laurel is considered to be a strong purification tree and along with breaking bad luck it is used in exorcisms and in cleansing rituals, mostly burned.

Magnolia Tree Legacy Protection Spell

Introduced to Europe in the 1700s, the Magnoliaceae family has 12 genera and over 200 species with many cultivars. These well-loved flowering trees have a native distribution across North America and Asia.

If you are creating anything that you consider to be a legacy, this is a strong and important spell that you can do to protect it. This can be anything that you envision will stay in your family or to be of continued benefit to others long-term, for example a body of work, a business, a family history record or property. Magnolia is the tree selected to assist as it is a wisdom-keeper itself, a very strong protector against negative and harmful energies and a provider of great strength.

Timings: New Moon, Saturday, Late Night

Tree Spells ✦ 261

Find and Gather

- a small branch of a Magnolia tree (*Magnolia* spp.) - any size
- secateurs
- an offering
- water
- a white fabric ribbon

The Spell

Magnolia trees seldom shed branches, but they do sometimes need pruning. You will need to respectfully harvest a branch for your spell. To do this, look carefully at the tree to select a branch that suits you and that feels ready to be harvested. Only take one. Your offering should be something biodegradable, perhaps a special small cake or biscuit you have made.

Once you have cut the branch with your secateurs, put your hand over the cut limb tightly and say:

Thank you, wise tree,
I honour and respect thee.

Pour the water at the base of the tree and say:

May you never be thirsty.

Place your offering at the base of the tree and say:

May you have all that you need.

Tie the white ribbon where you cut your branch from and say:

My legacy grows and my legacy will be,
Protect and guide with love, oh great mighty tree.

Place the branch above the front door of where your legacy is. This could be your home or your business.

To ensure a lover stays true to you, place a Magnolia shoot under the bed. They will always then be faithful. To keep a business partner honest and loyal, place a Magnolia shoot under their desk or work area.

Magnolia have long been considered a female tree, of being a vessel of goddess energy, and are symbolic of motherhood and feminine strength. This is perhaps due to its flower, which is a beautiful cup-like pink or white blossom.

Spindle Tree Shadow Self Spell

The Spindle tree is found throughout Europe. It grows along the edges of forests and hedgerows, creating a beautiful autumn display each year with the turning of its leaves from a pale green first to purple-red, then yellow, and striking red and orange fruit.

Spindle tree is the base of this spell as it is considered a tree that can unveil hidden knowledge, destiny and wisdom but also because it helps people examine their shadow self and understand how it may be impacting their lives.

Timings: Dark Moon, Saturday, Midnight/Late Night

Find and Gather

- a small piece of Spindle wood (*Euonymus europaeus*)
- a piece of string about 15 cm/6" long
- a pen/pencil and a sheet of paper - at least A3 size
- matches
- a fireplace or heat-proof dish

The Spell

You may like to carve the Spindle into a pendulum shape if you have the skill.

On the sheet of paper draw a circle as large as will fit. On the outside of the circle, equally spaced around it, write down all the shadow aspects of yourself. Be honest.

Tie the string to the Spindle wood and then hold the Spindle above the sheet of paper and say out loud what your challenges are. Let the Spindle spin and move as it will. Watch where it goes and what words it is pulled towards as these will be the shadow aspects of yourself that are most affecting your challenge. You might find some solutions or insights into how you can gain control or at least work a little better with your situation.

Once you have finished, burn the paper completely.

The Spindle tree was known as 'skewer wood' in Victorian times due to the practice of using its wood to make skewers. It has also been used to create spindles, clothes pegs and charcoal.

The tool of the Greek Fates that helped create the destiny of each human was a spindle made from the wood of the Spindle tree. They would spin a thread that represented the life, measure it and cut it.

White Poplar Tree Guidance Spell

The White Poplar is native to western Asia, North Africa and Europe. A very hardy tree, it is often used as a roadside city tree because it tolerates pollution well. White Poplars are fast growing and have white downy hairs on the underside of their leaves and covering their shoots. On windy days this gives the impression that the tree is covered in silver.

White Poplar is used in this guidance spell as it helps find guidance and to calm fears you may have in moving forward. You will be creating a simple dance ribbon for this spell and using it much the same way gymnasts do, by twirling it through the air around you – and, yes, you can dance!

Timings: New Moon, Monday, Late Night

Find and Gather

- a White Poplar stick or small branch (*Populus alba*)
- a 4 m/13' white ribbon

The Spell

Tie the ribbon to one end of the stick. Take this outside and think about the thing you are seeking guidance with. Walk around (*or dance!*), twirling the ribbon through the air as you do. When it feels right, safely toss the stick in the air and let the ribbon and stick fall where they may.

Examine the patterns you see in the ribbon and the way the stick is lying. You might like to take a photo for

reference so you can look at it again, but you really should try to tune in to the messages before you.

Look out for letters, numbers, crosses, arrows or circles as they can indicate very definite answers. You may like to see if there are shapes of animals, objects and so on as well, as these will all have meanings. Look up a tea-leaf reading dictionary for interpretations. Dream guides and magickal correspondences lists will also be helpful.

You could make a mini version of this divination dance stick by using a small White Poplar twig and thinner 'baby' ribbon cut to your desired length. Simply twirl in the air and let it land on a table.

Due to the way its leaves tremble in the slightest breeze, White Poplar is often regarded as a folklore remedy or an ingredient of magickal spells to cure diseases with the symptom of trembling, such as palsy. The trees also carry the common names of 'quivering tree', 'quaking tree' and 'trembling tree'.

According to Roman legend, Hercules wove a crown of Poplar leaves to protect himself from the flames of the Underworld on his journey there. They became scorched from the heat on the topside but turned light from the reflection of Hercules's face, as it possessed a god-like radiance.

Dragon's Blood Tree Hex Breaker Spell

The Dragon's Blood Tree is probably most noted for the incense made from its distinctive red resin but has an equally interesting appearance. This native to the Socotra Archipelago in Yemen has an overall structure similar to that of an open umbrella.

The combination of fire and ice in this hex-breaker is a very final way to resolve the issue. Using Dragon's Blood will give you complete protection, which is vital when going into the energies of a hex in order to break it. It also gives you courage when going into battle or facing challenges and it will increase your personal power.

Timings: Waning Moon, Tuesday, Midnight

Tree Spells ✦ 265

Find and Gather

- a pen and small piece of paper
- a heat-proof dish
- matches
- a small plastic container
- water
- a stick of Dragon's Blood incense or a few small pieces of resin (*Dracaena cinnabari*)

The Spell

Write down the hex as you believe it to be on the piece of paper. Burn it in the heat-proof dish and say:

Fire dissolve the words against me,
Fire break the hex that has been.

Let the ashes cool completely then place them in your plastic container. Pour in enough water to cover the ashes and stir with the Dragon's Blood incense stick. Break the stick up and throw it into the container. Place in the freezer. As you do say:

Frozen you are,
No longer you move.
Be gone from my life,
And never return.

Leave for 90 days and then bury off your property.

You can add Dragon's Blood resin or incense or in fact any botanical part to your spellwork for a turbo boost. This would be very helpful if you are redoing a spell because the first time it wasn't as affective as you had hoped.

Dragon's Blood can be used to create a red ink that is very powerful when used for writing spellwork. Mix one part powdered Dragon's Blood resin to one part Arabic gum and then 10 to 15 parts alcohol (*depending on consistency*).

Mangrove Tree Opportunity Spell

Growing in coastal areas, in salt or brackish water, Mangrove trees are found throughout the world in tropical and subtropical regions. They offer a home for young organisms and some protection against coastal erosion. Although there are many different types of trees and plants that can grow within the Mangrove forest, there are only a few that are actual 'Mangrove trees' and they are found in the plant family Rhizophoraceae.

The use of Mangrove tree in this spell is to tap into the energies of opportunity, adaptability, availability and the ability to put things to best use. If you do live near Mangroves then by all means go to the forest, but you will still need to do this spell the way it is set out. It relies on you imitating a Mangrove tree yourself.

Timings: Full/Waxing Moon, Thursday, Daytime

Find and Gather

+ a blue cup or jug
+ a jar with lid
+ a handful of small seashells/sand/pebbles
+ salt

The Spell

Take yourself to the seaside or a Mangrove forest if you're lucky enough to be near. If neither is available to you then a river, dam, stream or lake will do, and if no waterway is available to you at all stand in a basin or bath. You will then need enough water to cover your feet.

Standing with your feet covered in water and your toes splayed open say:

> *I stand as a Mangrove,*
> *Firm here on the shore*
> *Water comes in,*
> *Tide pulls you out,*
> *Within there lies chances,*
> *Here, there, all about.*

Scoop up a cupful of water and place in the jar. If possible, add a handful of small seashells/sand/pebbles to the water and if not near salt water, a good dash of salt. Seal and take home. Whenever you want new opportunities or for something to go your way, shake the jar and ask it:

Mangrove water,
Move for me now,
Water comes in,
Tide pulls you out,
Within there lies chances,
Here, there, all about.

To survive. Mangrove trees are not only tolerant of salt but also have a complex root system to withstand waves and tides. They are also able to live with very low oxygen supplies when growing in waterlogged mud.

Mangroves stand between two worlds. the sea and the land. and so can be helpful in any magickal work that requires two aspects of something to be balanced. changed or explored. Decisions especially around emotions (*water*) and the physical (*earth*) can benefit.

Elder Tree Evolution Spell

The Elder is actually a shrub, not a tree, but is included in this collection as it is often referred to as a tree in magickal traditions. Native to Europe and North America, it is also widely known as Elderberry. The flowers are used to make cordial and other drinks while the berries are used for syrup and jelly, and both are used for wine.

Elder flowers are used in this spell because flowers in general symbolise evolution and growth as they are the reproductive parts of a plant. If you use the flowers, you must cook them as they are toxic if consumed raw. Elder trees instil inner strength, self-esteem and courage. They will boost your vigour, impart good luck and nurture progress while giving you the fortitude to carry on. This spell works very well for those creating vision boards.

Timings: Waxing Moon, Saturday, Daytime

268 ✦ Earth Magick

Find and Gather

- your favourite cupcake recipe and ingredients
- a handful of Elder flowers (*Sambucus nigra*) - the spell can be completed without these
- elderflower cordial
- 2 beautiful glasses, one larger and grander than the other
- sparkling water
- your journal, diary or vision board

The Spell

Make the cupcake batter, then mix the Elder flowers into the batter and say:

> *Elder wise,*
> *Elder strong,*
> *Help me go from here,*
> *To evolve where I long.*

Bake your cupcakes and then set up a beautiful table with the glasses, sparkling water, elderflower cordial and a cupcake and have your diary/journal/vision board before you.

Place a dash of elderflower cordial in the smaller glass and fill with sparkling water. Pour this into the other glass and say:

> *Today I stand here,*
> *Tomorrow I rise,*
> *Evolving with passion,*
> *Becoming the wise.*

Eat the cupcake and drink the elderflower water.

Elder is connected with the White Goddess in Pagan traditions and brings healing and comfort. Planting one in a garden or working field is thought to bring good luck and protection.

Growing an Elder tree in your garden will ensure that the mother Elder protects it and it is also thought that doing so will ensure that the gardener dies in their own bed. As it is also said that having this tree growing in your garden might discourage friends from visiting you, perhaps a 'welcome friends' spell would help!

Tree Spells ✦ 269

Pine Tree Increase Intuition Spell

Any conifer in the Pinus *genus is considered a pine tree. They are long-living trees with age ranges recorded from 100 to more than 1,000 years. Native to the Northern Hemisphere and small tropical areas of the Southern Hemisphere, they are found in a vast range of climates from sea level to 5,200 m/17,100'. These include rainforests, deserts and the tropics.*

Pine will open up paths between worlds, especially above and below the earth. This tree also helps strengthen faith, imparts longevity and keeps things true. For this spell, a traditional witch bottle will be made. Also known as spell bottles, they have been in use since at least the early 17th century in the UK and USA. This is a way of capturing energies to be used time and again and so they must be created with great care.

Timings: New Moon, Monday, Late Night

Find and Gather

- a purple candle
- a candle holder
- matches
- a small handful of dried Pine needles (*Pinus* spp.)
- a beautiful clear bottle and seal
- any small crystals that you are drawn to
- water
- a purple ribbon

The Spell

Set the candle in the candle holder and light. Add your Pine needles to the bottle and then say:

Above and below,
Connect and inspire,
Intuition be sharp,
And alive in the fire.

Hold your bottle high above the flame as you say the last line.

Add the crystals and fill with water, then seal the bottle and tie the purple ribbon around the neck. Whenever you are seeking clearer intuition, simply shake your bottle then sit quietly and watch the contents completely settle. You should receive thoughts that will help you and you will naturally strengthen your intuitive powers.

The oldest living Pine tree can be found in California, USA. It is a Great Basin Bristlecone Pine (*P. longaeva*) that has been nicknamed 'Methuselah' and is around 4,600 years old.

If you collect a Pine cone that still contains Pine nuts on Midsummer Day and then eat one of the nuts each day until finished, you are said to become invincible.

Ash Tree Magickal Empowerment Spell

The common Ash tree grows wild in Europe from the Pyrenees through to the Caucasus. All Ash trees can be found growing in the temperate areas of the world but in particular Europe, Asia and North America.

Ash is selected as it symbolises power and mastery and will also increase psychic awareness. This spell requires the creation of a small and very simple doll, traditionally called a 'poppet', that is going to contain your spell and be something you can carry with you if needed.

Timings: Full Moon, Sunday, Midday

Find and Gather

- pins
- 2 pieces of red fabric
- a black felt-tip pen
- scissors
- a needle
- red thread
- shavings of pieces of Ash tree bark (*Fraxinus excelsior*)
- a clear quartz crystal

Tree Spells + 271

The Spell

Pin the fabric pieces together. With the black felt-tip pen, draw a simple human figure on the top piece. Cut out the figure. Sew the pieces together, leaving a small opening at the top of the head.

Fill the doll with the Ash tree bark and say:

> *Ash tree of power,*
> *Of magick and might,*
> *I call on your gifts,*
> *With a promise to do right.*

Add the crystal and sew up the opening. You can now carry this with you when you want a boost in magickal power, use it during other spells and rituals or leave it in places to inspire magick.

Ash trees grow well in soils that are calcareous limestone based. The timber is very strong, impact resistant and durable so has been used to create tools and ladders as well as horse-drawn coaches.

You can also boost your psychic abilities by placing an Ash leaf under your pillow at night. You should have prophetic dreams so be sure to keep a dream journal nearby.

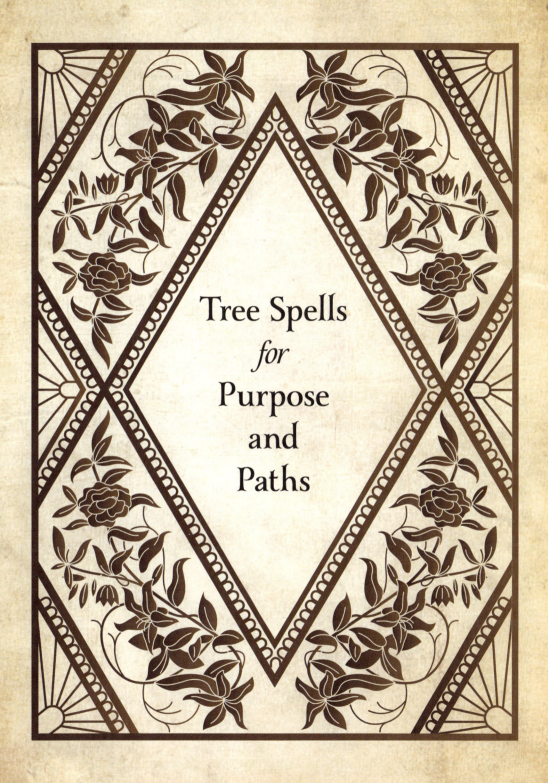

Tree Spells
for
Purpose
and
Paths

Spruce Tree Awaken My Passion Spell

Spruces grow in the colder regions of the Northern Hemisphere. They are pyramid-shaped trees, and although they look similar to Fir trees you can identify Spruces by the peg-like stump on each needle where it's attached to the twig.

Spruce is used to create this anointing oil. Use it daily to find and grow your life passion. Spruce instils boldness and passion and will help you let go of self-pity and any weakness that does you no good. This spell will help with those who may be finding it hard to define their purpose or fire up their passion, or perhaps feel they have lost their way a little.

Timings: Full Moon, Sunday, Midday

Find and Gather

- a red cloth
- a clear glass or crystal bowl
- a fire agate crystal
- 1 cup of sweet almond oil
- 11 drops of spruce essential oil
- a beautiful sterilised bottle
- organic cotton wool pads or balls

The Spell

Spruce oil is safe for most people to use on their skin but you should still allergy-test yourself first. If you are anointing surfaces with the oil, please do a test somewhere inconspicuous first.

In the place in your home which is most used by you, lay out your red cloth and place the bowl upon it. Place the fire agate crystal in the bowl, then gently pour in the almond oil and say three times:

> *Oil of Spruce,*
> *Stone of fire,*
> *Passion be found,*
> *Then take me higher.*

Pour the oil into the bottle. You can now help enliven your passion and find your purpose by lightly anointing the doorways of each room of your home/workspace with the oil or by placing a cotton wool pad/ball on a dish somewhere in each room. Place the fire agate near to the place where you work/create or generally are in your home or place of business.

The Norway Spruce (*Picea abies*) is the traditional Christmas tree of most European countries. It is also the tree from which timber is used to create the bodies of many stringed instruments, including the violin.

Most trees in the Northern Hemisphere shed their leaves during the colder months of the year so it was believed that the trees that held their leaves, like the Spruce, had power over death because they harboured good and pure spirits. Spruce branches and later the trees themselves were brought into homes in the winter to afford the same protection.

Hickory Tree Personal Path Spell

A member of the Juglandaceae (Walnut) family, the Hickory tree has large, aromatic leaves and is deciduous. It's native to North America, Mexico, China and Indochina. Hickory and Oak are the dominant trees of the hardwood forests of North America.

Hickory is used here because it will impart patience, flexibility and strength. This spell creates a magickal floor wash. These have been used since we have had floors. It makes sense that the place where we meet the earth and that we place our feet upon should be energetically cleansed and empowered. The addition of orange blossom to your floor wash water will effectively and positively lift your energy.

Timings: Waxing Moon, Thursday, Dusk/Twilight

Find and Gather

+ ½ bucket water
+ ½ cup Hickory leaves (*Carya* spp.)
+ ¼ cup orange blossom water
+ a bucket
+ a mop

Tree Spells ✦ 275

The Spell

Open all the windows and doors of your home. Pour the water into a clean bucket then toss in your Hickory leaves. Put the mop in, stir in a clockwise direction and say:

> *Hickory strong, patient and true,*
> *Find me a path that is right and is true.*

Stir in your orange blossom water and say:

> *Orange tree sweet,*
> *Happy and bright,*
> *Keep me uplifted,*
> *True, steady and right.*

Wash over the floor and as you do, work your way towards the front door. Go outside and throw the remaining water and the leaves on your front path.

If you do not have hard floors, you can create a mist with a smaller amount of water and Orange Blossom water in a misting bottle. Place a chopped up Hickory leaf inside and then spray on your floors.

Hickory is an exceptionally strong timber and is used to craft tools, walking sticks, sporting clubs and sticks, paddles and furniture. Having almost the strength of steel and yet a considerable amount of flexibility led the Native Americans to use it to make their bows.

You can predict the weather by looking at Hickory nuts. The thickness indicates what the coming winter will have in store. The thicker the shell, the more challenging the season will be for everyone.

Yew Tree Rebirth Spell

Found in North America, Asia and Europe, the Yew grows mostly in the middle latitudes, but a few are found in tropical highlands. Although they are poisonous, they are still favoured as a decorative garden tree.

The inclusion of Yew in this spell must be done carefully as it is highly poisonous. It is better to be in the presence of the actual tree and create a ritual to capture the energy; however, there are flower essences based on Yew that could be substituted for being in the presence of the tree.

Timings: Full Moon, Sunday, Morning

Find and Gather

- a beautiful wooden box
- a small mirror which will fit in the bottom of the box
- a Yew tree (*Taxus baccata*)
- a piece of green-coloured silk
- 2 teaspoons of dried Sacred Blue Lily flowers (*Nymphaea caerulea*)
- matches
- a fire or heat-proof dish
- 9 small clear quartz crystal points

The Spell

Take out the mirror and capture the image of the Yew tree in it. Place the green cloth loosely in the box, then the mirror and say:

> *Time has come for me to let go,*
> *Yew tree, now is the time,*
> *I do know.*

Place the Sacred Blue Lily flowers in the dish and light or toss into the fire and say:

> *Listen, tree, day and night,*
> *When I next open this box,*
> *A new birth sees the light.*

Place the crystals around in the box and as you add each say:

> *Protect and empower,*
> *The new life begun,*
> *May it strengthen and thrive,*
> *All its days in the sun.*

Take the box home and when you are ready to end something in your life and start anew, open the box. Leave it so for seven days and then bury it under the Yew tree or another strong, young (but long-lived) tree.

The Yew tree is sacred to the goddess Hecate. Ancient Romans would adorn black bulls with Yew branches and leaves and then sacrifice them to Hecate at Saturnalia to ensure a tolerable winter. It was thought that ghosts would feed on the bull and not the remaining herd.

To dream of Yew trees can mean an escape from a very serious accident or it can mean the passing of a friend from illness.

Mesquite Tree Awaken Creativity Spell

Mesquites are native to the south-western United States and Mexico (except Creeping Mesquite, which is from Argentina). Mesquite is a legume and is one of the very few sources of fixed nitrogen in the desert environments in which it grows.

Mesquite is included in this creativity opening spell as it has a natural energy-warming ability, inspires healing and will encourage abundance. I find my creativity is bound by my emotions so bringing the power of fire into the emotional element of water should help balance things. This water can be used any time you would like to stimulate creativity. If it is raining, collect rainwater for an added magickal boost.

Timings: Waxing Moon, Friday, Evening

Find and Gather

- a beautiful white cloth
- a large, beautiful bowl
- pure water
- a fire
- a handful of Mesquite wood (*Prosopis* spp.)
- a mirror
- a special bottle

The Spell

Find a place outside where you can see the moon. Lay the white cloth out on the ground and say:

> *Gently touched with cloth of white,*
> *Ground in Earth for magick tonight.*

Set the bowl upon the cloth. Pour in the pure water and say:

Water of heart, of love and of care,

Support and bring comfort to all that is there.

Toss your Mesquite wood into the fire and say:

Tree of warmth,

Inspiration bright,

Creativity open,

For me from this night.

Taking the mirror, angle it so you catch the reflection of the Moon and bounce it into the bowl of water. Tend the fire but let it burn out. Leave the bowl out for the night. The next morning, scoop a little of the Mesquite ash into the bottle and fill with the water. Use it sparingly as you would a flower essence mist by spritzing in the air when you need a creativity boost.

Mesquite is the most common tree and shrub of the south-western United States. It has been described as a gift from heaven by the early settlers. who used it as a primary food source when stocks ran out. The beans can be eaten. made into a flour and also roasted as a substitute for coffee.

To many of the Native American peoples. Mesquite is regarded as a Tree of Life. This is probably due to all parts of these hardy desert plants being useful.

Aspen Tree Overcome Obstacles Spell

Native to North America, Aspens live in areas of colder weather and particularly cool summers. Most Aspens grow in large colonies, coming from a single seedling, and then spread by means of root suckers.

Aspen trees connect with the yin and the yang of anything they are in the presence of. They represent the duality of a situation so that you are aware of what has been and what may be possible. Aspen will still and calm fears, inspire trust in love and will also work to provide opportunities for success and abundance so that you can move forward. This is a very simple spell but still very powerful. You will be jumping a stick of Aspen to jump your obstacle.

Tree Spells ✦ 279

Timings: New Moon, Tuesday, Twilight

Find and Gather

- 2 bricks (*or other objects to raise each end of the stick slightly*)
- a stick or branch of Aspen (*Populus tremula, P. tremuloides*) at least 0.5 m/20" long
- a pen and paper
- 2 red candles
- 2 candle holders
- matches
- a heat-proof dish

The Spell

Set the bricks on the ground, spaced out so that you can rest an end of the Aspen stick on each. The Aspen stick only has to be raised slightly off the ground so you can step over it.

Take your paper and write down your obstacle. Put a candle holder with a red candle in it on the ground at each end of the Aspen stick. Make sure they are a safe distance away, so you do not set your clothing on fire while performing this spell.

Light each candle and say:

With fire I fight and burn away what is stopping me.

Stand on one side of your stick, holding the paper, and say:

These obstacles are ashes on the side that I leave.

Walk over to a candle and light the paper, dropping it into the heat-proof dish to burn.

Step or jump over the Aspen stick and say:

A new path I've taken,

A new start begun,

May the blocks that have barred me,

Be forever now done.

Clap your hands loudly to send the energy forward. Bury all your ingredients except your holders, bricks and the tray under a tree.

Aspen trees are aligned with the New Moon and are considered the Virginal Goddess tree. Any magickal ritual or spell cast at this time would be empowered by the addition of Aspen, so closely connected is this tree.

Known as the 'whispering tree', a messenger and also associated with the god Mercury, communication is another strong aspect of the Aspen. If you wish to increase your own powers of communication, place an Aspen leaf under your tongue.

Silver Fir Progress Spell

Native to the mountain regions of Europe, this is a popular Christmas tree in the north-east of North America and Canada. It can live for more than 30 years and this makes it the longest lived of the conifers.

Silver Fir is a wonderful tree to engage when you want to move your progress along a little faster. It also helps with checking in on how you are going, as it imparts great clarity in all things.

Timings: Waxing Moon, Wednesday, Daytime

Find and Gather

- a large bowl
- a watering can with a sprinkler head to mimic rain
- water
- silver fir essential oil
- orange food colouring/dye
- a stick or twig of Silver Fir (*Abies alba*) if possible - if not, any twig

The Spell

Place the bowl on a table in a quiet room. Using the watering can, fill it with water to about the halfway point and as you do say:

> Rain of the season,
> Come down and now see,

How well I am doing,
And what I may need.

Add 8 drops of silver fir essential oil and say:

Tree of silver,
Guide my way.

Now add a small dash of the orange food colouring, stir with the twig and say:

Empower my progress,
Make it faster and fresh,
Ensure each step that I take,
Is always the best.

This spell can also be used to divine ways for added success and progress by examining any patterns or symbols that you see in the water.

The Silver Fir is the tree of the Winter Solstice day and is also strongly aligned with the moon and the triple aspect of the goddess. It is also sacred to Diana, Artemis, Osiris and Attis.

To farewell a friend who is leaving, a gift or a wearable talisman created from the pine cones of the Silver Fir will ensure good luck and safe journeys. Burning the needles of the tree around the bed of a newborn baby is said to similarly bless the child with a safe and lucky life journey.

Fig Tree Magickal Power Booster Spell

Cultivated throughout the world in temperate regions for its fruit, the Fig tree was originally from south-west Asia and the Middle East. This tree has been cultivated since ancient times and can grow wild from sea level to 1,700 m/5,577').

This is a spell which will have you creating a very easy Fig jam. Use it to boost your spellcasting by taking a spoonful yourself or you could use it as your offering to the trees that you are working with. Figs are aligned with the energies of longevity, fertility and love.

Timings: Full Moon, Sunday, Midday

Find and Gather

- 4 cups of sliced Figs (*Ficus carica*)
- 1 ½ cups of granulated sugar
- ¼ cup water
- ¼ cup lemon juice
- a pinch of salt
- a saucepan
- sterilised jars

The Spell

Place all the ingredients in the saucepan and say:

> *Fig of abundance,*
> *I honour your power,*
> *Simmer here in my brew,*
> *For just a wee hour.*

Bring to a boil until the sugar dissolves, stirring occasionally. Reduce the heat and cook, continuing to stir occasionally. This should take between 40–60 minutes depending on the Figs, but the liquid should be thick and sticky. Remove from the heat. Gently mash any large pieces of Figs with a fork.

As you mash say:

> *The brew is done!*
> *The magick released,*
> *Now into my jars,*
> *To safely keep!*

Pour into warm jars, leaving a small space, and seal.

Let cool, then store the jam in the refrigerator for up to two months.

The Bible does tell us that the forbidden fruit was an Apple, but these days botanists agree that it was more likely a Fig. Apples did not grow in the region described in the story of Genesis at that time, but the Fig did, and the attributes could align with the biblical story.

Fig leaves can be used for simple divination answers. Write your question on a fresh Fig leaf in pen. If the Fig leaf seems quick to dry out, then the answer is negative or not. If the leaf is slow to dry, then the answer is yes.

Tree Spells ✦ 283

Silver Birch Tree Find Your Way Spell

One of the first trees to colonise northern Europe after the last ice age was the Silver Birch. This tree is one of the hardiest trees on earth: it can live through drought and withstand extreme cold. It seeds abundantly. This tree is included in this spell as the name is thought to have come to us from the Sanskrit word 'bhurg', meaning the continuous phases of life and describing the energies that Silver Birch imparts.

Timings: New Moon, Friday, Sunrise

Find and Gather

- a large map - can be of any place
- 4 candles - 1 of each colour: red, pink, white and blue
- holders for the candles
- matches
- 11 small Silver Birch sticks (*Betula pendula*) - similar in shape and size as 'pick-up-sticks'

The Spell

Find a protected space and place your map upon a flat surface. Set the candles up at each corner of the map. Light each, saying:

> Red is for action that I might have to take,
> Pink for the healing I am yet to make.
> White is for that which I need to let go,
> Blue for the things I am yet to know.

Hold your Silver Birch sticks over the middle of the map and drop them, asking:

> What do I need?
> Where shall I go?
> Tell me, Silver Birch, what it is I must know.

Look at where most of the sticks are pointing because this will indicate what it is you need to do in order to find your way at the moment.

Traditionally, babies' cradles were made from Birch as it was considered to be the most protective of all the woods when it came to children. Such a cradle would ensure no harm would come to the child. Birch leaves were also placed under the pillows of sick children and babies to give them the strength to shake off the illness.

Birch trees are used in some regions as a type of living May Pole during Beltane celebrations of the Pagan calendar. The bonfires are typically lit with Birch branches but are made from Oak.

Hemlock Tree Secret Reveal Spell

*The Hemlock tree is a long-lived conifer found naturally in North America and Asia. It has earned its common name because the leaves, when crushed, smell very like the poisonous Hemlock plant (*Conium maculatum*) but it is not related.*

Hemlock tree is used in this spell because it has the energies of transformation, revelation and offering assistance. Because it is rather easy to find small lower branches of Hemlock trees suitable to use as wands as they are, in this spell you will be crafting a wand that you can use forever to find the answers to secrets, unfold mysteries and even help you learn esoteric knowledge.

Timings: New Moon, Monday, Late Night

Find and Gather

- a small branch of a Hemlock tree (*Tsuga canadensis*) - sized to suit you
- 1 cup of Hemlock tree needles
- 1 cup of boiling water
- a teapot and 2 cups

The Spell

Clean and trim the branch as you like and if you desire, carve or decorate it. It is perfectly okay for you to leave the branch exactly as you found it as it is to create something crafty. This is your wand, so do what feels right for you.

Set a lovely tea service for two, somewhere quiet in your home. Put your new Hemlock tree wand on the table behind one teacup, as if it were joining you for tea, which it is!

Tree Spells ✦ 285

Crush the Hemlock needles in your hands and drop into the teapot, saying:

Hemlock tree,

Warm and unlock for me,

Secrets and answers,

Of mysteries deep.

Pour over the boiling water and let steep for 5 minutes. Pour a cup for you and your wand and ask the wand:

What is your name, my new wand friend?

You should give the wand the first name that pops into your head.

Drink your tea, take the wand outside, pour its cup over it and say:

(Insert name), *together we shall be,*

I'll honour and protect,

My word you shall have

Of my utmost respect.

Use the wand by waving it over rituals, spells, books – anything that you are trying to decipher. Make sure you always ask the wand by name to help you and thank it.

The needles of the Hemlock tree are sometimes used to make a tea and perfume. The resin can be burned to produce a lovely incense that also imparts the energetic qualities of the Hemlock tree.

Hemlock tree features in many Native America myths and stories and all seem to carry the message that the tree provides a refuge. a way of escape and a solution to adversity.

Olive Tree Inner Peace Spell

The Olive is a small tree that grows naturally in the Mediterranean, the Arabian Peninsula, southern Asia and the Canary Islands. This tree produces the fruit, also called olive, that is a major agricultural crop of the Mediterranean region.

This spell creates a relaxing hair oil treatment that will impart the peaceful qualities of Olive tree to you all day long and give you beautifully shiny, healthy hair and a healthy scalp. Use as much as your hair will tolerate. Thick, dry or damaged hair will probably need the entire mixture while normal or oily hair will only require a small amount.

Timings: Waning Moon, Friday, Dusk/Late Night

Find and Gather

- a white cloth
- a white candle
- a candle holder
- matches
- a small bowl
- a sprig of Rosemary (*Rosmarinus officinalis*)
- 4 tablespoons of virgin olive oil
- 4 drops of rosemary essential oil
- an Olive wood stick (*optional*) or a wooden spoon

The Spell

Lay out your white cloth and white candle in the holder and light it.

Into the bowl place the Rosemary, then pour over the olive oil and set it before the candle.

Lift it up and say:

Tree of peace,
Of inner strength and harmony,
Surround me with your blessings.

Put the bowl down and add the drops of rosemary essential oil, and with each say:

Carry the blessings,
Remember the peace.

Stir with the Olive tree stick or a wooden spoon. With your hair dry, massage the oil mixture into your scalp and comb through your hair, right through to the ends. Wrap up your hair in a damp, warm towel and leave for 15–30 minutes. Wash and condition.

Olive has been used throughout time as an anointing oil and as lamp oil to provide light in holy temples. Olive oil also provides the base of 'Holy Oil'. This oil represents the wisdom of God. The other oils included are myrrh, galangal and cinnamon.

To dream of eating Olives means that you are going to receive a really wonderful gift and could also rise in your status. If you dream of gathering Olives then the omen is very much in your favour for happiness, joy and peace.

Tree Spells ✦ 287

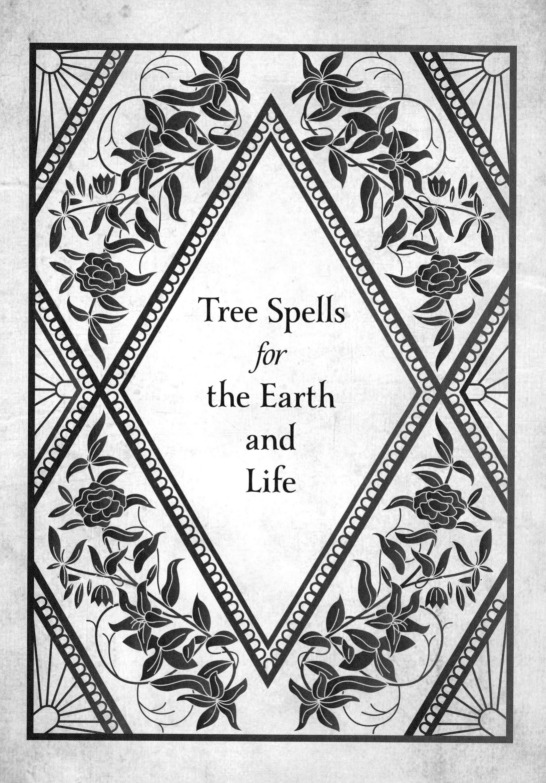

Tree Spells *for* the Earth and Life

A Tree-Planting Spell

This spell is for any tree you plan on growing anywhere. It assists the tree to take root and thrive but also to send out energies to protect others of its kind and trees in general.

The offering that you will be gathering to put inside the jar must correspond with the characteristics of your tree. Research crystal correspondences to find suitable crystals, symbols, animals (so you can include their images), other plants and so on.

Timings: Full Moon, Monday, Morning

Find and Gather

- your tree
- gardening tools and supplies as suggested for your tree
- a lovely glass jar and lid
- offerings for your tree
- milk
- honey
- water

The Spell

When planting a tree, the usual rule is to dig a hole twice as deep and as wide as the pot your tree came out of, but check with the nursery for exact instructions. You will perhaps also need extra suitable soil, fertiliser, mulch and so on, and you will need to make sure the position you select is suitable for the tree.

Plant your tree and as you do, speak to it: encourage it to grow strong and tell it why you selected it, what you hope for it and give it promises of your commitment to its care.

Fill the jar with your offerings. Dig a hole nearby. Tell the tree why you selected these gifts, listing each, and then bury it near the tree and say:

If ever I am not here,
These gifts will keep you company,

Tree Spells ✦ 289

I hope they remind you that you are loved,
And respected in this place.

Pour a little milk and honey on the ground around the tree and say:

May you never go thirsty or hungry,
And may the good spirits of this place welcome you.

Water the tree well.

Knocking on a wooden piece of furniture or object to counter any bad luck that might befall you once you mention something with negative possibilities comes from the ancient belief that pagan gods lived inside trees. If you knocked on the tree you could awaken the gods and then ask for their assistance.

You should avoid planting very large or tall trees to the east or the north-east of your home as according to many traditions and to Feng Shui advice they will emit negative energies in such positions.

American Sycamore Gardener Success Spell

Sycamore is a common name which refers to many different types of trees across the world and across different genera. The American Sycamore is found naturally growing in eastern and central North America and north–eastern Mexico.

Use this spell when planting a new garden or a new bed or crop. It will ensure added protection for your plants and more vigorous growth. Moss agate is known as the 'gardener's crystal' or stone. It will not only increase your own gardening skills if worn, the crystal will also improve the growth of any plant if placed in the soil alongside it.

Timings: Full/Waxing Moon, Thursday, Morning

Find and Gather

- 4 sticks fashioned from Sycamore branches or wood (*Platanus occidentalis*)
- 1 cup of milk
- 4 green moss agate crystals
- 4 leaves of American Sycamore
- 4 gold coins

290 ✦ Earth Magick

The Spell

Mark out the corners of your garden space that you are creating the spell for. It could be the entire garden or block, a bed or a crop area.

Dip the end of each of the Sycamore sticks into the milk and say:

> *Blessed with milk,*
> *Blessed with the life,*
> *Go into the ground,*
> *And make everything thrive.*

Stake a stick firmly in the ground at each corner of your defined space. Wrap each green moss agate in a Sycamore leaf and push one down in the earth next to each stick. Push down a gold coin with each as well and say:

> *I pay thee well,*
> *I pay thee true,*
> *Now set about,*
> *Do what you do.*

Some Native American tribes consider Sycamores to be the ghosts of the forest, due to their twisted limbs. One story tells of a great chief who ruled over the evil spirits. He was angry with two of his tribe and so cast them down to earth. They crashed into a Sycamore tree, turning it twisted with their evil spirits.

In Ancient Egyptian times, Sycamore trees were considered to be the connectors between the lands of the living and the world of the dead. It was believed to be from the Sycamore tree that the sun was released each morning.

Palo Santo Tree Sacred Space Spell

The common name of this tree is Spanish for 'holy stick'. It is native to Mexico, Peru and Venezuela. Palo Santo is a member of the same family as Myrrh and Frankincense and is a favourite folk medicine for a variety of complaints.

Palo Santo is used in this spell because it is a powerful purifier and positive energy bringer. The wood enhances creativity, instils universal love and strengthens spiritual connections. It also helps create a sacred space for you to work within. The combination of making a tea and a mojo bag out of the same stick is an important step because the energy of the shared experience will strengthen the bond between self and space.

Timings: Full Moon, Sunday, Evening

Find and Gather

- a sharp knife
- 1 stick of Palo Santo heartwood (*Bursera graveolens*)
- a teapot
- 2 cups of boiling water
- a strainer
- a teacup
- honey
- a small mojo bag
- string or ribbon

The Spell

With the sharp knife, very carefully shave off about 2 teaspoons of Palo Santo wood. Place 1 teaspoon in your teapot and pour in the boiling water. As you do say:

Wood of Palo Santo,
Healer divine,
Clear this space and make sacred,
From now for all time.

Pour through a strainer into your teacup and sweeten with a little honey.

Put the other teaspoon of Palo Santo shavings into the mojo bag and say again:

Wood of Palo Santo,
Healer divine,
Clear this space and make sacred,
From now for all time.

Once you have finished your tea, use the string or ribbon to hang the mojo bag above the main entrance to your space.

The wood of Palo Santo will purify, remove negative energy and impart positive energy at the same time. This is a trait that not many other plants share. The smoke can also help people focus better and is a very powerful meditation supporter.

Palo Santo sticks that are of a yellow colour are from the female trees and those that are white are male. Both have the same qualities and uses but there are additional aspects you might like to consider in magickal work that is closely associated with gender.

Chestnut Tree Nature Regeneration Spell

Chestnuts are trees with edible nuts that are within the botanical family of Fagaceae (Beech). They are native to temperate areas of the Northern Hemisphere. Most are large trees that are very long lived. They do best in dry soils and tolerate drought and shallow soils very well.

Chestnuts are used in this spell because they provide solid grounding energy while promoting longevity and boosting energy – perfect for regeneration to occur. If you are feeling zapped of strength, motivation and physical, mental or even emotional ability, then try these delicious chocolate chestnut magick truffles.

Timings: New Moon, Monday, Late Night

Find and Gather

- 1 cup of plain sweet biscuits (*cookies*)
- a large bowl
- 1 cup of cocoa powder
- a large, clean, plastic, food-grade bag
- 1 cup of finely chopped Chestnuts (*Castanea sativa*)
- 1 cup of desiccated coconut
- a wooden spoon
- 395 g/14 oz can of condensed milk
- a flat plate
- 1 cup finely grated dark chocolate

The Spell

Place the biscuits into the plastic bag and hit with a rolling pin to crush finely. Put these in the bowl along with the cocoa powder, desiccated coconut and chopped nuts. Slowly pour in the condensed milk while mixing with the wooden spoon and say three times:

> *Chocolate treat,*
> *Energy sweet,*
> *Chestnut divine,*
> *Strong energy mine.*

Place in the fridge for half an hour so that the mixture firms. Spread out the grated chocolate on the flat plate. Roll tablespoons of the mixture into balls and then roll in the grated chocolate to coat.

These will keep in an airtight container in the fridge for up to four days. Eat one (or two!) when you need regenerating energies.

The Japanese eat Chestnuts on New Year's Day to ensure success and to give them the strength needed for the coming year. They are considered symbolic of difficulties and overcoming them in Japan.

Eating Chestnuts encourages fertility and carrying them will increase desire for you from others. Bowls of Chestnuts around the home are said to increase abundance for the household, but you must eat them.

Sequoia Tree Spell for Those in Need

All Sequoia trees (also known as Redwoods) have very distinctive red fibrous bark and the species includes some of the oldest and tallest trees in the world. Many of the species are now extinct and have only been named after the discovery of their fossils. They are found in the Northern Hemisphere.

Not everyone will have access to a Sequoia tree for this spell, but you can find the tallest tree in your neighbourhood and still bring the energy of this mighty giant to you. Their power and majesty really can reach around the world! This spell is based loosely on the wish-

294 ✦ Earth Magick

granting Clootie Tree. In the UK, Ireland and particularly Cornwall these magickal trees are known by many names including May Bushes, Rag Trees and Faerie Trees.

Timings: Full Moon, Sunday, Night

Find and Gather

+ a Sequoia tree (*Sequoia* spp.) or a proxy tree (*see page 211*)
+ a pink ribbon, any length (*for healing*)
+ a red ribbon, any length (*for strength*)
+ a green ribbon, any length (*for new paths*)

The Spell

Sit on the ground with your back against the tree. Take some time to just sit and listen to the tree and get to know it. Talk to the tree, telling it who and what your request for help from the tree is all about. When you feel ready, take the three ribbons, stand before the tree and say:

> *For you, great Sequoia,*
> *The ribbons of three,*
> *I ask that you help,*
> *Those I know in need.*

Tie the pink ribbon to the tree (to a branch if possible) and say:

> *Pink is for healing,*
> *Complete and true.*

Tie the red ribbon to the tree and say:

> *Red is for strength,*
> *Courage and faith.*

Tie the green ribbon to the tree and say:

> *And green for new growth,*
> *For us and for you.*

Giant Sequoias (*Sequoiadendron giganteum*), or Giant Redwoods, are the world's largest single trees and they usually grow to an average height of 50-85 m/164-279' and 6-8 m/20-25' in diameter. There have been trees recorded at 948 m/311' in height.

Almond Tree Grief Support Spell

Almond trees are widely distributed throughout the world due to the popularity of their nuts (also called almond), which have been cultivated for over 2,000 years. They are native to the Middle East, particularly Mediterranean climate regions.

This is a very gentle and soothing bath spell that you can create for yourself or another to support and comfort during times of grief. Almond tree is included as it has rejuvenation qualities and can help gently with any unresolved issues or feelings.

Timings: Full Moon, Sunday, Dusk

Find and Gather

- 2 white candles and holders
- matches
- 4 tablespoons of sweet almond oil
- 2 tablespoons of sea salt
- 8 drops of rose oil
- 1 rose quartz crystal

The Spell

Set the candles safely on, or very close to, your bath.
    Light them and say:
        White light of protection,
        Surround in your grace.
    Run your bath, add the sweet almond oil and say:
        Heal and glow.
    Then add the sea salt and say:
        Ground and balance.
    Add the rose oil and say:
        Love and protect.
Once the bath is filled to your liking, take your rose quartz crystal with you and immerse yourself in the healing and replenishing waters for as long as you like.

Carrying almonds in your pockets is supposed to lead you to reassurance. Dreaming of eating them foretells that a journey is imminent and eating them will increase your wisdom. If you are looking for success in business, climb an Almond tree.

The almond shape is found repeatedly in mediaeval art, quite often surrounding God, Christ and the Virgin Mother. In Christianity the almond shape symbolises the intersection of the circles between heaven and earth.

Myrtle Tree Celebration Spell

Common Myrtle is native to the Mediterranean region in southern Europe, western Asia, Macaronesia, the Indian subcontinent and North Africa. There are many trees with 'Myrtle' in their name because they share similar characteristics but only one true Myrtle: Myrtus communis.

Group spells create amazing magick and are a perfect way to tap into the energies and make something long lasting with all those present at a gathering. This spell can be done at any type of get-together but works well to channel the good will, joy and atmosphere of celebrations. Planting a tree is a time-honoured tradition at such times and the use of Myrtle will ensure longevity and love. Myrtle also has close associations with marriage and relationships, so this would be the perfect engagement celebration spell.

Timings: Full Moon, Friday, Any Time

Find and Gather

- ribbons, each 1 m/40" long
- gardening tools
- a very small quartz crystal for each person
- a Myrtle plant (*M. communis*) - a cutting or sapling
- water

The Spell

Ask each guest to bring a ribbon to your celebration and have some extras on hand for those who might have forgotten. Dig a hole for the Myrtle. Have each person lay their ribbon with one end touching the hole and the rest stretched out flat on the ground, with a small quartz crystal at the other end. The ribbons should all fan out around the central hole like a sunburst. You can ask the guests to make a wish for the celebration or themselves or share something.

All stand around the starburst and if you can, hold hands and say:

Together we stand and energy raise,

The love and hope,

To last for all coming days.

You might like to edit this to suit your celebration or gathering.

Plant the Myrtle and water well.

Have each person take their ribbon and crystal home. This will contain the magick of the spell for them personally. If your gathering is a recurring event, they may like to bring the ribbon and crystal back with them. In the years that follow, cuttings from the Myrtle can be shared with those who were present as a way to continue the energy and hopes of the original day.

The Common Myrtle is one of the four species used by those observing the Jewish faith during the festival of Sukkot (*Feast of Tabernacles*). Celebrated on the 15th day of the seventh month, it marks the end of the harvest time in the Land of Israel.

Drinking Myrtle tea once every three days, or wearing Myrtle, is said to ensure you remain young-looking. This old folk tradition has been proven at least partly correct as it has been shown that certain Myrtles contain antioxidants that benefit the skin.

Acacia Tree Morning Ritual

There are over 1,000 species of Acacia, with more than 900 of these being native to Australia, and they make up that country's largest flowering genus. They are also found in Africa. On both continents Acacias are found in all types of terrestrial habitats, from woodland, alpine and coastal dunes to rainforests, grasslands and deserts.

Wattleseed tea is a zingy botanical brew that will bring the energies of new beginnings, hope and joy to your day. It can be brewed alone in a coffee plunger, added to your regular coffee or tea as in this spell, or added to a warm glass of water with a slice of lemon. Dedicate a special cup or mug just for this ritual. Make sure it is brightly coloured.

Timings: Any Moon Phase, Any Day, Morning

Find and Gather

- roasted ground wattleseed (*Acacia* spp.)
- your usual tea or coffee
- a special morning ritual cup or mug
- a journal
- a pen

The Spell

I have a journal that I keep everything in. It's overflowing with spells, sketches, shopping lists and to-do lists as well as my daily journals. You might do this too or perhaps you have a special journal dedicated to your morning ritual. Have it ready in the place that you will take your coffee or tea. Set this time away from computers and phone, somewhere lovely.

Make your morning beverage and as you complete the task say:

Today I awake,
To a day that is new,
Possibilities positive,
In all I may do.

In as jaunty manner as you can, throw in a dash of wattleseed and say:

Grow little suns,
Glow and shimmer with glee.
Bring a day that is bright,
And happy for me.

Grab your journal and drink. Sit in your lovely place and make some positive notes on what could unfold today. I have a dried Wattle leaf as my journal bookmark and I often find myself sketching a few Wattle flowers each morning, too. It all helps to bring their uplifting energies into my day.

The Acacia is a symbol of eternal life and of protection across many cultures. The final resting place of the god Osiris, lord of the Underworld, is said be an Acacia and this is why he is also known as 'lord of the Acacia'. The Freemasons use the Acacia as a symbol of eternal life.

Acacia is worn by Buddhists and Hindus, as the tree is considered sacred by them and is believed to offer them protection. Hindus sometimes wear a sprig in their turbans for this reason.

Sandalwood Evening Blessing Ritual

Sandalwood, also known as Indian Sandalwood, is a small tree native to India, Indonesia and the Malay Archipelago. The fragrance and medicinal qualities of the wood of this tree are important to many cultures and faiths.

Sandalwood helps clear negativity. It also sharpens mental focus onto what really matters and will help wishes come true – all good qualities for a night-time ritual. This spell creates a lightly fragrant balm that you can dab lightly on yourself before retiring for the night.

Timings: Full Moon, Saturday, Night

Find and Gather

- 2 tablespoons of vegetable wax
- a saucepan
- a heat-proof bowl
- 2 drops of rose essential oil
- a wooden spoon
- 2 drops of sandalwood essential oil
- 2 tablespoons of grapeseed oil
- a beautiful sterilised jar with a lid

The Spell

Carefully melt the wax over a low heat in the saucepan and then pour into the heat-proof bowl. Add the rose oil and, stirring with the wooden spoon, say:

> *Sweetly cleanse away the day,*
> *Of things that here,*
> *Should really stay.*
> *Calm so sweetly,*
> *Calm so sweetly.*

Earth Magick

Add the sandalwood and grapeseed oil and, stirring, say:

Negativity be gone and be done,
Tonight I lie softly,
Until tomorrow's new sun.

Pour into the warm jar and let cool. Once set, put the lid on and store in a cool, dry, dark place for up to six months. To use, dab a little on your pulse points.

According to folklore. wishes can be granted by Sandalwood. The best way is to write your wish on a piece of Sandalwood and then burn it. The smoke should rise and release. finding ways to grant your wish.

Sandalwood and Lavender together create a powerful spirit world connector. You could create a spell using both plants or you could replace the rose oil in this spell with lavender essential oil to make a balm that will help deepen your spirit communication experiences.

European Beech Ancient Wisdom Awakening Spell

The European Beech is the most dominant tree in the woodlands of southern Britain. It is also a popular street and park tree in temperate areas of the world, especially North America. The Beech is often clipped into a hedge.

This spell will increase your awareness while studying ancient wisdom and assist you to find ways to use it. European Beech not only helps open paths to wisdom, it imparts the energies of luck and success. By creating the bookmark in this spell, you will have a long-lasting guide and energy booster to carry with you as you study. Select your old book in a subject that you are passionate about as the wisdom within it will also carry into the bookmark.

Timings: Full Moon, Wednesday, Dusk

Find and Gather

- 4-6 leaves of European Beech (*Fagus sylvatica*)
- a large, heavy, old book
- a piece of cardboard - bookmark-sized to your preference
- glue (*suitable for paper crafts*)
- clear contact paper or wide, clear packing tape
- scissors
- paper towels

The Spell

Open your book and say:
> *Old friend of wisdom,*
> *Keeper of power,*
> *Press my leaves of Beech,*
> *To help me also empower.*

Place a paper towel on the page and lay your leaves out flat and spaced well so they are not touching each other. You can use more than one page if you need. Make sure you cover the leaves with an additional paper towel.

Close the book and add a few more heavy books on top so it is weighted down to press the leaves. Store in a cool, dry place for three weeks, then check on your leaves: if they are dried out then proceed; if not, leave for a while longer.

Place and glue the dried leaves as you desire on your cardboard bookmark, then cover neatly with contact or packing tape. Use in books when you study, in your journal or lean up against computers you are researching on.

There are many indications for the use of Beech in spellwork including sprinkling some ground Beech powder in your right shoe to lead you to success and fortune, carrying pieces in your pocket for luck and making wishes come true by burying pieces.

The botanical name for Beech comes to us from the Ancient Celts, who resided in what is now France. They worshipped a god named Fagus, the god of babies and childbirth. Concoctions created from the Beech tree have been used as a disinfectant throughout Europe for hundreds of years.

How to Create Your Own Spells

Personal spells are incredibly powerful because they are so personal. Creating spells from plants that have special meanings and memories to you, and ones you feel a strong affinity for, can enhance their energies incredibly.

After experiencing and practising some of the spells from my collection you may like to create your own based on the methods I have shown you, or to explore other practices. Just remember to also be respectful, safe and focused.

Magickal Correspondences

You may wish to create a bath, essence, tea, mandala – anything at all that will be in itself an action related to the energy of the spell. Items required for this should be aligned with your outcome. These are usually called *correspondences* or *magickal correspondences*. Expand your knowledge in areas that you do not have experience with by seeking out resources that specialise in the correspondence you wish to include, such as Astrological, Crystal, Colour and so on. Following is a brief list of such correspondences to get you started:

COLOUR

You can use colour in cloths to set your spell upon, in the tools that you use, candles and in the flowers themselves and in additional ingredients.

Red: passion, power, strength, courage, renewal, health, motivation, self-esteem, confrontation, ambition, challenge, purchases

Pink: healing, calming, emotions, harmony, compassion, self-love, romance, relaxation, new beginnings, partnerships

Orange: opportunities, legal matters, obstacles, abundance, gain, power, happiness

Yellow: friendship, returns, productivity, creativity, education, healing

Green: wellness, new beginnings, marriage, home, planning, peace, harmony, birth, rebirth, fertility, affection, luck, change, creativity, socialising

Blue: self-improvement, opportunity, charity, study, growth, travel, insight, patience, meditation, sports, religion, social standing, expansion, higher education, wisdom

Brown: focus, lost items, grounding, harvest, security, generosity, endurance

Violet: psychic growth, divination, spiritual development, self-improvement

Purple: spirit, ambition, protection, healing, intuition, business, occultism

White: protection, safety, transformation, enlightenment, connection to higher self, becoming more outgoing, relieving shyness, the cycle of life, freedom, health, initiation

Black: divination, rebirth, material gain, discoveries, truth, sacrifice, protection, creation, death, karma, absorbing energies, binding, neutralising, debts, separation

TIMINGS

These are the times that you put spells together and when they are cast. They add an energetic boost to your spells by bringing alignment to what you are doing in the space you are creating it. I'm sharing simple ones here for you but you can also explore deeper seasonal timings, ones associated with traditional pagan celebrations and observances and ones that are unique to the area and people of where you live and are open to others.

Moon Phases

Waxing: new projects, beginnings, growth

Full: empowerment, healing, attainment

Waning: banishing, cleansing, letting go

New: divination, revelations

Day of the Week

Monday: home, family, dreams, emotions, female energies, gardens, medicine, psychic development, travel

Tuesday: courage, strength, politics, conflict, lust, endurance, competition, surgical procedures, sports, masculine energies

Wednesday: communication, divination, self-improvement, teaching, inspiration, study, learning

Thursday: luck, finances, legal matters, desires, honour, accomplishments, prosperity, material gain

Friday: friendship, pleasure, art, music, social activities, comfort, sensuality, romance

Saturday: life, protection, self-discipline, freedom, wisdom, goals, reincarnation

Sunday: spirituality, power, healing, individuality, hope, professional success, business

Time of Day

Dawn: beginnings, awakening, cleansing, new ideas, change, love

Morning: growth, home, gardening, finances, harmony, generosity

Midday: health, willpower, physical energy, intellect

Afternoon: communication, business, clarity

Dusk/Twilight: reduction, change, receptiveness

Night: pleasure, joy, socialising, gatherings, play

Midnight: endings, release, recuperation

CRYSTALS

The addition of crystals in the form of whole pieces, tumble stones, balls and jewellery can add the energies of each to your spell. Not all crystals are suitable for all types of spells as some are not safe when coming in contact with items you use for consumption or topically.

You will need to check these as you create your spells with a reliable specialised crystal usage resource.

Agate: courage, longevity, love, protection, healing, self-confidence

Agate, Black: success, courage

Agate, Black and White: physical protection

Agate, Blue Lace: peace, consciousness, trust, self-expression

Agate, Green Moss: healing, longevity, gardening, harmony, abundance
Amazonite: creativity, unity, success, thought process
Amber: protection, luck, health, calming, humour, spell breaker, manifestation
Amethyst: peace, love, protection, courage, happiness, psychic protection
Apache Tear: protection from negative energy, grief, danger, forgiveness
Apatite: control, communication, coordination
Aquamarine: calm, strength, control, fears, tension relief, thought processes
Aventurine: independence, money, career, sight, intellect, sport, leadership
Azurite: divination, healing, illusions, communication, psychic development
Bloodstone: healing, business, strength, power, legal matters, obstacles
Calcite: purification, money, energy, spirituality, happiness
Carnelian: courage, sexual energy, fear, sorrow release, action, motivation
Chalcedony: emotions, honesty, optimism
Chrysocolla: creativity, female energies, communication, wisdom
Citrine: detox, abundance, regeneration, cleansing, clarity, initiative
Dioptase: love attracter, prosperity, health, relaxation
Emerald: wealth, protection, intellect, artistic talent, tranquillity, memory
Epidote: emotional healing, spirituality
Fluorite: study, intellect, comprehension, balance, concentration
Garnet: protection, strength, movement, confidence, devotion
Gold: power, success. healing, purification, honour, masculine energy
Hematite: divination, common sense, grounding, reasoning, relationships
Herkimer Diamond: tension soothing, sleep, rest, power booster
Iolite: soul connection, visions, discord release
Jade: justice, wisdom, courage, modesty, charity, dreams, harmony
Jasper: healing, health, beauty, nurturing, travel
Jet: finances, anti-nightmares, divination, health, luck, calms fears
Kunzite: addiction, maturity, security, divinity
Kyanite: dreams, creativity, vocalisation, clarity, serenity, channelling
Labradorite: destiny, elements
Lapis Lazuli: love, fidelity, joy, healing, psychic development, inner truth
Larimar: confidence, depression, serenity, energy balance
Malachite: money, sleep, travel, protection, business
Moldavite: changes, transformation, life purpose

Moonstone: youth, habits, divination, love, protection, friends

Obsidian: grounding, production, peace, divination

Onyx: stress, grief, marriage, nightmare protection, self-control

Opal: beauty, luck, power, money, astral projection

Pearl: faith, integrity, innocence, sincerity, luck, money, love

Peridot: wealth, stress, fear, guilt, personal growth, health

Prehnite: chakras, relationships

Pyrite: memory, focus, divination, luck

Quartz, Clear: protection, healing, power, psychic power

Quartz, Rose: love, peace, happiness, companionship

Quartz, Smoky: depression, negativity, tension, purification

Rhodochrosite: new love, peace, energy, mental powers, trauma healing

Ruby: wealth, mental balance, joy, power, contentment, intuition

Sapphire: meditation, protection, power, love, money, wisdom, hope

Sardonyx: progression, finances, self-protection

Selenite: decisions, reconciliation, flexibility, clarity

Silver: stress, travel, invocation, dreams, peace, protection, energy

Sodalite: wisdom, prophetic dreams, dissipates confusion

Sugilite: physical healing, heart, wisdom, spirituality

Sunstone: sexual healing, energy, protection, health

Tanzanite: magick, insight, awareness

Tiger's Eye: courage, money, protection, divination, energy, luck

Topaz: love, money, sleep, prosperity, commitment, calm

Tourmaline: friendship, business, health, astral projection

Tourmaline, Black: grounding, protection

Tourmaline, Blue: peace, stress relief, clear speech

Tourmaline, Green: success, creativity, goals, connection with nature

Tourmaline, Pink: friendship, love, creativity

Tourmaline, Red: projection, courage, energy

Turquoise: protection, communication, socialising, health, creative solutions

Botanical Meanings

FLOWER MEANINGS

To use a flower in a spell you should understand its energy. To do this, you need to know its meaning. You can discover this by exploring the properties it has or look to resources such as aromatherapy, flower essence guides and flower meaning resources that are based on the language of flowers as well as the actual properties of the plants themselves.

I have included an excerpt from another of my titles, *Flowerpaedia: 1,000 flowers and their meanings,* which shares with you the meanings of some of the flowers in this book. I have sourced these meanings through years of researching the properties of plants.

African Violet (Saintpaulia): spirituality, protection, higher learning

Agapanthus (Agapanthus praecox): love letters, magickal love, my love has not faded, never-fading love

Azalea (Rhododendron sect. Tsutsusi): take care of yourself for me, romance, womanhood, temperance, stay true

Camellia, Japanese (Camellia japonica): my destiny is in your hands, excellence, concentration, peace, calm

Carnation, Red (Dianthus caryophyllus): love, compassion, romance, be mine, abundance, progression, life force, yes

Chrysanthemum, White (Chrysanthemum): tell me the truth, trust me, I promise, you are sweet, innocence, purity, honesty

Chrysanthemum, Yellow (Chrysanthemum): I cannot be with you, no, refusal, boundary protection

Cornflower (Centaurea cyanus): knowledge, protection of home, new friends, friendship, new love, new-home blessings, delicacy

Dahlia (Dahlia): you can do this, encouragement, dignity, confidence, vitality, inner strength, creativity, generosity, faith, resilience, instability

Dandelion (Taraxacum officinale): I am faithful to you, your wish is granted, long-lasting happiness, healing, intelligence, warmth, power, clarity, survival

310   +   Earth Magick

Delphinium (*Delphinium*): anything is possible, I have new feelings for you, possibility, new opportunity, protection, new feelings, leadership, communication, true voice

Elder (*Sambucus nigra*): inner strength, self-esteem, courage, fortitude, calm fears, nurturing, stabilise inner energy, vigour, resilience, joy, recovery, renewal of energy, protection from evil, good luck, release sins, prolong life, peaceful sleep

Freesia (*Freesia*): I trust you, life is worthwhile, trust, inner guidance, friendship, innocence, optimism, hope, thoughtfulness

Fuchsia (*Fuchsia magellanica*): true feelings, freeing deep emotions, amiability, confiding love, good taste

Gardenia (*Gardenia jasminoides*): awareness, secret love, divine message

Geranium (*Geranium*): I want to meet you, peace of mind, elegance, comfort, I prefer you, I miss you, fertility, love, virility

Gladiolus (*Gladiolus*): never give up, strength of character, constancy, faith, boundary setting, creative growth, ego

Hibiscus (*Hibiscus*): you are perfect, delicate beauty, youth, fame, joy, happiness, personal glory

Hydrangea (*Hydrangea*): you are unfeeling, please understand, perseverance, understanding, interconnectedness, wholeness

Iris, Blue Flag (*Iris versicolor*): I believe in you, faith, wisdom, valour, purification, spirit messages, creativity, inspiration, ability to be happy, release blocks, eliminate negative feelings

Jasmine (*Jasminum officinale*): abundance, victory, congratulations, hope

Jonquil (*Narcissus jonquilla*): returned desire, ease of worry, desire, power, sorrow, death

Lavender (Lavandula stoechas): cleansing, protection, grace, trust, I admire you

Lemon (*Citrus limon*): I promise to be true, discretion, prudence, fidelity in love, cleansing, space cleansing, banish negative thoughts, zest

Lisianthus (*Eustoma grandiflorum*): will you marry me?, I appreciate you, outgoing nature, appreciation, calming, romantic desire, wedding, gratitude, comfort

Madonna Lily (*Lilium candidum*): healing, secrets revealed, encouragement, I promise, protection against negativity

Magnolia (*Magnolia campbellii*): wisdom, acceptance, strength, female energies, changes, I will always love you

Morning Glory (*Ipomoea purpurea*): habit breaking, consistency, mortality, love in vain, affection, enthusiasm, vitality, love

How to Create Your Own Spells ✦ 311

Nasturtium (*Tropaeolum majus*): I believe you can succeed, I support you, let's have fun, creative freedom, vitality, fun challenges, independence, over-thinking, jest

Passion Flower (*Passiflora incarnata*): I am pledged to another, belief, passion, religious superstition, religious work, stability, spiritual balance, higher consciousness

Peony (*Paeonia officinalis*): I wish you a happy marriage, happy wedding anniversary, wealth, honour, good health, prosperity, romance, compassion, shame, female fertility, nobility

Peruvian Lily (*Alstroemeria*): I wish you success, I am devoted to you, I am your friend, strength, wealth, good fortune, abundance, prosperity, friendship, devotion

Poppy, Field (*Papaver rhoeas*): memory, continuance, sacrifice, revelations, you are always in my memory

Red Clover (*Trifolium pratense*): good fortune, good luck, fertility, domestic virtue, protection from danger, psychic protection, cleansing, clear negativity, balance, calmness, clarity, enhance self-awareness

Rose, Red (*Rosa*): I love you, I respect you, you are beautiful, respect, love, courage, passion, lust, relationship, beauty

Rose, Wild (*Rosa acicularis*): I trust you, will you marry me?, new path, trust, promises, contracts, betrayal

Rose, Yellow (*Rosa*): I am your friend, can we be friends? I am falling in love with you, falling in love, welcome back, I will return, friendship, new beginning

Rosemary (*Rosmarinus officinalis*): I remember you, your presence revives me, psychic awareness, mental strength, accuracy, clarity, remembrance, memory

Sacred Blue Lily (*Nymphaea caerulea*): rebirth, sacredness, victory, second chance, disconnection, I understand you

Snapdragon (*Antirrhinum majus*): I'm sorry for what I did, grace under pressure, inner strength, expression of emotions, increased perception, spell breaker, deviousness, grace

Snowdrop (*Galanthus nivalis*): I am here for you, hope, new beginnings, illumination, inner peace, self-neglect, renewal, solutions

Stargazer Lily, Pink (*Lilium orientalis*): expanded horizons, abundance, spontaneity, wealth, prosperity, ambition

Sunflower (*Helianthus annuus*): get well, be strong, strength, happiness, male healing, confidence, self-esteem, assertiveness

Sweet Pea (*Lathyrus odoratus*): you are beautiful, good luck, gratitude, greed, harmony, protection, responsibility, comfort, social responsibility

Sweet Violet (*Viola odorata*): steadfastness, loyalty, humility, constancy, shyness, protection from deception, protection from inebriation, love potions

Thistle, Scotch (*Onopordum acanthium*): retaliation, integrity, truth, pride, self-respect

Tuberose (*Polianthes tuberosa*): I desire you, dangerous pleasures, sex, intimacy, protection, strength

Water Lily (*Nymphaea*): unity, creation, enlightenment, resurrection, purity, gracefulness, separation

OTHER FLOWERS

Most herbs and trees also have flowers, and you can use floral references that explore meanings and uses to develop your own spells. Flowers hold the same energy as the rest of the plant. In fact, they offer an additional boost to the plant's energy because it is in the process of reproduction.

Below is a sample of flowering plants featured in this book, but you can find many more in my book *Flowerpaedia, 1,000 Flowers and Their Meanings* (Cheralyn Darcey, Rockpool Publishing, Sydney, Australia, 2017).

Agrimony (*Agrimonia eupatoria*): do not worry, inner fears and worries

Allspice (*Pimenta dioica*): you are worthy, self-value, self-nurture

Angelica (*Angelica archangelica*): inspiration, spiritual protection, facing the unknown, protection

Basil (*Ocimum basilicum*): travel well, open heart, compassion, strengthen faith, spirituality, peace, love, fidelity, virtue, preservation, mourning, courage in difficulties, harmony

Burdock (*Arctium*): do not touch me, protection, healing, persistence, importunity, core issues, release anger

Catnip (*Nepeta cataria*): calm hysteria, clarity, focus, female healing

Chamomile, German (*Matricaria chamomilla*): equilibrium, relax, calm down, release tension, soothing, ease nightmares, energy, patience in adversity, nervous system support, love, attract love

Chamomile, Roman: (*Chamaemelum nobile*): I admire your courage, do not despair, love in austerity, patience, abundance, attract wealth, fortitude, calm

How to Create Your Own Spells ✦ 313

Chicory (Cichorium intybus): I love you unconditionally, removal of obstacles, invisibility, momentum, release of tension, favours, frigidity, unconditional love

Chives (Allium schoenoprasum): protection from evil spirits, protection of house, weight loss, protection, long life

Cinnamon (Cinnamomum verum): forgiveness of hurt, clairvoyance, creativity, defence, divination, dreams, healing, love, mediation, psychic development, purification, spirituality, success, wealth, power

Cloves (Eugenia caryophyllata): protection, dignity, exorcism, love, money

Coltsfoot (Tussilago farfara): I am concerned for you, maternal love, concern, children, new challenges, vitality, physical stamina, immunity

Comfrey (Symphytum officinale): healing, fusion

Dill (Anethum graveolens): lust, luck, protection from evil, finances

Echinacea (Echinacea purpurea): higher self, strength, physical strength, immunity, healing, dignity, wholeness, integrity

Foxglove (Digitalis purpurea): I believe in you, beware, stateliness, communication, insincerity, magick, confidence, creativity, youth

Frankincense (Boswellia sacra): faithful heart, blessing, consecration, courage, divination, energy, exorcism, love, luck, meditation, power, protection, purification, spiritual growth, spirituality, strength, success, visions

Garlic (Allium sativum): good fortune, protection, strength, courage, aphrodisiac, wholeness, immunity

Ginger (Zingiber officinale): you are loved, clarity, determination, intelligence, courage, warm feelings, tension relief, sensitivity, perception, sensory awareness

Ginkgo (Ginkgo biloba): beauty, business, calling spirits, dreams, fertility, longevity, love

Ginseng (Panax): love, wishes, beauty, protection, lust, grounding, balance, disconnection, longevity, mental powers

Goldenseal (Hydrastis canadensis): healing, money

Gotu Kola (Hydrocotyle asiatica): self-awareness

Guarana (Paullinia cupana): wishes, energy

Hawthorn (Crataegus monogyna): balance, duality, purification, sacred union, hope, heart protection

Honeysuckle (Lonicera): be happy, I am devoted to you, happiness, sweet disposition, sweet life, end arguments, homesickness, intimacy, unity

Hop (*Humulus lupulus*): apathy, injustice, passion, pride, healing, sleep, mirth

Hyssop (*Hyssopus officinalis*): I forgive you, cleanliness, sacrifice, breath, forgiveness, purification, shame, guilt, pardon, repentance

Juniper (*Juniperus*): journey, protection, anti-theft, love, exorcism, health, healing, cleansing, purifying spaces

Laurel (*Laurus nobilis*): I change but in death, I admire you but cannot love you, victory, protection from disease, protection from witchcraft, merit, glory

Lemon Balm (*Melissa officinalis*): lift spirits, renewed youth, calm, strengthen mind, restore health, vigour, balance emotions, relax, courage, inner strength

Lemon Verbena (*Aloysia triphylla*): attractiveness, love, protection from nightmares, sweet dreams, marriage, purification

Lemongrass (*Cymbopogon citratus*): friendship, lust, psychic awareness, purification, protection from snakes

Marshmallow (*Althea officinalis*): to cure, humanity, dispel evil spirits, attract good spirits, beneficence, mother, maternal energies, protection

Meadowsweet (*Filipendula ulmaria*): healing, love, divination, peace, happiness, protection from evil, balance, harmony

Motherwort (*Leonurus cardiaca*): concealed love, female healing, inner trust, spiritual healing, astral travel, immortality, longevity, relationship balance, mothering issues, sedation, calm anxiety

Mugwort (*Artemisia vulgaris*): prophecy, protection, strength, psychic abilities, prophetic dreams, healing, astral projection, awkwardness, creative visualisation, visions, clairvoyance, divination

Nettle (*Urtica*): you are cruel, you are spiteful, cruelty, pain, slander, clear choices, decision-making, protection against evil spirits, health recovery

Onion (*Allium cepa*): protection, purification, detox, hibernation, potential

Oregano (*Origanum vulgare*): joy, happiness, honour

Parsley (*Petroselinum crispum*): entertainment, feast, protection of food, festivity, to win, useful knowledge

Patchouli (*Pogostemon cablin*): defence, fertility, releasing, love, wealth, sexual power

Peppermint (*Mentha x piperita*): friendship, love, clarity, refreshment, concentration, clear thinking, inspiration, energy, alert mind, study support

Rosemary (*Rosmarinus officinalis*): I remember you, your presence revives me, psychic awareness, mental strength, accuracy, clarity, remembrance, memory

Sage (Salvia officinalis): purification, longevity, good health, long life, wisdom, cleansing, protection, higher purpose, reflection, inner peace, esteem, domestic virtue

Sandalwood (Santalum album): clear negativity, mental focus, reincarnation, wishes

Scottish Primrose (Primula scotica): I love you completely, I'm sorry, compassion, acceptance, anxiety, forgiveness, unconditional love, patience

Skullcap (Scutellaria): relaxation, psychic healing, relaxation of nerves, self-esteem, ability to cope

Slippery Elm (Ulmus rubra): stop gossip

Sweet Marjoram (Origanum majorana): let go of fear, self-reliance, comforting, relieve physical tension, relieve mental tension, consolation, protection from lightning, comfort grief, fertility, love, joy, honour, good fortune, long life

Thyme (Thymus vulgaris): bravery, affection, courage, strength, let's do something, activity

Wormwood (Artemisia absinthium): do not be discouraged, absence, authenticity, sorrowful parting

Yarrow (Achillea millefolium): friendship, war, elegance, banishing, relaxation

Flowerpaedia can also be used to look up energies and themes and so find flowers, herbs and plants that you wish to include in your spell. Following is a small sample from the book:

Change: Bee Balm (*Monarda* spp.), Scarlet Pimpernel (*Anagalis arvensis*), Mayflower (*Epigaea repens*), Fireweed (*Chamerion angustifolium*), Snowplant (*Sarcodes sanguinea*)

Clarity: Boronia (*Boronia ledifolia*), Grass Tree (*Xanthorrhoea resinosa*), Sweet Alyssum (*Alyssum maritimum*), Hemp (*Cannabis sativa*), Angel's Trumpet (*Brugmansia candida*), Dandelion (*Taraxacum officinale*), Petunia (*Petunia*), Hippeastrum (*Hippeastrum*), Rosemary (*Rosmarinus officinalis*), Trout Lily (*Erythronium americanum*), Greater Celandine (*Chelidonium majus*), Peppermint (*Mentha piperita*), Catnip (*Nepeta cataria*), Clary Sage (*Salvia sclarea*), Red Clover (*Trifolium pretense*), Ginger (*Zingiber officinale*), Carrot (*Daucus carota* subsp. *sativus*), Grapefruit (*Citrus parasisi*), Coffee (*Coffea arabica*)

Clarity, emotional: Love-in-a-Mist (*Nigella damascene*), Gerbera Daisy, Yellow (*Gerbera jamesonii*)

Deceit: Mock Orange (*Philadelphus*), Venus Flytrap (*Dionaea muscipula*), Lewis Mock Orange (*Philadelphus lewisii*), Dogbane (*Apocynum cannabinum*), Fly Orchid (*Ophrys insectifera*), Rocket (*Eruca sativa*)

Encouragement: Madonna Lily (*Lilium candidum*), Carnation, Pink (*Dianthus caryophyllus*), Dahlia (*Dahlia* spp.), Goldenrod (*Solidago virgaurea*), Black-Eyed Susan (*Rudbeckia hirta*), Campion, Red (*Silene*), Bayberry (*Myrica*), Watermelon (*Citrullus lanatus*), Butterfly Lily (*Hedychium coronarium*)

Release: Lechenaultia (*Lechenaultia formas*), Henbane (*Hyoscyamus niger*), Calendula (*Calendula officinalis*), Skunk Cabbage (*Symplocarpus foetidus*), Alder (*Alnus*), Rose, Meadow (*Rosa blanda*), Butterfly Weed (*Asclepias tuberosa*), Moneywort (*Bacopa monnieri*), Melilot (*Melilotus officinalis*), Air Plant (*Tillandsia* spp.)

Release anger: Burdock (*Arctium* spp.), Firethorn (*Pyracantha* spp.)

Release attachments: Trumpet Creeper (*Campsis radicans*)

Release barriers: Lady's Mantle (*Alchemilla vulgaris*)

Survival: Waratah (*Telopea speciosissima*), Dandelion (*Taraxacum officinale*), Tropic Bird Orchid (*Angraecum eburneum*), Texas Bluebonnet (*Lupinus texensis*), Kapok (*Ceiba pentandra*)

Glossary

apothecary: a storehouse or shop containing magickal supplies

basal: arising from the root crown of a plant

bract: a modified leaf that sometimes looks like a petal

bracteole: leaf-life projections

bulb: underground stem with modified leaves that contains stored food for plant shoot within

cardinal points: directions on a compass

cast: to create and release magick

compound leaf: a leaf with a division of two or more small leaf-like structures

corm: the underground bulb-like part of some plants

corona: a ring of structures that rise like a tube from a flower

cultivar: a plant that has agricultural and/or horticultural uses and whose unique characteristics are reproduced during propagation

cut flower: a flower used as decoration

dominant hand: the hand you are more proficient with using

endemic: native or restricted to a certain place

floret: one of the small flowers making up a flower head

flower head: a compact mass of flowers forming what appears to be a single flower

Full Moon: when the moon is fully visible as a round disc

grounding: to bring yourself back into the everyday world

hermaphrodite (n): having both male and female reproductive parts

hermaphroditic (adj.): having both male and female reproductive parts

hex: a spell cast to cause harm

inflorescence: several flowers closely grouped together to form one unit, or the particular arrangement of flowers on a plant

lobe: a rounded or projected part

lanceolate: shaped like a lance, tapering to a point at each end *leaflet:* a small leaf or leaf-like part of a compound leaf

leguminous: an erect or climbing bean or pea plant

magick: metaphysical work to bring about change

mojo bag: a magick bag into which magickal items are placed and worn on the person

New Moon: the moon phase when the moon is not visible

oracle: a person who translates divination messages between people and the Other Worlds

ovate: egg-shaped with a broader end at the base

pagan: originally meaning people who lived in the countryside and now meaning those who follow nature-based spirituality and hold beliefs other than the main religions of the world

panicle: a loose cluster of flowers on a branch

parasitic: gains all or part of its nutritional needs from another living plant

perennial: a plant that lives for three or more years

pericarpel: the cup-like structure of a flower on which the petals or stamens sit

pinnate: feather-like

pollarding: pruning a tree of the upper branches to promote a dense head of foliage and branches

pseudanthium: a flower head consisting of many tiny flowers

raceme: inflorescence in which the main axis of the plant produces a series of flowers on lateral stalks

ray flower: a flower that resembles a petal

ritual: a ceremony that combines actions and sometimes words and music

scrying: using a reflective surface or a body of water to gaze into during divination

sessile: attached without a stalk

spent: flowers that have died

stamen: the pollen-producing reproductive organ of a flower

staminal column: a structure, in column form, containing the male reproductive organ of a plant

steep: to leave in hot water so that properties are imparted via heat into the water

stem: the main part of a plant, usually rising above the ground

tepal: a segment in a flower that has no differentiation between petals and sepals

thermogenic: the ability to generate and maintain heat

tuber: a thickened part of an underground stem

Vodoun: a religion created by African ethnic groups in colonial Saint-Domingue and then blended with Christianity in the 16th and 17th centuries

Waning Moon: when the moon is getting smaller, towards Dark/New

Waxing Moon: when the moon is getting larger, towards Full

witch bottle: a bottle filled with items then sealed and usually buried to create a spell

Bibliography

Benzakein, Erin and Waite, Michele M., *Floret Farm's Cut Flower Garden* (Chronicle Books 2007)

Byczynski, Lynn, *The Flower Farmer* (Chelsea Green Publishing 2008)

Clarke, Ian and Lee, Helen, *Name That Flower* (Melbourne University Press 1987)

Cook, Will, *Indoor Gardening* (TCK Publishing 2013)

Coombes, Allen J., *Dictionary of Plant Names* (Timber Press 2002)

Cunningham, Scott, *Encyclopedia of Magical Herbs* (Llewellyn Publications 2010)

Graves, Julia, *The Language of Plants* (Lindisfarne Books 2012)

Hall, Dorothy, *The Book of Herbs* (Angus & Robertson 1972)

Hanson, J. Wesley, *Flora's Dial* (Jonathan Allen 1846)

Harrison, Lorraine, *RHS Latin for Gardeners* (Mitchell Beazley 2012)

Hemphill, John and Rosemary, *Myths and Legends of the Garden* (Hodder & Stoughton 1997)

Hill, Lewis and Hill, Nancy, *The Flower Gardener's Bible* (Storey Publishing 2003)

Jay, Roni, *Sacred Flowers* (Thorsons 1997)

Kear, Katherine, *Flower Wisdom* (Beyond Words 2000)

Kelly, Frances, *The Illustrated Language of Flowers* (Viking O'Neil 1992)

Mac Coitir, Niall, *Irish Wild Plants* (The Collins Press 2008)

Macoboy, Stirling, *What Flower Is That?* (Lansdowne Press 2000)

Newbery, Georgie, *The Flower Farmer's Year* (UIT Cambridge Ltd 2015)

Olds, Margaret, *Flora's Plant Names* (Gordon Cheers 2003)

Pavord, Anna, *The Naming of Names: The Search for Order in the World of Plants* (Bloomsbury 2005)

Phillips, Stuart, *An Encyclopaedia of Plants in Myth, Legend, Magic and Lore* (Robert Hale Limited 2012)

Potter, Jennifer, *Seven Flowers and How They Shaped Our World* (Atlantic Books 2013)

Richardson, Fern, *Small-Space Container Gardens* (Timber Press 2012)

Sanders, Jack, *The Secrets of Wildflowers* (Lyons Press 2014)

Shipard, Isabell, *How Can I Use Herbs In My Daily Life?* (David Stewart 2003)

Sulman, Florence, *A Popular Guide to Wild Flowers of New South Wales* (Angus & Robertson Ltd 1926)

Telesco, Patricia, *A Floral Grimoire* (Citadel Press 2001)

Thomsen, Michael and Gennat, Hanni, *Phytotherapy Desk Reference* (Global Natural Medicine 2009)

Vickery, Roy, *A Dictionary of Plant-Lore* (Oxford University Press 1995)

Ward, Bobby J., *A Contemplation Upon Flowers* (Timber Press 1999)

White, Ian, *Australian Bush Flower Healing* (Bantam Books 1999)

About the Author

Cheralyn Darcey is a botanical alchemist, organic gardener, artist and presenter. Inspired by her pagan family upbringing and her passion for nature and magic, Cheralyn focuses on the spiritual, cultural, therapeutic and physical connections between humans and plants.

She hosts a talkback radio show on the 2SM Super Radio Network and is also the bestselling author of many books and oracle decks including *The Australian Wildflower Reading Cards, Flower Reading Cards, Florasphere Calm* and *Florasphere Inspired, Flowerpaedia: 1000 Flowers and Their Meanings, Flower Petals* and *Flowers of the Night Oracle.*

cheralyndarcey.com
Instagram: cheralyn
Facebook: cheralyn.darcey
TikTok: cheralyndarcey